Second Edition

deutsch aktuell 1

Wolfgang S. Kraft

Consultants

Chief Consultant
Hans J. König
The Blake Schools
Hopkins, Minnesota

Monika Devrient
Städtisches Gymnasium
Mülheim, Germany

Karl-Heinz Gabbey
Buffalo Grove High School
Buffalo Grove, Illinois

Richard C. Helt
University of Arizona, Tucson

Anthony Jung
University of Nebraska at Omaha

Peter Klose
Grand Blanc High School
Grand Blanc, Michigan

Hildegard S. Morrell
Bellevue Senior High School
Bellevue, Washington

Roland Specht
Ruhr-Universität Bochum
Bochum, Germany

EMC Publishing, Saint Paul, Minnesota

ISBN 0-8219-0070-6

Published by EMC Publishing
300 York Avenue
St. Paul, Minnesota 55101

Printed in the United States of America
0 9 8 7 6 5 4 3

A Word to the Student

Many often ask, "Why study German? — What do I need it for?" Did you know that Germans make up the largest single ethnic group in this country and that most major U.S. companies have subsidiaries or branch offices in Germany? When you apply for a job, knowledge of a foreign language will be a great advantage for you with many companies. Knowledge of German will give you a better chance to get that job.

Studying German in our increasingly complex world has become an important asset for anyone who desires to learn more about today's world. But it is not just learning the language that will open the door to German-speaking countries — it is the knowledge and insight into the German culture. Understanding the German language and culture will help you to know your own language and culture better.

The strength of *Deutsch: Aktuell* is its realistic and up-to-date treatment of the German language and culture. As the word *aktuell* implies, it is a topical, contemporary program in which you will explore *all* German-speaking countries (West and East Germany, Austria and Switzerland). You will be exposed to topics that have been carefully selected on the basis of how typical they are or how frequently they occur in the daily lives of the people in the German-speaking countries.

Deutsch: Aktuell will teach you to communicate in German in everyday situations. Don't be afraid to express yourself. It's natural to make mistakes, but your language skills will become much stronger as you use the language. You will acquire the desire and confidence to communicate in German.

And now, I wish you the best of success and lots of fun, or as we say in German...
Viel Erfolg und viel Spaß!

Wolfgang Kraft

Lektion 1

Lektion 2

Lektion 3

Lektion 4

Lektion 5

Lektion 8

Lektion 9

Deutsches Sprachgebiet

Nordsee

Ostsee

Helgoland

Flensburg
Schleswig
Fehmarn
Rügen

Kiel
Holstein

Lübeck
Rostock

Inseln
Bremerhaven
Schwerin

Emden
Wilhelmshaven
Hamburg

DEUTSCHE
DEMOKRATISCHE
REPUBLIK

Oldenburg
Bremen

Niedersachsen

Berlin (Ost)

Elbe

Osnabrück
Hannover
Braunschweig

Potsdam
Magdeburg

Oder

Münster
Bielefeld
Goslar

Dessau

Dortmund
Nordrhein-Westfalen

Cottbus

Essen
Wuppertal
Harz

Saale

Halle

Duisburg

Kassel

Leipzig

Düsseldorf

BUNDES-
REPUBLIK
DEUTSCHLAND

Dresden

Köln

Erfurt

Gera

Karl-Marx-
Stadt

Aachen
Bonn

Thüringer Wald

Jena

Rhein

Fulda

Hessen

Erzgebirge

Zwickau

Koblenz

Rheinland-Pfalz

Wiesbaden
Frankfurt/Main

LUXEMBURG

Mainz

Würzburg

Bayreuth

Trier

Darmstadt

Bayern

Saarland
Mannheim

Nürnberg

Heidelberg

Saarbrücken

Neustadt
Rothenburg

Karlsruhe

Regensburg

Donau

Baden-Baden

Stuttgart

Passau

Baden-Württemberg

Schwarzwald

Augsburg
München

Linz

Freiburg

Konstanz
Chiemsee

Salzburg

Wien

Neusiedlersee

Titisee
Oberammergau
Zugspitze

ÖSTERREICH

Basel
Bodensee

Garmisch-
Partenkirchen

Aare
Zürich

Vaduz

Watzmann

Graz

Rhein

LIECHTENSTEIN
Innsbruck

Luzern

Bern

Grossglockner

SCHWEIZ

Rhone

Genf

Monte Rosa

Alpen

Dialog

Wo wohnst du?

ANDREAS:	Grüß dich, Monika!
MONIKA:	Grüß dich, Andreas! Wie geht's?
ANDREAS:	Nicht schlecht.
ANDREAS:	Kennst du Ingo?
MONIKA:	Nein.
ANDREAS:	Ingo ist mein Freund.
INGO:	Grüß dich, Monika! Wohnst du auch hier in Buchenau?
MONIKA:	Ja. Ich wohne da drüben. Und du?
INGO:	Ich wohne gleich hier um die Ecke.
MONIKA:	Was machst du jetzt, Andreas?
ANDREAS:	Ingo und ich gehen in die Stadt.
MONIKA:	Ich gehe auch in die Stadt.
INGO:	Komm doch mit!
MONIKA:	Gut, das ist mir recht.

Fragen über den Dialog (Questions about the Dialog)

1. Kennt Monika Ingo?
2. Wo wohnt Monika?
3. Wo wohnt Ingo?
4. Was machen Andreas und Ingo?
5. Was macht Monika?

Where Do You Live?

ANDREAS:	Hi, Monika!
MONIKA:	Hi, Andreas! How are you?
ANDREAS:	Not bad.
ANDREAS:	Do you know Ingo?
MONIKA:	No.
ANDREAS:	Ingo is my friend.
INGO:	Hello, Monika! Do you live here in Buchenau, too?
MONIKA:	Yes. I live over there. And you?
INGO:	I live right around the corner.
MONIKA:	What are you doing now, Andreas?
ANDREAS:	Ingo and I are going downtown.
MONIKA:	I'm going downtown, too.
INGO:	Why don't you come along?
MONIKA:	O.K., that's all right with me.

Nützliche Ausdrücke (Useful Expressions)

Grüß dich, Monika!*	Hi, Monika!
Wie geht's?	How are you?
Gleich um die Ecke.	Right around the corner.
Was machst du?	What are you doing?
Ich gehe in die Stadt.	I'm going downtown.
Komm doch mit!	Why don't you come along?
Das ist mir recht.	That's all right with me.

Grüß dich! is commonly used in Southern Germany.

Wie geht's?

2

Ergänzung (Supplement)

1. Tag, Andreas!
   Guten Tag, Monika!
   Grüß dich, Ingo!

2. Wie heißt du?   Ich heiße Helga.
   Wie heißen Sie?   Ich heiße Herr Lehmann.
        Ich heiße Frau Schmidt.
        Ich heiße Fräulein Meier.
   Wie heißt er?   Er heißt Hans.
   Wie heißt sie?   Sie heißt Tina.

3. Wie geht es dir, Kurt?   Nicht schlecht.
   Wie geht es Ihnen, Herr Müller?   Danke, gut.

4. Heißt er Ralf?   Ja, er heißt Ralf.
        Nein, er heißt nicht Ralf.
        Er heißt Walter.

5. Wo wohnst du?   Ich wohne da drüben.
        Ich wohne gleich um die Ecke.
        Ich wohne in Hamburg.
   Wohin geht Sabine?   Sie geht in die Stadt.

6.

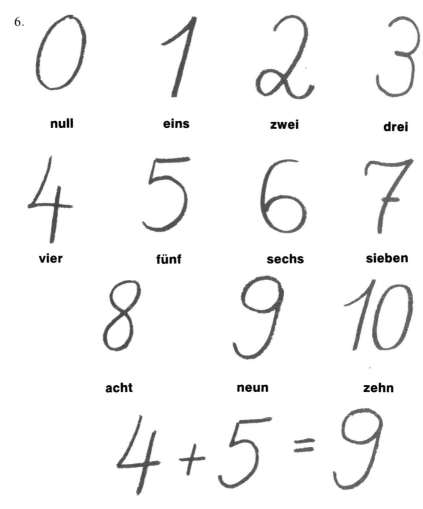

null	eins	zwei	drei
vier	fünf	sechs	sieben
acht	neun	zehn	

Vier plus fünf ist neun.

Das Alphabet		
a ah	**k** kah	**u** uh
b beh	**l** ell	**v** fau
c tseh	**m** emm	**w** weh
d deh	**n** enn	**x** iks
e eh	**o** oh	**y** üpsilon
f eff	**p** peh	**z** tset
g geh	**q** kuh	**ä** äh
h hah	**r** err	**ö** öh
i ih	**s** ess	**ü** üh
j jot	**t** teh	**ß** ess-tset

Namen für Jungen		Namen für Mädchen	
Achim	Jörg	Alexandra	Katja
Alexander	Jürgen	Andrea	Katrin
Andreas	Kai	Angelika	Kerstin
Axel	Karsten	Anja	Manuela
Benjamin	Klaus	Annette	Maren
Bernd	Lars	Barbara	Marianne
Björn	Manfred	Beate	Marlis
Boris	Manuel	Bettina	Martina
Carsten	Marc	Bianca	Melanie
Christian	Marco	Birgit	Michaela
Daniel	Marcus	Britta	Miriam
Dennis	Martin	Carmen	Monika
Dieter	Matthias	Christa	Nadine
Dirk	Michael	Christiane	Nadja
Erich	Nils	Christine	Natalie
Felix	Norbert	Claudia	Natascha
Florian	Oliver	Cornelia	Nicole
Frank	Patrick	Daniela	Nina
Franz	Peter	Diana	Petra
Fritz	Rainer	Doris	Renate
Georg	Ralf	Elke	Rita
Gerd	Rudolf	Erika	Ruth
Gerhard	Rüdiger	Eva	Sabine
Günter	Sebastian	Gabi	Sandra
Hans	Simon	Gerda	Sibylle
Harald	Stefan	Gisela	Sigrid
Hartmut	Steffen	Heidi	Silke
Heiko	Sven	Heike	Silvia
Helmut	Thomas	Helga	Simone
Herbert	Thorsten	Ilse	Sonja
Hermann	Timo	Inge	Stefanie
Holger	Tobias	Ingrid	Stephanie
Ingo	Torsten	Irene	Susanne
Jan	Udo	Jennifer	Tanja
Jens	Uwe	Jessica	Tina
Joachim	Volker	Julia	Ursula
Jochen	Walter	Jutta	Waltraud
Johannes	Wolfgang	Katherina	Yvonne

Ausspracheübung (Pronunciation Exercise)

short /a/		long /a/	
machst	Hans	Tag	Helga
Stadt	acht	da	Tina
das	Hamburg	ja	
was	Walter	Fragen	
Andreas	danke	Monika	
Ralf			

Übungen (Exercises)

The Familiar Form: *du* (singular) and *ihr* (plural)

The familiar form is used when you speak to relatives, close friends, children and animals.

Examples: (Ingo's mother is speaking to her son.) *Kennst du Monika?* Do you know Monika?
(Andreas is talking to his friends.) *Was macht ihr?* What are you doing?

The Formal Form: *Sie* (singular and plural)

The formal form is used when you speak to adults and to those you are not addressing by their first name.

Examples: (Thomas is talking to his teacher.) *Gehen Sie in die Stadt, Herr Schulz?* Are you going downtown, Mr. Schulz? (Mrs. Müller talks to some customers.) *Wo wohnen Sie jetzt, Herr und Frau Meier?* Where are you living now, Mr. and Mrs. Meier?

NOTE: The formal form *Sie,* in both the singular and plural, is capitalized.

Personal Pronouns

	Singular	Plural
1st person	ich I	wir we
2nd person	du you	ihr you
3rd person	er he sie she es it	sie they
formal form	Sie you	Sie you

Present Tense Verb Forms

In the present tense in English, there are basically two different verb forms for all persons. For instance, *come* can be used for all persons, except third person singular where it is *come(s).* In German, however, the verb has more forms, as can readily be seen in the chart.

To use the proper verb form, you need to know the infinitive of the particular verb. The infinitive of the English verb *went, gone* or *goes* is *to go.* The infinitive of a German verb ends with *-en* (in a few cases *-n*) as in geh*en*, mach*en*, or wohn*en*. The infinitive is a combination of the stem of the verb and the ending (INFINITIVE = STEM + ENDING).

Example: INFINITIVE = STEM + ENDING
                gehen   =   *geh*   +   *en*

When the stem of a verb is known, you need to know the appropriate ending for the particular singular or plural form.

The present tense of regular verbs is characterized by the endings indicated below.

Singular	ich geh-e du geh-st er sie } geh-t es	I go you go he goes she goes it goes
Plural	wir geh-en ihr geh-t sie geh-en Sie geh-en (sg. & pl.)	we go you go they go you go

NOTE: Should the stem of the verb in the 2nd person singular end in *s, ß, x or z,* then the *s* of the ending is dropped.

Examples: *du heiß-t* (your name is)
du putz-t (you are cleaning)
du mix-t (you are mixing)
du lös-t (you are loosening)

The Letter *ß (ess-tset)*

The letter *ß* is equivalent to *ss.* The *ß* is used in these positions:
a. at the end of a word (Grüß dich!)
b. before a consonant (heißt)
c. after a long vowel or vowel combination (Straße, weiß)
The *ß* is never used when all the letters in a word are capitalized.

Example: *Straße* but *STRASSE*

Nouns

All nouns in German are capitalized.
Examples: *die Stadt, der Tag*

Folgt den Beispielen! (Follow the examples.)

1. Ich wohne hier.   Ich wohne hier.
   Andreas   Andreas wohnt hier.
   Andreas und Monika
   wir
   du
   Frau Meier

2. Wie heißt sie? (Monika)   Sie heißt Monika.
   Wie heißt er? (Andreas)
   Wie heißt sie? (Frau Schmidt)

Wie heißt er? (Herr Lehmann)
Wie heißt sie? (Fräulein Meier)
Wie heißt er? (Ingo)

3. Was machst du jetzt?   Was machst du jetzt?
   wir   Was machen wir jetzt?
   Monika
   Ingo und Andreas
   Herr Schmidt
   ihr
   er

4. Andreas kennt Ingo.   Andreas kennt Ingo.
   Monika   Monika kennt Ingo.
   Herr und Frau Meier
   ich
   wir
   Herr Lehmann

5. Change each of the following sentences from the familiar to the formal form.

    1. Wie heißt du?
    2. Wohnst du da drüben?
    3. Wie geht's?
    4. Du kennst Frau Meier.
    5. Du gehst in die Stadt.
    6. Was machst du jetzt?
    7. Wo wohnst du?

6. Beantwortet diese Fragen! (Answer these questions.)

    1. Wie geht's?
    2. Wo wohnst du?
    3. Wie heißt du?
    4. Was machst du jetzt?
    5. Kennst du Monika? Ja,…
    6. Wohnst du gleich um die Ecke? Ja,…
    7. Gehst du in die Stadt? Ja,…

7. Select one of the words from the list to complete each sentence.

    1. Wie _____?
    2. Ingo _____ mein Freund.
    3. Ich _____ in die Stadt.
    4. Frau Lehmann _____ gleich um die Ecke.
    5. Er _____ Andreas.

6. Was _____ ihr jetzt?

7. _____ Sie da drüben, Herr Schmidt?

8. Das ist mir _____.

heißt	recht
macht	ist
gehe	wohnt
wohnen	geht's

8. Provide an appropriate response in German.

1. Grüß dich! Wie geht's?
2. Wohnst du hier?
3. Was machst du?
4. Wohnt Monika in Buchenau?
5. Heißt er Herr Meier?

Erweiterung (Expansion)

Folgt den Beispielen!

9. Eins plus drei ist…? Eins plus drei ist vier.
   Fünf plus zwei ist…?
   Acht plus eins ist…?
   Drei plus drei ist…?
   Zwei plus acht ist…?
   Vier plus fünf ist…?

10. Kennt er Monika? Ja, er kennt Monika.
    Wohnt sie hier?
    Geht Andreas in die Stadt?
    Wohnt Ingo gleich um die Ecke?
    Heißt er Herr Meier?
    Heißt sie Fräulein Lehmann?

11. Write out each problem and answer in German.

1. 2 + 5 = _____
2. 3 + 3 = _____
3. 8 + 1 = _____
4. 4 + 1 = _____
5. 2 + 2 = _____

12. Wie heißt das auf deutsch?

1. What's your name?
2. Where do you live?
3. Andreas is my friend.
4. That's O.K. with me.
5. Do you know Mrs. Meier?
6. I live over there, too.
7. Hello, Monika!
8. Why don't you come along.
9. Three plus six is nine.
10. Five plus one is six.

13. Decide whether or not the response to each question or statement is appropriate. If it is inappropriate, write a response that makes sense.

1. Wie geht's?
   Nein.
2. Wo wohnst du?
   Da drüben.
3. Was machst du?
   Das ist mir recht.
4. Wie heißt er?
   Er heißt Elke.
5. Guten Tag, Frau Meier!
   Gut.
6. Kennen Sie Fräulein Lehmann?
   Ja.
7. Vier und fünf ist…?
   Nein.
8. Was macht ihr jetzt?
   Wir gehen in die Stadt.
9. Wie geht es Ihnen, Herr Schmidt?
   Nicht schlecht.
10. Wohnen Sie hier?
    Ja, gut.

14. Beantwortet diese Fragen!

Was machst du jetzt?
Wie heißt du?
Wo wohnst du?
Wie geht es dir?
Gehst du in die Stadt?
Wie heißt er?
Wie heißt sie?

Kulturecke 1 (Culture Corner)

Greetings, Farewells and Introductions

"Hello" and "Hi" have become almost international greetings these days, and many younger Germans use them when dealing with each other. Their own language, however, did not originally include such short, informal greetings. The normal German greeting is *"Guten Tag."* Often the first word is dropped, and you'll simply hear *"Tag"* or people just mumble *"n' Tag."* In Southern Germany you will rarely hear *"Guten Tag"* but rather *"Grüß Gott."* Young people in Southern Germany will also greet each other with *"Grüß dich."* In Austria people often greet each other with *"Servus."*

In the morning, most Germans greet each other with *"Guten Morgen,"* or simply *"Morgen"* whereas in the evening they say *"Guten Abend"* or again just mumble *"n' Abend."* It is quite customary for strangers in smaller towns to greet each other. Men will even tip their hats. When entering a town or city, the visitors are often greeted with a sign that says *"Willkommen."*

"Auf Wiedersehen" or simply *"Wiedersehen"* means *"good-bye." "Tschüs"** is a very casual form of *"Wiedersehen,"* primarily used in Northern Germany. It comes closest to the American "See you!" or "So long!" Ending a telephone conversation, most Germans say *"Auf Wiederhören"* or simply *"Wiederhören."* It means "Hope to hear you again," just as *"Auf Wiedersehen"* means "Hope to see you again." If a German says *"Bis bald!"* (until soon) or *"Bis dann!"* (until then), he or she usually has a specific time in mind. A German does not need to say "Good-bye, hope to see you again," because *"Auf Wiedersehen"* means exactly that.

On leaving a party at night, when Americans would say "Good night," most Germans will not say *"Gute Nacht"* but *"Auf Wiedersehen."* People living in the same house would say *"Gute Nacht."* And, of course, family members say it when they go to bed.

*The standard way of spelling "Tschüs" is with "s." However, Germans will also spell it with "ss" (Tschüss) or with "ß" (Tschüß).

Bis bald!

Auf Wiederhören!

Servus!

Germans do a lot more handshaking than Americans. Germans not only shake hands when being introduced but many still consider a handshake as part of the everyday greeting. To a German, it means little more than saying "Hello." A nod of the head usually accompanies the handshake. When meeting acquaintances in the street, in shops or elsewhere in public, Germans usually shake hands only if they intend to have a little chat.

What do you say when introducing people to each other in Germany? You say *"Darf ich bekannt machen?"* or *"Darf ich vorstellen? — Herr Meier — Herr Schmidt."* The two shake hands, smile and say *"Guten Tag, Herr Meier"* and *"Guten Tag, Herr Schmidt"* to each other. A friendly nod of the head when shaking hands would be in order, too.

Americans who are used to saying "How are you?" when being introduced, may be tempted to say *"Wie geht es Ihnen?"* when being introduced to a German. This is not customary, however, unless you are at the doctor's office and he inquires about your health. *"Wie geht es Ihnen?"* or short *"Wie geht's?"* is a greeting for someone you already know.

Kulturecke 2

„Du" oder „Sie"?

Both words *"du"* and *"Sie"* mean "you." However, *"du"* is considered the informal mode and *"Sie"* the formal mode of address. For Germans, there is nothing stiff about *"Sie."* For instance, people may work in an office for years and still call each other *"Sie,"* yet the atmosphere can be very friendly and pleasant. So, who calls each other *"du"*? Primarily blue-collar workers, students and military personnel or the police force say *"du"* to each other.

In social life, people you know well — called *"Bekannte"* (acquaintances) — are addressed with *"Sie,"* while close, personal friends — called *"Freunde"* — are addressed with *"du."* Young people, too, quickly tend to use the *"du"* form among each other.

All members of a family say *"du"* to each other. Children are always addressed with *"du"* until mid-adolescence. Among each other, children use the *"du"* form as well. The *"du"* form is also used in prayers and church services. Finally, you always address animals with *"du,"* regardless of whether they are small or large.

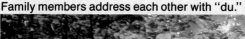

Family members address each other with "du."

Vokabeln

acht eight
auch also, too
da there
   da drüben over there
danke thanks
das the, that
deutsch German
drei three
du you (familiar singular)
die **Ecke,-n** corner
eins one
er he
es it
die **Frau,-en** Mrs., woman
das **Fräulein,-** Miss
der **Freund,-e** boyfriend, friend
fünf five
gehen to go
   Wie geht's? How are you? (familiar)
gleich immediately, right away
   gleich um die Ecke right around the
   corner
gut good, well, O.K.
heißen to be called, named
   Wie heißt du? What's your name?
der **Herr,-en** Mr., gentleman
hier here
ich I
ihr you (familiar plural)
in in
ist is
ja yes
jetzt now
der **Junge,-n** boy
kennen to know (someone)
kommen to come
   Komm doch mit. Why don't you
   come along?
machen to do, make
das **Mädchen,-** girl
mein my
der **Name,-n** name
nein no
neun nine
nicht not
null zero
plus plus
recht right
   Das ist mir recht. That's all right
   with me.
schlecht bad
sechs six
Sie you (formal)
sie she, they
sieben seven

die **Stadt,¨e** city
der **Tag,-e** day
   Tag! Hello! (conversational), Hi!
   Guten Tag! Hello!
um around
   um die Ecke around the corner
und and
vier four
was what
wie how
Wie geht's? How are you? (familiar)
wir we
wo where
wohnen to live
zehn ten
zwei two

Wo wohnen Sie?

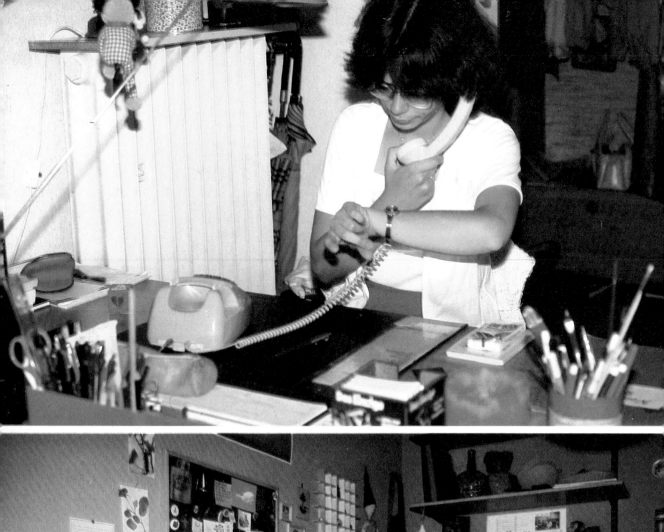

Dialog

Zu Hause

am Telefon

HEIKE: Heike Gruber.

SVEN: Tag, Heike. Hier ist Sven. Ich komme bald rüber.

HEIKE: Um wieviel Uhr?

SVEN: Um vier.

HEIKE: Ich habe dann keine Zeit.

SVEN: Schade. Na, dann bis morgen.

HEIKE: Tschüs bis morgen.

im Zimmer

BIRGIT: Warum bleibst du zu Hause?

HEIKE: Ich habe heute viel zu tun.

BIRGIT: Wie langweilig! Du, ich brauche etwas Geld.

HEIKE: Schon wieder? Wieviel denn?

BIRGIT: Zehn Mark. Petra und ich gehen zur Eisdiele.

HEIKE: Du hast Glück. Ich habe noch etwas Geld.

BIRGIT: Keine Angst! Du bekommst das Geld morgen zurück.

HEIKE: Bis später.

Fragen über den Dialog

1. Wo ist Heike?
2. Hat Heike heute Zeit?
3. Warum bleibt Heike zu Hause?
4. Was braucht Birgit?
5. Wieviel Geld bekommt Birgit?
6. Was machen Birgit und Petra heute?

At Home

on the telephone

HEIKE: Heike Gruber.

SVEN: Hello Heike. This is Sven. I'm coming over soon.

HEIKE: What time?

SVEN: At four.

HEIKE: I won't have time then.

SVEN: Too bad. Well, then 'til tomorrow.

HEIKE: See you tomorrow.

in the room

BIRGIT: Why are you staying at home?

HEIKE: I have a lot to do today.

BIRGIT: How boring! Say, I need some money.

HEIKE: Again? How much?

BIRGIT: Ten marks. Petra and I are going to the ice cream parlor.

HEIKE: You're lucky. I still have some money.

BIRGIT: Don't worry. You'll get the money back tomorrow.

HEIKE: See you later.

Nützliche Ausdrücke

Er kommt rüber.	He's coming over.
Um wieviel Uhr?	At what time?
Schade.	Too bad.
Ich bleibe zu Hause.	I'm staying home.
Hast du viel zu tun?	Do you have a lot to do?
Wie langweilig!	How boring!
Du hast Glück.	You're lucky.
Keine Angst!	Don't worry! Don't be afraid!
Sie geht auf ein Gymnasium.	She goes to a secondary school.
Ich bin pünktlich.	I'm punctual. I'm on time.
Was ist los?	What's the matter?
Schreibt ihr heute eine Arbeit?	Are you taking a test today?
Sie sprechen über…	They talk about…
Hast du Lust?	Would you like to?
Ist es möglich?	Is it possible?
Steigen Sie ein?	Are you getting in(to)?

Ergänzung

1. Welcher Tag ist heute? Heute ist Montag.

2. die Sekunde, die Minute, die Stunde, der Tag, die Woche, der Monat, das Jahr

3.

11	12	13	14	15
elf	zwölf	dreizehn	vierzehn	fünfzehn

16	17	18	19	20
sechzehn	siebzehn	achtzehn	neunzehn	zwanzig

4. Wieviel Uhr ist es? (Wie spät ist es?)

Es ist zwölf.
Es ist zwölf Uhr.

Es ist zehn.
Es ist zehn Uhr.

Es ist eins.
Es ist ein Uhr.

Es ist vier.
Es ist vier Uhr.

Es ist sieben.
Es ist sieben Uhr.

5. Wieviel ist acht plus fünf? Acht plus fünf ist dreizehn.
   Wieviel ist elf minus sieben? Elf minus sieben ist vier.

Aussprcheübung

short / i /	long / i /
ich	viel
mit	wie
in	wieviel
ist	Eisdiele
bis	sie
immer	die
nicht	wir
Monika	vier

Übungen

Formation of Questions

To form a question you must use the so-called inverted word order. The subject and the verb of the sentence are interchanged.

Examples: *Kommen Sie später?* Are you coming later?
Gehen wir in die Stadt? Are we going downtown?
Heißt sie Christine? Is her name Christine?
Geht Thomas nach Hause? Is Thomas going home?

You can readily see that the formation of questions in German is simpler than in English where most questions use the form of "to do" (do you?, does he?, etc.).

The inverted word order is also used with such question words as those listed below:

Wie? (how)   *Wie* heißen Sie?
Wo? (where)   *Wo* wohnst du?
Wohin? (where to)   *Wohin* gehen Sie?
Was? (what)   *Was* machst du jetzt?
Woher? (where from)   *Woher* kommt er?

Folgt den Beispielen!

1. Du hast keine Zeit.   Hast du keine Zeit?
   Monika wohnt da drüben.
   Andreas geht in die Stadt.
   Ihr bekommt das Geld.
   Heike bleibt zu Hause.
   Herr Schmidt kennt Sven.

2. München ist eine Stadt.   Ist München eine Stadt?
   Wir haben viel zu tun.
   Ich brauche etwas Geld.
   Sie gehen zur Eisdiele.
   Sven kommt bald rüber.
   Er wohnt in Buchenau.

3. Kennst du Katrin?   Ja, ich kenne Katrin.
   Gehst du in die Stadt?
   Wohnst du hier?
   Bleibst du zu Hause?
   Brauchst du Geld?
   Hast du viel zu tun?

4. Habt ihr fünf Mark?   Ja, wir haben fünf Mark.
   Fragt ihr Heike?
   Habt ihr etwas Zeit?
   Bleibt ihr hier?
   Bekommt ihr Geld?
   Wohnt ihr da drüben?
   Kommt ihr um sieben?

5. Change each statement to a question.

1. Susanne ist heute nicht pünktlich.
2. Sie haben viel zu tun, Herr Gruber.
3. Wir gehen nicht in die Stadt.
4. Sven kommt um zwei Uhr aus der Schule.
5. Ihr wohnt in München.
6. Du brauchst etwas Geld.
7. Er hat keine Angst.
8. Monika kennt Susanne.
9. Herr und Frau Lehmann gehen zur Eisdiele.
10. Wir warten eine Weile.

6. Beantwortet diese Fragen!

1. Wo wartest du?
2. Um wieviel Uhr kommst du aus der Schule?
3. Warum gehst du in die Stadt?
4. Brauchst du etwas Geld?
5. Hast du viel zu tun?
6. Wieviel Uhr ist es jetzt?
7. Warum hast du keine Zeit?
8. Warum bleibst du zu Hause?

Present Tense of *haben* (to have)

Although most verbs show the regular pattern of conjugation (stem + ending), there are several verbs which do not follow this pattern, as in the case with *haben*.

Singular	ich habe du hast er sie } hat es	I have you have he has she has it has
Plural	wir haben ihr habt sie haben Sie haben (sg. & pl.)	we have you have they have you have

Folgt den Beispielen!

7. Heike hat zehn Mark. Und Monika?   Monika hat auch zehn Mark.
   Wir haben zwölf Mark. Und du?   Ich habe auch zwölf Mark.
   Andreas hat fünf Mark. Und Sabine?
   Herr und Frau Lehmann haben zwanzig
       Mark. Und ihr?
   Ich habe zwei Mark. Und Peter?
   Wir haben fünfzehn Mark. Und ihr?

8. Hast du viel zu tun?   Hast du viel zu tun?
      Frau Meier   Hat Frau Meier viel zu tun?
      ihr
      Sven
      wir
      Heike und Birgit

9. Haben Sie Glück?   Hast du Glück?
   Haben Sie etwas Geld?
   Haben Sie eine Cola?
   Haben Sie zwanzig Mark?
   Haben Sie keine Angst?
   Haben Sie eine Idee?

10. Supply the correct form of *haben*.

1. Wir _____ keine Zeit.
2. Ich _____ viel zu tun.
3. _____ du etwas Geld?
4. Monika _____ eine gute Idee.
5. _____ ihr keine Angst?
6. Herr und Frau Schmidt _____ keine Lust.
7. _____ Sie fünfzehn Mark?

The Definite Article (Nominative Singular): *der, die, das* (the)

In German there are three variations of the definite article in the nominative singular, i.e. *der, die* and *das*. The nominative is used to identify the subject.

Examples: *Der Junge heißt Peter. Die Idee ist gut. Das Gymnasium ist in der Nähe.*

It is extremely important to learn these articles that accompany the individual nouns. You should refer to these as masculine *(der)*, feminine *(die)*, and neuter *(das)*. Be aware, however, that the *nouns* associated with either of the three articles are not necessarily "masculine" or "feminine" or "neuter" by context—i.e., the article for a man's tie *(die Krawatte)* is feminine.

	Singular		
	masculine	*feminine*	*neuter*
nominative	der	die	das

Folgt dem Beispiel!

11. *der, die* oder *das?*

Tag	der Tag
Name	
Zeit	
Uhr	
Geld	
Eisdiele	
Mark	
Ecke	
Freund	
Gymnasium	

12. Supply the proper definite article.

1. Wie heißt _____ Junge?
2. Wo ist _____ Schule?
3. _____ Idee ist gut.
4. _____ Telefon ist da.
5. _____ Frau wohnt gleich um die Ecke.
6. Wie heißt _____ Mädchen?
7. _____ Stadt ist langweilig.
8. _____ Herr kommt pünktlich.

zu Hause and *nach Hause*

There is a distinct difference in using these two phrases. *Zu Hause* means *at home;* whereas *nach Hause* has the meaning *(going) home.*

Examples: *Wo ist Heidi? Sie ist **zu Hause**.*
  *Wohin geht Uwe? Er geht **nach Hause**.*

13. *zu Hause* oder *nach Hause*?

1. Wann gehen Sie _____?
2. Katrin kommt um fünf Uhr _____.
3. Warum bleibst du heute _____?
4. Heike ist nicht _____.
5. Auf dem Weg _____ sprechen sie über die Schule.
6. Ich warte _____.
7. Hast du etwas Geld _____?

Cognates

Words that look alike in German and English and have the same meaning are called *cognates*. Although you can look them up in the vocabulary section, you won't have any problem identifying the meaning of a cognate. Here are some examples of cognates:

Telefon	*Diskothek*	*Butter*	*Hotel*	*Bank*
Chance	*Bus*	*Englisch*	*Eis*	*Amerika*

die Diskothek

das Eis

das Hotel

Lesestück (Reading Selection)

Susanne geht nach Hause

Monika geht auf ein Gymnasium° in Buchenau. Buchenau ist eine Stadt in der Nähe° von München. Jeden° Tag kommt Monika um ein Uhr aus der Schule°.

Monika wartet° oft, bis Susanne und Katrin aus der Schule kommen. Alle drei gehen dann zusammen° nach Hause. Katrin ist immer pünktlich. Beide warten eine Weile. Endlich° kommt Susanne. Sie kommt oft zu spät°. Susanne ist heute nicht froh°. Sie ist verärgert°.

Katrin fragt° Susanne: ,,Was ist los?" Susanne sagt°: ,,Ich habe heute viel zu tun. Wir schreiben morgen° eine Arbeit." Auf dem Weg° nach Hause sprechen sie oft über die Schule. Monika fragt: ,,Warum gehen wir nicht in die Stadt?" Katrin sagt: ,,Das ist eine gute Idee." Susanne hat auch Lust, aber heute ist es nicht möglich°.

Alle drei gehen jetzt schnell zur Haltestelle°. Die S-Bahn° kommt in fünf Minuten. Monika sagt zu Susanne und Katrin: ,,Ich kaufe° noch schnell° eine Cola." Ein Kiosk ist gleich in der Nähe. Da kommt auch schon° die S-Bahn. Susanne sagt zu Monika und Katrin: ,,Tschüs bis morgen." Sie steigt ein°, und Monika und Katrin gehen in die Stadt.

secondary school
nearby/every
from school
waits
together
finally
late/happy
angry
asks/says
tomorrow
on the way

possible
to the stop/train

buy/quickly
already
gets in

Tschüs bis morgen!

Fragen über das Lesestück

1. Wo ist Buchenau?
2. Um wieviel Uhr kommt Monika aus der Schule?
3. Warum wartet Monika?
4. Wer kommt zu spät?
5. Warum ist Susanne verärgert?
6. Was ist eine gute Idee?
7. Was kommt in fünf Minuten?
8. Was kauft Monika?
9. Was macht Susanne jetzt?
10. Was machen Monika und Katrin?

Erweiterung

14. What words are missing?

elf, _____, dreizehn, vierzehn, _____, sechzehn, _____, achtzehn, neunzehn, _____
Montag, _____, Mittwoch, _____, Freitag, Sonnabend, _____
Sekunde, _____, Stunde, _____, Woche, _____, Jahr

15. *Wieviel Uhr ist es?* Use a complete sentence to answer.

1. 1:00
2. 8:00
3. 12:00
4. 3:00
5. 6:00
6. 9:00

16. Select one of the words from the list below and supply the correct form.

1. Ich _____ um zwei Uhr aus der Schule.
2. _____ du Katrin?
3. Wir _____ eine Arbeit.
4. Herr Lehmann _____ in München.
5. _____ ihr jetzt nach Hause?
6. Birgit _____ zehn Mark.
7. Er _____ keine Angst.
8. Sie _____: ,,Was ist los?"
9. Sven _____ heute zu Hause.
10. Heike _____: ,,Tschüs bis morgen."

kommen	haben	gehen
fragen	schreiben	heißen
sagen	bleiben	brauchen
wohnen		

Folgt den Beispielen!

17. *Wieviel Uhr ist es?*
    Wieviel Uhr ist es? (zwei)   Es ist zwei Uhr.
    Wieviel Uhr ist es? (zehn)
    Wieviel Uhr ist es? (fünf)
    Wieviel Uhr ist es? (zwölf)
    Wieviel Uhr ist es? (sieben)
    Wieviel Uhr ist es? (neun)

18. *Wieviel ist...?*
    Wieviel ist zwei plus drei?   Zwei plus drei ist fünf.
    Wieviel ist sechs plus fünf?
    Wieviel ist vierzehn plus fünf?
    Wieviel ist acht plus sieben?
    Wieviel ist vier plus neun?
    Wieviel ist eins plus elf?

19. Wieviel ist zehn minus vier?   Zehn minus vier ist sechs.
    Wieviel ist zwölf minus neun?
    Wieviel ist siebzehn minus sieben?
    Wieviel ist zwanzig minus zehn?
    Wieviel ist acht minus fünf?
    Wieviel ist dreizehn minus elf?

20. Wie heißt das auf deutsch?

  1. Don't be afraid!
  2. Stay at home!
  3. That's a good idea.
  4. He is angry.
  5. How boring!
  6. We have a lot to do.
  7. How much money do we have?
  8. She is always on time.
  9. It's not possible.
 10. What's the matter?

21. Complete the conversation by providing appropriate responses.

  1. Um wieviel Uhr kommst du aus der Schule?
  2. Was machen wir dann?
  3. Das ist eine gute Idee.
  4. Ja, morgen schreiben wir eine Arbeit.

22. Welcher Tag ist es?

1. Heute ist Sonntag. Morgen ist _____.
2. Morgen ist Donnerstag. Heute ist _____.
3. Heute ist Freitag. Morgen ist _____.
4. Morgen ist Mittwoch. Heute ist _____.
5. Heute ist Donnerstag. Morgen ist _____.
6. Morgen ist Montag. Heute ist _____.

23. *Beantwortet die Fragen!* Use the cues provided. Be sure to write out the numbers.

1. Wieviel Geld brauchst du? (ich / 10 Mark)
2. Wieviel Geld braucht Sven? (er / 17 Mark)
3. Wieviel Geld braucht ihr? (wir / 8 Mark)
4. Wieviel Geld brauchen Sie? (ich / 20 Mark)
5. Wieviel Geld braucht Susanne? (sie / 12 Mark)

Beantwortet diese Fragen!

24. Wo wohnst du? (gleich um die Ecke)   Ich wohne gleich um die Ecke.

Was brauchst du?
  (etwas Geld)

Was macht ihr um drei Uhr?
  (zur Eisdiele gehen)

Um wieviel Uhr kommst du aus der
  Schule? (zwei Uhr)

Was schreibt ihr?
  (eine Arbeit)

Was macht Katrin?
  (nach Hause gehen)

25. Wieviel Uhr ist es jetzt?

Warum bleibst du zu Hause?

Hast du viel zu tun?

Wo wartest du?

Um wieviel Uhr gehst du nach Hause?

Was fragst du?

Warum gehst du in die Stadt?

Was brauchst du?

26. *Um wieviel Uhr kommst du?* Indicate when you are coming by using these periods of time: *heute morgen, heute vormittag, heute mittag, heute nachmittag*, or *heute abend*.

1. Ich komme um 11 Uhr.
2. Ich komme um 20 Uhr.

3. Ich komme um 16 Uhr.
4. Ich komme um 12 Uhr.
5. Ich komme um 9 Uhr.
6. Ich komme um 14 Uhr.
7. Ich komme um 6 Uhr.

Sprachspiegel

Answer these questions with as much detail as possible, using the vocabulary and expressions you have learned so far.

1. Warum gehst du am Montag in die Stadt?
2. Was machst du am Sonntag?
3. Wer kommt rüber? Und warum?
4. Wer ist am Telefon?
5. Brauchst du etwas Geld? Warum?
6. Was ist schade?
7. Warum haben wir Glück?
8. Was ist nicht möglich?

Wie sagt man's? (How is it said?)

Ich heiße Silvia. Und du?
Anja.

Tag, Volker. Wie geht's?
Danke, gut.

Mein Name ist Christine Weber. Wie heißen Sie?
Herr Schneider.

Heißt du Birgit?
Nein, Inge. Birgit ist da drüben.

Hast du etwas Zeit?
Nicht jetzt.
Und später?
Dann schon.

Gehst du in die Stadt?
Ja, heute nachmittag.

Was kaufst du?
Eine Cola.
Ich auch.

Zungenbrecher (Tongue Twister)

Fritz fischt frische Fische.
(Fritz catches fresh fish.)

Kulturecke

What Time Is It?

In ancient times, people were just as interested in determining the time of the day as we are today. Different methods such as a sundial were used. Today, of course, we have a more sophisticated way of telling time, not only in our country but all over the world.

One of the most important phrases to know in any language is "What time is it?" In Germany you will find many clocks that will answer your question immediately. However, sometimes you will need to ask someone for the time. The most common ways to ask the time are *"Wieviel Uhr ist es?"* or *"Wie spät ist es?"* Here are some examples of expressing time in German:

6:00 = *Es ist sechs Uhr.*
9:00 = *Es ist neun.*
3:30 = *Es ist halb vier.*
8:30 = *Es ist acht Uhr dreißig.*
9:15 = *Es ist Viertel nach neun.* or *Es ist ein Viertel zehn.* or *Es ist neun Uhr fünfzehn.*
12:45 = *Es ist Viertel vor eins.* or *Es ist drei Viertel eins.*
8:05 = *Es ist fünf Minuten nach acht Uhr.* or simply *Es ist fünf nach acht.*
1:20 = *Es ist zwanzig Minuten nach eins.* or *Es ist ein Uhr zwanzig.*
11:50 = *Es ist zehn Minuten vor zwölf Uhr.* or *Es ist elf Uhr fünfzig.*
9:55 = *Es ist fünf vor zehn.* or *Es ist neun Uhr fünfundfünfzig.*
11:33 = *Es ist elf Uhr dreiunddreißig.* or *Es ist drei Minuten nach halb elf.*

A city hall clock. (Ulm)

die Weltzeituhr (Ost-Berlin)

Germans use a 24-hour system. (Bremen)

Germans do not use the *A.M./P.M.* system. The traveler will have to become familiar with the 24-hour system in a hurry, particularly when dealing with the official language used on radio and TV or at train stations. The 24-hour system is used primarily to avoid misunderstandings. There is no problem with the numbers 1 to 12, as they designate the *A.M.* period of time. Figures 13 to 24 indicate the hours that we call *P.M.* A Rhine steamer leaving at 1:20 P.M., for instance, would be announced as *13.20 (dreizehn Uhr zwanzig).*

An old-fashioned clock seller. (Schwarzwald)

Wieviel Uhr ist es? (Mainz)

Vokabeln

der **Abend,-e** evening
aber but
achtzehn eighteen
alle all
am (or: **an dem**) at the, on the
die **Angst,-̈e** fear
    Keine Angst! Don't worry! Don't be afraid!
die **Arbeit,-en** work
    eine Arbeit schreiben to take a test
auf to, on
aus from, out of
bald soon
beide both
bekommen to get, receive
bis until
bleiben to stay, remain
brauchen to need
die **Cola,-s** cola

dann then
denn used for emphasis
    Wieviel Geld brauchst du denn? Well, how much money do you need?
der **Dienstag** Tuesday
der **Donnerstag** Thursday
dreizehn thirteen
ein(e) a, an
einsteigen to get in(to), board
die **Eisdiele,-n** ice cream parlor
elf eleven
endlich finally
etwas some, a little
fragen to ask
der **Freitag** Friday
froh happy, glad
fünfzehn fifteen
das **Geld** money

das **Glück** luck
    Glück haben to be lucky
das **Gymnasium,-sien** secondary school
    Sie geht auf ein Gymnasium.
    She goes to a secondary school.
    haben to have
die **Haltestelle,-n** stop (for
    bus, streetcar or train)
das **Haus,¨er** house
    nach Hause gehen to go home
    zu Hause at home
    heute today
    heute abend this evening
die **Idee,-n** idea
    immer always
das **Jahr,-e** year
    jeden (form of **jeder**) each, every
    kein no
    keine Zeit no time
der **Kiosk,-e** kiosk
    langweilig boring
    los: was ist los? What's the matter?
die **Lust** pleasure, joy
    Sie hat Lust… She would like to…
die **Mark** German monetary unit
    minus minus, less
die **Minute,-n** minute
der **Mittag,-e** noon
der **Mittwoch** Wednesday
    möglich possible
der **Monat,-e** month
der **Montag** Monday
der **Morgen** morning
    heute morgen this morning
    morgen tomorrow
    na well
der **Nachmittag,-e** afternoon
die **Nähe** nearness, proximity
    in der Nähe nearby
    neunzehn nineteen
    noch still, yet
    oft often
    pünktlich punctual, on time
    rüberkommen (colloquial)
    to come over
die **S-Bahn,-en** city train, suburban express
    train
    sagen to say
der **Samstag** Saturday
    schade too bad
    schnell fast, quick(ly)
    schon already
    schreiben to write
die **Schule,-n** school
    sechzehn sixteen
die **Sekunde,-n** second
    siebzehn seventeen
der **Sonnabend** Saturday

der **Sonntag** Sunday
    spät late
    Wie spät ist es? What time is it?
    How late is it?
    später later
    sprechen to speak, talk
    sprechen über to talk about
    steigen: Sie steigt ein. She gets in(to).
die **Stunde,-n** hour
das **Telefon,-e** telephone
    Tschüs! See you! (sometimes spelled
    Tschüss! or **Tschüß!**)
    tun to do
die **Uhr,-en** clock, watch
    Wieviel Uhr ist es? What time is it?
    Es ist vier Uhr. It's four o'clock.
    um at
    Um wieviel Uhr? At what time?
    verärgert angry
    viel much
    vierzehn fourteen
    von from, of
der **Vormittag,-e** forenoon
    wann when
    warten to wait
    warum why
der **Weg,-e** way
    auf dem Weg on the way
die **Weile** while
    eine Weile a while
    welcher which
    wer who
    wieder again
    wieviel how much?
    Um wieviel Uhr? At what time?
die **Zeit,-en** time
das **Zimmer,-** room
    zu at, too, to
    zur (or: **zu der**) to the
    zurückbekommen to get back
    zusammen together
    zwanzig twenty
    zwölf twelve

Dialog

Auf dem Bahnhof

HERR MEISTER: Wir haben zu viel Gepäck.

FRAU MEISTER: Ja, du hast recht.

HERR MEISTER: Warte!…Hier ist ein Koffer-Kuli.

FRAU MEISTER: Prima. Um wieviel Uhr fahren wir denn nach Dortmund?

HERR MEISTER: Hier ist der Fahrplan. Abfahrt nach Dortmund: 8 Uhr 28, Gleis 7.

FRAU MEISTER: Es ist schon Viertel nach acht. Beeilen wir uns!

HERR MEISTER: Immer mit der Ruhe, Schatz! Wir bekommen die Fahrkarten am Schalter 2.

HERR MEISTER: Zwei Fahrkarten nach Dortmund, bitte.

BEAMTER: Zweiter Klasse?

HERR MEISTER: Nein, erster Klasse.

BEAMTER: Hin und zurück?

HERR MEISTER: Nein, nur einfach.

BEAMTER: Einen Moment. Mal sehen, was der Computer zeigt. Ja, alles ist klar. Das macht 80 Mark.

HERR MEISTER: Hier ist Gleis 7.

FRAU MEISTER: Der Zug ist noch nicht da.

HERR MEISTER: Ah, dort kommt er schon. Ich trage die Tasche und den Koffer.

FRAU MEISTER: Warte! Nicht so schnell!

HERR MEISTER: Dieser Platz ist sehr bequem.

FRAU MEISTER: Wir haben wieder einmal Glück.
Der Zug ist auch nicht zu voll.

HERR MEISTER: Ja, wie sagt man doch: „Ende gut, alles gut!"

Fragen über den Dialog

1. Haben Meisters viel Gepäck?
2. Wohin fahren sie?
3. Um wieviel Uhr fahren sie?
4. Wo bekommen Meisters die Fahrkarten?
5. Fahren Herr und Frau Meister zweiter Klasse?
6. Ist der Zug schon da?
7. Wie ist der Platz?
8. Ist der Zug zu voll?

At the Railroad Station

MR. MEISTER:	We have too much luggage.
MRS. MEISTER:	Yes, you're right.
MR. MEISTER:	Wait!…Here is a luggage cart.
MRS. MEISTER:	Great. What time are we going to Dortmund?
MR. MEISTER:	Here is the schedule. Departure to Dortmund: 8:28 A.M., track 7.
MRS. MEISTER:	It's already a quarter after eight. Let's hurry!
MR. MEISTER:	Take it easy, dear! We'll get the tickets at counter 2.
MR. MEISTER:	Two tickets to Dortmund, please.
OFFICIAL:	Second class?
MR. MEISTER:	No, first class.
OFFICIAL:	Round trip?
MR. MEISTER:	No, just one-way.
OFFICIAL:	One moment. Let's see what the computer is showing. Yes, everything is O.K. That's 80 marks.
MR. MEISTER:	This is track 7.
MRS. MEISTER:	The train isn't here yet.
MR. MEISTER:	Ah, there it is already. I'll carry the bag and the suitcase.
MRS. MEISTER:	Wait! Not so fast!
MR. MEISTER:	This seat is very comfortable.
MRS. MEISTER:	We're lucky again. The train is not too crowded.
MR. MEISTER:	Yes, as they say, "All is well, that ends well."

Nützliche Ausdrücke

Du hast recht.	You're right.
Prima.	Great.
Beeilen wir uns!	Let's hurry!
Immer mit der Ruhe!	Take it easy!
Alles ist klar.	Everything is O.K.
Das macht 10 Mark.	That's 10 marks.
Ich habe Glück.	I'm lucky.
Die Matheaufgaben sind ganz leicht.	The math problems are quite easy.
Das glaube ich nicht.	I don't believe that.
Sie ist sehr klug.	She is very smart.
Er weiß es.	He knows it.
Es dauert ein paar Minuten.	It takes a few minutes.
Gehst du zu Fuß?	Are you walking?

Sie gehen zu Fuß.

Die Aufgaben sind ganz leicht.

Weiß sie es?

Ergänzung

1.

10	*20*	*30*	*40*	*50*
zehn	**zwanzig**	**dreißig**	**vierzig**	**fünfzig**
60	*70*	*80*	*90*	*100*
sechzig	**siebzig**	**achtzig**	**neunzig**	**hundert, einhundert**
21	*22*	*23*	*24*	
einundzwanzig	**zweiundzwanzig**	**dreiundzwanzig**	**vierundzwanzig**	

2. Wieviel Uhr ist es?

Es ist halb drei.

Es ist Viertel vor zehn.

Es ist fünf Minuten vor vier.

Es ist Viertel nach sechs.

Es ist zehn Minuten nach zwölf.

3. Wie heißen die Nachbarländer von Deutschland?
   Dänemark, Holland (die Niederlande), Belgien, Luxemburg, Frankreich,
   die Schweiz, Österreich, die Tschechoslowakei, Polen

4. Nord, Ost, Süd, West *oder*: der Norden, der Osten, der Süden, der Westen

Ausspracheübung

short / o /	long / o /
komm	wohne
doch	so
von	Monat
Woche	Montag
noch	Bahnhof
Bonn	Dialog
bekommst	schon
oft	Cola
dort	froh
Ost	ohne
Nord	groß

Übungen

The Definite Article (Accusative Singular)

In the sentence *Ich frage das Mädchen* (I ask the girl.) *Ich* is called the subject (nominative), *frage* the verb, and *das Mädchen* the direct object (accusative) of the sentence.

	Singular		
	masculine	*feminine*	*neuter*
nominative	der	die	das
accusative	den	die	das

NOTE: From the chart above, you can readily see that the *die* and *das* articles do not change in the accusative and that *der* changes to *den*.

An *n* is added to certain masculine nouns when they are direct objects (accusative). In this category, the following nouns have been introduced so far: *der Herr, der Junge, der Beamte.*

Examples: *Seht ihr Herrn Meister? Wir brauchen den Jungen. Karin fragt den Beamten.*

Folgt den Beispielen!

1. Was liegt da drüben? (Tasche)   Die Tasche liegt da drüben.

   Fahrplan   Der Fahrplan liegt da drüben.
   Geld

Uhr
Vorort
Stadt

2. Wo ist der Schalter?   Wo ist der Schalter?
   Gepäck   Wo ist das Gepäck?
   Eisdiele
   Herr
   S-Bahn
   Platz
   Mädchen

3. Wo ist der Zug?   Der Zug ist in Dortmund.
   (in Dortmund)
   Wo ist der Koffer-Kuli?   Der Koffer-Kuli ist da drüben.
   (da drüben)
   Wo ist die Eisdiele?
   (um die Ecke)
   Wo ist das Geld?
   (hier)
   Wo ist der Koffer?
   (dort)
   Wo ist die Frau?
   (zu Hause)

4. Sehen Sie den Bahnhof?   Ja, ich sehe den Bahnhof.
   Fahrplan   Ja, ich sehe den Fahrplan.
   Computer
   Zug
   Platz
   Schalter

5. Was hast du? (Tasche)   Ich habe die Tasche.
   Uhr
   Mark
   Cola
   Fahrkarte
   Arbeit

6. Wir sehen das Geld.   Wir sehen das Geld.
   Junge   Wir sehen den Jungen.
   Telefon
   Gymnasium
   Mädchen
   Gleis

7. Kaufst du die Fahrkarte?   Kaufst du die Fahrkarte?
   Tasche   Kaufst du die Tasche?
   Koffer

Computer
Cola
Fahrplan

8. Was kennst du? (Platz)   Ich kenne den Platz.
 Stadt   Ich kenne die Stadt.
 Haltestelle
 Vorort
 Mädchen
 Schule

9. Was brauchst du?   Ich brauche den Fahrplan.
 (Fahrplan)
 Was kaufst du?   Ich kaufe die Tasche.
 (Tasche)
 Was hast du?
 (Geld)
 Was bekommst du?
 (Fahrkarte)
 Was brauchst du?
 (Koffer)

10. Supply the correct form of the words given in parentheses.

 1. Wir tragen (the luggage) _____.
 2. Fragen Sie doch (the official) _____!
 3. Um wieviel Uhr kommt (the train) _____?
 4. Seht ihr (the ticket counter) _____?
 5. Ich brauche (the luggage cart) _____.
 6. Die Jungen bekommen (the money) _____.
 7. (The streetcar) _____ kommt gleich.
 8. Wann beginnt (the school) _____?
 9. (The telephone) _____ ist da drüben.
 10. Er fragt (the girl) _____?

11. Beantwortet diese Fragen!

 1. Wer kommt um acht Uhr?
 2. Was brauchst du denn?
 3. Warum bist du verärgert?
 4. Wen fragst du?
 5. Warum hast du Glück?
 6. Was dauert ein paar Minuten?
 7. Wo ist die Haltestelle?
 8. Wann kommt der Zug?

9. Was ist eine gute Idee?

10. Wohin gehst du?

12. Provide the appropriate form of the definite article (*der, die, das*).

1. Wo ist _____ Fahrplan?
2. Fragen Sie doch _____ Beamten!
3. Ich trage _____ Koffer.
4. Wie ist _____ Platz?
5. Hast du _____ Gepäck?
6. Wir brauchen _____ Geld.
7. Wann kommt _____ Straßenbahn?
8. Er fragt _____ Mädchen.

Question Words: *Wer? Wen? Was?*

Both question words *wer* (who) and *wen* (whom) ask about a person. To inquire about objects, you must use the question word *was* (what).

Wer inquires about the subject of the sentence, whereas *wen* asks about the direct object of the sentence. You can use either word whether masculine, feminine or neuter.

Examples: *Karin wohnt da drüben. **Wer** wohnt da drüben?*
*Ich frage **den Beamten**. **Wen** frage ich?*
*Wir brauchen **etwas Geld**. **Was** brauchen wir?*

Folgt den Beispielen!

13. Wer wohnt da drüben?   Herr Meister wohnt da drüben.
    (Herr Meister)
    Wer hat Glück? (ich)
    Wer geht auf das Gymnasium?
    (Katrin und Susanne)
    Wer kennt Heike? (Birgit)
    Wer hat viel zu tun? (wir)
    Wer bleibt zu Hause? (ihr)

14. Wen fragt sie? (Junge)   Sie fragt den Jungen.
    Wen sehe ich? (Gabi)
    Wen brauchen wir?
    (Beamter)
    Wen kennt ihr?
    (Herr Gruber)
    Wen fragst du?
    (Frau)
    Wen seht ihr?
    (Mädchen)

15. Du bekommst *acht Mark.*   Was bekommst du?
    Ich frage *den Beamten.*   Wen frage ich?
    Herr Meister kauft *die Fahrkarte.*
    Wir haben *viel Zeit.*
    Andreas kennt *das Mädchen.*
    Die Jungen tragen *den Koffer.*
    Ich sehe *Birgit.*
    Er hat *viel Glück.*
    Wir schreiben *die Arbeit.*

16. *Herr und Frau Meister* gehen in die Stadt.   Wer geht in die Stadt?
    Ich frage *Susanne.*   Wen frage ich?
    Mein Freund wohnt in Deutschland.
    Wir haben die Tasche.
    Petra fragt *Frau Meier.*
    Sven kommt heute nicht.
    Ich sehe *Herrn Gruber.*
    Du bleibst zu Hause.

17. **Change the following sentences to questions. Use the correct question word — *wer,***
    ***wen* or *was* — in your questions.**

    1. Frau Schmidt kauft *die Tasche.*
    2. Ich kenne *Herrn Meister.*
    3. *Andreas* kommt um vier Uhr nach Hause.
    4. *Mein Freund* geht heute in die Stadt.
    5. Wir brauchen *etwas Geld.*
    6. Ihr seht *die S-Bahn.*
    7. *Die Stadt* ist nicht weit von hier.
    8. *Der Beamte* hat den Fahrplan.
    9. Ich sehe *Kerstin.*
    10. Sven fragt *die Frau.*

Present Tense of *sein* (to be)

The conjugation of *sein* is irregular.

Singular	ich bin	I am
	du bist	you are
	er ⎫	he is
	sie ⎬ ist	she is
	es ⎭	it is
Plural	wir sind	we are
	ihr seid	you are
	sie sind	they are
	Sie sind (sg. & pl.)	you are

Folgt den Beispielen!

18. Katrin ist immer pünktlich.
    Monika und Susanne

    ich
    ihr
    Herr und Frau Meister
    wir

    Katrin ist immer pünktlich.
    Monika und Susanne sind immer
       pünktlich.

19. Sind Sie heute abend zu Hause?
    ihr
    du
    Herr Schmidt
    wir
    die Mädchen
    ich

    Sind Sie heute abend zu Hause?
    Seid ihr heute abend zu Hause?

20. **Supply the correct form of** *sein*.

    1. Warum _____ Heike verärgert?
    2. _____ du um acht Uhr zu Hause?
    3. Herr und Frau Lehmann _____ nicht da.
    4. Der Bahnhof _____ sehr weit von hier.
    5. _____ Sie Frau Meier?
    6. Ihr _____ immer so pünktlich!
    7. Ich _____ sehr froh.
    8. Das _____ eine gute Idee.
    9. Wo _____ ihr denn, Andreas und Susanne?
    10. Wieviel _____ drei und sechs?

kennen and wissen

Both words, *kennen* and *wissen*, mean "to know." However, *kennen* means "to know a person or a place," whereas *wissen* means "to know something" (as a fact).

Examples: *Kennst du Sabine?* but: *Weißt du, wer Sabine ist?*
        Wir kennen Hamburg. but: *Wir wissen, wo Hamburg liegt.*

The verb *wissen* has irregular forms when it is used with *ich, du* and *er (sie, es)*.

ich weiß	wir wissen
du weißt	ihr wißt
er ⎫	sie wissen
sie ⎬ weiß	Sie wissen
es ⎭	

Folgt dem Beispiel!

21. Weißt du das nicht?   Weißt du das nicht?
     der Junge   Weiß der Junge das nicht?
     ihr
     der Beamte
     Kerstin und Gabi
     ich
     wir

22. *kennen* oder *wissen?* **Provide the correct form of the appropriate verb.**

1. _____ Sie, um wieviel Uhr der Zug kommt?
2. Ich _____ Peter. Er ist sehr klug.
3. _____ du den Beamten?
4. Ich _____ nicht, was er macht.
5. _____ Kerstin die Matheaufgaben?
6. Wir _____, wo Peter wohnt.
7. _____ ihr das Mädchen?
8. Ja, wir _____ Herrn Schulz.

Telling Time (A.M. or P.M.)

Germans use the numbers 1 to 12 for A.M. and 13 to 24 for P.M. The 24-hour system is used particularly with official time announcements (radio, television, schedules, for example). However, when you ask someone on the street what time it is and the time of the day is obvious, then only the numbers 1 to 12 are used.

Examples: It's 4 P.M. *Es ist 16 Uhr.* (radio announcer)
               Es ist 4 Uhr. (your friend answering)
When dealing with official time announcements, you will not hear the words *halb, (ein) Viertel, vor* or *nach,* but instead the announcer first will indicate the last full hour and then the minutes.

Examples: It's 8 P.M. *Es ist 20 Uhr.*
               It's 9:18 P.M. *Es ist 21 Uhr 18.*

Words Used for Emphasis

A number of German words are used strictly for emphasis. Such words are *aber, auch, denn, doch* and *ja.* These words cannot be translated but are particularly important in conversational usage.

Examples: *Komm um sieben Uhr!* Come at seven o'clock.
               *Komm **doch** um sieben Uhr!* Why don't you come at seven o'clock.
               Wohin gehst du? Where are you going?
               *Wohin gehst du **denn?*** Where *are* you going? or Tell me, where are you going?

Lesestück 1

Kerstins Schulweg

Kerstin wohnt in Mülheim, einem Vorort° von Köln. Jeden Tag,   *suburb*
von Montag bis Freitag, geht Kerstin um halb acht zur Schule. Bis
zur Haltestelle sind es nur° fünf Minuten zu Fuß. An einem Auto-   *only*
maten kauft sie Fahrkarten° für die Straßenbahn°.   *tickets/streetcar*

    Gabi, Kerstins Freundin, kommt auch immer pünktlich. Ker-
stin begrüßt° Gabi. Sie kennt Gabi schon ein paar Jahre. Beide sind   *greets*
gute Freundinnen. Sie warten nicht sehr lange. Dann kommt auch
schon die Straßenbahn und beide Mädchen steigen ein.

    Gabi und Kerstin sprechen oft über die Schule. ,,Sind die
Matheaufgaben nicht wieder einmal sehr schwer°?" fragt Gabi.   *hard*
,,Das glaube ich nicht. Sie sind eigentlich ganz leicht," antwortet°   *answers*
Kerstin. ,,Du bist ja auch sehr klug. Du weißt immer so viel," sagt
Gabi.

    Beide Mädchen fahren drei Haltestellen mit° der Straßen-   *with*
bahn. Das dauert nur acht Minuten. Von der Haltestelle gehen sie
noch zwei Ecken zu Fuß. Sie gehen jetzt etwas schneller. Sie haben
nicht viel Zeit. Die Schule beginnt um acht Uhr.

Kerstin kauft Fahrkarten an einem Automaten.

Die Straßenbahn kommt.

Sie gehen zur Schule.

Fragen über das Lesestück

1. Was ist Mülheim?
2. Um wieviel Uhr geht Kerstin zur Schule?
3. Wie weit ist es bis zur Haltestelle zu Fuß?
4. Was kauft Kerstin dort?
5. Kommt Gabi zu spät?
6. Was kommt bald?
7. Sind die Matheaufgaben für Kerstin schwer?
8. Fahren Kerstin und Gabi lange?
9. Wie weit gehen sie dann zu Fuß?
10. Um wieviel Uhr beginnt die Schule?

Erweiterung

23. Use the appropriate word from the list below to complete each sentence.

1. Gehst du in die Stadt? Heute ist es nicht _____!
2. Ich weiß das nicht. Die Matheaufgaben sind zu _____ .
3. Fahren Sie hin und zurück? Nein, nur _____ .
4. Angelika kommt um drei Uhr. Sie ist immer _____ .
5. Ich habe jetzt keine Zeit. Das ist aber _____ .
6. Komm mit! Wir fahren nach Bonn. Das ist mir _____ .
7. Warum bist du so _____ ? Wir schreiben heute eine Arbeit.
8. Wir haben viel zu tun. Wie _____ !

recht	verärgert
schade	möglich
langweilig	einfach
pünktlich	schwer

24. Wie heißt das auf deutsch?

1. Four tickets to Germany, please.
2. The seat is not comfortable.
3. Why is she so smart?
4. I'm walking.
5. Mr. Meier believes that.
6. It takes only five minutes.
7. Are you buying the suitcase?
8. What does the computer show?

25. Respond to each question or statement with a complete sentence that is meaningful.

1. Die Schule beginnt um acht Uhr.
2. Warum bist du so froh?

3. Die Matheaufgaben sind ganz leicht.

4. Ich habe viel zu tun.

5. Wie weit ist die Haltestelle zu Fuß?

6. Was fragt er?

7. Da kommt schon die Straßenbahn.

8. Der Platz hier ist sehr bequem.

9. Hast du immer so viel Glück?

10. Ich fahre hin und zurück.

26. Supply the missing words.

1. Fahren Sie hin und zurück? Nein, nur (one-way) _____ .

2. Wo ist (track five) _____ ?

3. (Let's hurry!) _____ ! (The train) _____ ist schon da.

4. Ich kaufe (the ticket) _____ .

5. Gabi ist Kerstins (girlfriend) _____ .

6. Wir haben (much time) _____ .

7. Brauchen Sie (the telephone) _____ ?

8. Hast du (the luggage cart) _____ ?

27. Beantwortet die Fragen!

Wo bekommst du die Fahrkarten?

Was zeigt der Computer?

Warum haben wir Glück?

Wohin fahren wir?

Wie weit gehst du zu Fuß?

Warum wartest du?

Kommst du oft zu spät nach Hause?

Was kaufst du?

Rückblick (Review)

I. Provide the proper form of *haben* or *sein*.

1. Warum _____ Sie so verärgert?

2. _____ du etwas Zeit?

3. Endlich _____ ihr da!

4. Wir _____ oft Glück.

5. Die Idee _____ sehr gut.

6. Helmut und Stefan _____ immer pünktlich.

7. Monika _____ eine Cola.

8. _____ ihr das Geld?

9. Welcher Tag _____ morgen?

10. Du _____ ganz klug.

II. Write the complete answer (including numbers) to the question: *Wieviel Uhr ist es?*
Use the 24-hour system.

1. 6:00 P.M.
2. 10:00 A.M.
3. 11:30 A.M.
4. 3:15 A.M.
5. 11:15 P.M.
6. 2:26 P.M.
7. 7:12 A.M.
8. 9:55 A.M.
9. 4:13 P.M.

III. Write out the answer to the question: *Wieviel ist...?*

1. $5 + 8 = ?$
2. $26 - 17 = ?$
3. $15 + 18 = ?$
4. $60 - 20 = ?$
5. $100 - 91 = ?$
6. $31 + 25 = ?$

IV. *Wer? — Wen? — Was? — Wie? — Wo?* **Use the appropriate question word to form a question about each sentence. Be sure to ask the complete question.**

1. Sie kennt *Julia und Christa* sehr gut.
2. Er heißt *Jörg.*
3. Achim und Renate wohnen *in der DDR.*
4. Wir schreiben *eine Arbeit.*
5. *Mein Freund und ich* gehen in die Stadt.
6. Hamburg liegt *im Norden.*
7. Ihr fragt *Fräulein Müller.*
8. Heike braucht *das Geld.*

Er kennt das Mädchen gut.

Lesestück 2

Deutschland — Land und Fläche

Deutschland hat ungefähr° 78 Millionen Einwohner°. Über 61 Millionen wohnen in der BRD (Bundesrepublik Deutschland), fast° 17 Millionen in der DDR (Deutsche Demokratische Republik).

approximately/inhabitants
almost

Deutschland paßt° 22 mal in die Vereinigten Staaten, ohne° Alaska und Hawaii. Die BRD ist ungefähr so groß wie° der Staat Oregon. Die DDR ist ungefähr so groß wie der Staat Tennessee. In der Bundesrepublik ist die weiteste Entfernung° von Norden nach Süden 830 km (Kilometer), von Osten nach Westen 450 km. Die weiteste Entfernung von Norden nach Süden in der Deutschen Demokratischen Republik ist 500 km und von Osten nach Westen 350 km.

fits/without
as big as
farthest distance

Bonn ist die Hauptstadt° der Bundesrepublik. Diese Stadt liegt im Westen der BRD. Ost-Berlin ist die Hauptstadt der Deutschen Demokratischen Republik und liegt im Osten der DDR.

capital

Bonn ist die Hauptstadt der BRD.

Ost-Berlin ist
die Hauptstadt der DDR.

Fragen über das Lesestück

1. Wie viele Einwohner hat Deutschland?
2. Wie groß ist die Bundesrepublik und wie groß ist die DDR?
3. Was ist die weiteste Entfernung von Norden nach Süden in der DDR und in der BRD?
4. Wo liegt Ost-Berlin? Und Bonn?

Sprachspiegel

I. **Create your own dialog by using the information given. Be as creative as possible.**

You and your friend have arrived at the railroad station one hour before your train is leaving. You have plenty of time. You've got a lot of luggage, and you suggest to your friend that you get a cart. S/he suggests that you carry the luggage instead. You give your friend money so that s/he can buy the tickets. S/he tells the clerk at the window that you want to buy a second class ticket for yourself and your friend. S/he asks where both of you are going. You tell him/her that you are going to Köln. S/he tells your friend the total amount, and s/he pays. Since you've got some time, your friend suggests that you go to the kiosk around the corner to buy a cola.

II. **Pretend to be an official at a railroad station answering questions of tourists who are not familiar with the station or the German train system.**

1. Wo steht der Zug nach Hamburg, bitte?
2. Wo bekomme ich Fahrkarten?
3. Wie viele Haltestellen sind es bis München?
4. Um wieviel Uhr kommt der Zug aus Österreich?
5. Wo ist Gleis 10?
6. Ist der Platz so bequem wie erste Klasse?
7. Was ist die Entfernung von hier nach Bonn?
8. Wie viele Einwohner hat diese Stadt?

Wie sagt man's?

Ja, bitte?
Nach München bitte, hin und zurück.
Erster oder zweiter Klasse?
Zweiter Klasse, bitte.

Wann kommt der Zug?
In zwanzig Minuten. Gleis fünf.
Dann habe ich ja noch Zeit.

Wieviel kostet die Fahrkarte?
50 Mark.
Und nach Hamburg?

Zwei Fahrkarten, bitte.
Wohin denn?
Nach Köln.
Das macht 92 Mark.

Wo ist die Haltestelle?
Dort drüben.
Wann kommt die Straßenbahn?
In fünf Minuten.

Gehst du zu Fuß?
Zur Schule?
Nein, in die Stadt.
Das ist zu weit.

Sie weiß so viel.
Sie ist ja auch sehr klug.
Glaubst du das?
Nein, das weiß ich.

Zungenbrecher

Es klapperten die Klapperschlangen bis die Klappern schlapper klangen.
(The rattlesnakes rattled until the rattles sounded weaker.)

Kulturecke

Traveling by Train

Traveling by train in Germany can be rewarding or frustrating for the foreign traveler. If you're well prepared, you won't have any problems coping with this new and exciting adventure. When traveling between major cities, look for the main railroad station (*Hauptbahnhof*), usually located in the heart of the city. Should you depart from a small station, simply ask for the *Bahnhof*.

Upon entering a main station, become acquainted with the facilities. If you need information about a certain train, look for the schedules usually posted in a prominent location behind a glass window. There are normally two such schedules. One is marked "*Abfahrt*" (departure), the other "*Ankunft*" (arrival). The first schedule gives destinations, times of departure and other valuable information. In case you want to study these details in more privacy and at leisure, you should look for the information office, marked either "*Reiseauskunft*" or "*Information.*" There you can buy a printed train schedule for a nominal fee. For information on local train travel, many major stations have automats marked "*Reisezugauskunft*" that will provide you with requested information after you have pushed the proper buttons. The major stations have begun to install large overhead departure schedules that indicate the departure time, type of train, destination and other information such as possible changes. If you are in a hurry or need speedy personal attention, look for an official wearing a dark blue cap with a golden band marked "*Information.*" This official usually has a detailed train schedule and will have an answer to your question at his finger tips.

The facilities at train stations are generally well marked. Know the German names and you'll have no difficulty finding your way around. Buy your ticket at any window marked "*Fahrkarten.*" Let's assume you want to travel to Frankfurt. To ask for a ticket, simply say to the clerk, "*Nach Frankfurt, bitte.*" If your ticket is to be one-way, add the word "*einfach,*" which means literally "simple." If you want a round-trip ticket, say "*hin und zurück,*" which means "there and back."

After you have purchased your ticket, you may decide to check your luggage instead of taking it directly to the train. Look for a sign which is marked "*Reisegepäck-Annahme.*" Many travelers, however, prefer to take their luggage with them on the train. To check your luggage temporarily until departure, you should look for coin-operated lockers marked "*Schließfächer.*"

Every station, large or small, usually has some eating facilities. In major stations you may find the words "*Cafeteria,*" "*Imbiß,*" which is a snack bar, and "*Restaurant.*" If you don't want to sit down at a table, try to locate a snack bar that offers hot dogs, cold sandwiches and beverages. Those who would like to take some of the delicious German chocolates or candies on their trip can buy these goodies at specialty stands. Would you like to read some newspapers, magazines or books? Look for a stand marked "*Zeitschriften-Bücher.*" Germans rarely go to visit friends or relatives in other towns without taking a small gift along, such as candy or more typically flowers. It is quite common to find flower shops at the station.

If you have little luggage to carry, you won't have any problems taking it directly to the train. However, if you have more luggage than you can carry easily, look for a luggage cart marked "*Koffer-Kuli.*" You can place the luggage on the cart and wheel it right to the train. There is no charge for the use of these carts. Be sure to give yourself plenty of time to get to the train. The trains of the German Railroads (*Deutsche Bundesbahn*) are punctual and won't wait for you.

Most Germans travel second class (*Zweite Klasse*). Second class usually has vinyl seats; it's not luxurious but fairly comfortable. First class seats (*Erste Klasse*) are more plush and rather expensive. These accommodations are recommended only if you want to assure your-

Traveling by train is quite popular in Germany.

The *Intercity (IC)* trains connect major cities.

The *Abfahrt* schedule lists departing trains.

der Hauptbahnhof (München)

A specialty stand. (München)

self a seat during the rush period. If you're not sure, you can purchase a second class ticket and pay the difference after you have boarded the train. Check also to determine whether your car is a *Raucher* (smoker) or a *Nichtraucher* (non-smoker). Most cars have sections for both. Shortly before departure there will be the final call over the loudspeaker and a warning to step back and close the doors. Except at the major railroad stations, an official still blows the whistle to give the signal that the train is about to pull out.

Once the train has left the station, you can relax and examine your surroundings. You will find the compartment and the other facilities quite comfortable. Remember, most Germans travel by train and not by plane as in the U.S. Therefore, special care is taken to assure a pleasant environment on trains. If you don't want to bring your own sandwiches, you can have a warm or cold meal in the *Speisewagen* (dining car). Don't be surprised if someone else sits down at your table after asking you "*Ist hier noch frei?*" This is quite common in most German restaurants. If you want to take a nap, you can recline your seat. On a longer trip, you can reserve sleeping quarters in the *Schlafwagen* (sleeper) or in a *Liegewagen* (couchette) for an additional fee.

There are several types of trains, differing in the distance and speed of their runs. Most foreigners want to cover distances quickly. Therefore, you may prefer to travel in a *D-Zug*. A D-Zug makes fewer stops and connects more than 70 German cities. The fastest trains are the *Intercity* and the *TEE* (*Trans-Europa-Express*). These never stop in smaller towns. The Intercity trains link 40 major German cities and usually run at two-hour intervals. And, finally, should you fly in or out of Frankfurt — coming from or going to the area of Köln — Lufthansa, the German Airlines, will transport you in their Airport Express. This true adventure takes you past fairy tale-like castles along the Rhine.

Lufthansa Airport Express. (Köln)

Compartments are very comfortable.

Train travel can be relaxing.

Vokabeln

alles everything
an at
antworten to answer
der **Automat,-en** automat
der **Bahnhof,-̈e** (train) station
sich **beeilen** to hurry
    Beeilen wir uns! Let's hurry.
beginnen to begin
begrüßen to greet
Belgien Belgium
bequem comfortable
bitte please
bitte schön here you are
die **Bundesrepublik Deutschland**
    Federal Republic of Germany
der **Computer,-** computer
Dänemark Denmark
dauern to last
die **Deutsche Demokratische Republik**
    German Democratic Republic
Deutschland Germany
diese (form of **dieser**) this
dieser this
doch used for emphasis
dort there
eigentlich actual(ly), real(ly)
einfach simple, one-way
einmal once
    wieder einmal once again
das **Ende** end
fahren to drive, go
die **Fahrkarte,-n** ticket
der **Fahrplan,-̈e** schedule
die **Fläche,-n** area, surface
Frankreich France
die **Freundin,-nen** girlfriend
für for
der **Fuß,-̈e** foot
    zu Fuß on foot, walk
    zu Fuß gehen to walk
das **Gepäck** luggage, baggage
glauben to believe, think
das **Gleis,-e** track
groß big, large
halb half
hin und zurück round trip
kaufen to buy
der **Kilometer,-** kilometer
klar clear, O.K.
die **Klasse,-n** class
    zweiter Klasse second class
klug smart
der **Koffer,-** suitcase
der **Koffer-Kuli,-s** luggage cart

das **Land,-̈er** country, land
lange long
leicht easy
liegen to lie, be located
Luxemburg Luxembourg
mal times
man one, they, you people
die **Matheaufgaben** (pl.) math problems
die **Million,-en** million
mit with
der **Moment,-e** moment
nach to, after
das **Nachbarland,-̈er** neighboring country
die **Niederlande** Netherlands
der **Norden** north
nur only, just
der **Osten** east
Österreich Austria
paar: ein paar a few, some
der **Platz,-̈e** seat, place
prima great, splendid
die **Ruhe** peace, silence
    Immer mit der Ruhe! Take it easy.
der **Schalter,-** (ticket) counter
der **Schulweg,-e** way to school
die **Schweiz** Switzerland
schwer difficult, hard
sehen to see, look
    Mal sehen… Let's see…
sehr very
sein to be
so so
der **Staat,-en** state
die **Straßenbahn,-en** streetcar
der **Süden** south
die **Tasche,-n** bag
tragen to carry
die **Tschechoslowakei** Czechoslovakia
über over, above
die **Vereinigten Staaten** United States
das **Viertel,-** quarter
    Es ist Viertel nach acht. It's a
    quarter after eight.
voll full, crowded
der **Vorort,-e** suburb
der **Westen** west
wie viele how many
wissen to know
zeigen to show
der **Zug,-̈e** train

Dialog

In der Schule

STEFAN: Wo bleibt denn der Schlaukopf wieder?

DIRK: Keine Angst! Er kommt schon.

ELKE: Ihr seid so ungeduldig. Immer mit der Ruhe! Wir lösen die Physikaufgaben auch ohne Oliver. Seht mal, wer da kommt!

OLIVER: Na, ihr drei? Seid ihr sauer?

STEFAN: Verlier keine Worte! Wir brauchen deine Hilfe.

DIRK: Ich hab' mein Buch hier. Die Aufgabe steht auf Seite 97.

STEFAN: Ich verstehe die Formeln gar nicht.

ELKE: Lerne sie doch auswendig!

STEFAN: Dein Vorschlag ist wirklich praktisch.

OLIVER: Die Aufgabe ist doch ganz einfach! Lest die Beschreibung gründlich! Dann gebraucht diese Formel hier.

DIRK: Warum bist du denn so klug?

OLIVER: Ja, ich lerne eben fleißig. Man sagt ja: „Übung macht den Meister!"

Fragen über den Dialog

1. Warum ist Stefan ungeduldig?
2. Wer kommt?
3. Was brauchen Stefan, Dirk und Elke?
4. Wo steht die Aufgabe?
5. Was versteht Stefan nicht?
6. Was sagt Oliver? Ist die Aufgabe einfach oder schwer?
7. Warum weiß Oliver so viel?

At School

STEFAN: Where is the genius?

DIRK: Don't worry. He'll come.

ELKE: You're so impatient. Take it easy. We'll solve the physics problems without Oliver. Look who's coming!

OLIVER: Well, you three? Are you angry?

STEFAN: Don't waste any words! We need your help.

DIRK: I've got my book here. The problem is on page 97.

STEFAN: I don't understand the formulas at all.

ELKE: Why don't you memorize them?

STEFAN: Your suggestion is really practical.

OLIVER: The problem is quite simple. Read the description carefully. Then use these formulas here.

DIRK: Why are you so smart?

OLIVER: Well, I just study hard. They say, "Practice makes perfect."

Nützliche Ausdrücke

Du Schlaukopf!	You genius!
Sei nicht so ungeduldig!	Don't be so impatient!
Verlier keine Worte!	Don't waste any words!
Es steht auf Seite…	It's on page…
Ich verstehe das nicht.	I don't understand that.
Lerne es auswendig!	Memorize it!
Lest es gründlich!	Read it carefully!
Ich lerne fleißig.	I'm studying hard.
Übung macht den Meister!	Practice makes perfect!
Er wohnt in einer Wohnung.	He is living in an apartment.
Er klingelt an der Tür.	He is ringing the doorbell.
Sie gehen lieber zu Fuß.	They prefer to walk.
Der Blick ist besonders schön.	The view is especially beautiful.
Ich spreche gern Deutsch.	I like to speak German.
Sie sitzt auf einer Bank.	She is sitting on a bench.
Sie besprechen ein Buch.	They discuss a book.
Sie üben Englisch.	They practice English.

Der Blick ist
sehr schön.
(Kaiserstuhl)

Ergänzung

1. Wie heißen die zwölf Monate?

Herbst*
September, Oktober,
November

Sommer*
Juni, Juli, August

Winter*
Dezember, Januar, Februar

Frühling*
März, April, Mai

*All names of the months and seasons are "**der**" words.*

2. Was für Fächer haben die Schüler?
   Deutsch, Englisch, Mathematik (Mathe), Geschichte, Erdkunde, Chemie, Biologie,
   Physik, Musik, Kunst, Sport.

Stundenplan

Klasse: **8 b**   Zimmer: _____   Klassenleiter: *Schröder*

Zeit	Montag	Dienstag	Mittwoch	Donnerstag	Freitag	Sonnabend
8⁰⁰-8⁴⁵	Mathe	Chemie	Deutsch	Erdkunde	Geschichte	Deutsch
8⁵⁰-9³⁵	Deutsch	Biologie	Deutsch	Musik	Geschichte	Mathe
9³⁵-9⁵⁰	Große	Pause				Schwimmen
9⁵⁰-10³⁵	Englisch	Sport	Englisch	Kunst	Latein	Schwimmen
10⁴⁰-11²⁵	Latein	frei	Biologie	Englisch	Latein	
11²⁵-11⁴⁰	Große	Pause				
11⁴⁰-12²⁵	Latein	Mathe	Französisch	Französisch	Deutsch	
12³⁰-13¹⁵		Französisch	Physik	Chemie	Französisch	

3. Was für Noten bekommen die Schüler?

4. Wie alt bist du? Ich bin sechzehn (Jahre alt).

Ausspracheübung

/ x /	/ ch /
doch	ich
noch	nicht
Buch	recht
auch	gleich
acht	Mädchen
machen	sprechen
Woche	pünktlich
nach	gründlich
brauche	dreißig
einfach	sechzig

Übungen

The Indefinite Article (Nominative and Accusative Singular)

	Singular		
	masculine	*feminine*	*neuter*
nominative	ein	eine	ein
accusative	einen	eine	ein

The articles in the *ein*-group are called indefinite because they do not specifically identify the noun with which they are associated. All articles you have learned so far, i.e., *der, die, das*, are "*der*-words" (definite articles). In English the indefinite article is either *a* or *an*.

Examples: *ein Buch* (a book)

NOTE: You will see from the above that only the accusative of the masculine article differs from the nominative (*ein, einen*). This is also true of the definite article.

Folgt den Beispielen!

1. Der Student wohnt hier.   Ein Student wohnt hier.
    das Mädchen
    der Herr
    die Freundin
    der Schüler
    die Frau

2. Wo ist der Bahnhof?   Wo ist ein Bahnhof?
    Telefon
    Straßenbahn
    Schule
    Fahrplan
    Buch

3. Brauchen Sie einen Fahrplan?   Brauchen Sie einen Fahrplan?
    Telefon   Brauchen Sie ein Telefon?
    Fahrkarte
    Computer
    Uhr
    Koffer
    Tasche

4. Lernst du die Formel?   Lernst du eine Formel?
    Findet Katrin die Eisdiele?
    Die Mädchen lesen das Buch.

Ich verstehe die Aufgabe.

Wir gebrauchen das Wort.

Fragen Sie den Beamten?

Kauft Jürgen die Fahrkarte?

5. Ich lerne das Wort auswendig.　　　　　　　Ich lerne ein Wort auswendig.

　　Formel

　　Aufgabe

　　Übung

　　Buch

　　Beschreibung

6. Complete the following sentences.

　　1. Er sucht (a schedule) _____.

　　2. Fragen Sie doch (an official) _____!

　　3. Kaufst du (a cassette) _____?

　　4. Löst ihr (a problem) _____?

　　5. Dirk und Stefan gebrauchen (a formula) _____.

　　6. Wir sehen (a train) _____.

　　7. Die Mädchen lesen (a book) _____.

　　8. Wann schreibst du (a test) _____?

　　9. Ich verstehe (an exercise) _____.

　10. Brauchen Sie (a suitcase) _____?

7. Form complete sentences using the indefinite article.

　　　Beispiel: *ich / haben / Buch*
　　　　　　　Ich habe ein Buch.

　　1. wir / tragen / Tasche

　　2. wer / kaufen / Computer

　　3. Haltestelle / sein / um die Ecke

　　4. wo / stehen / Straßenbahn

　　5. verstehen / Sie / Wort

　　6. Katrin / Heike / kaufen / Cola

　　7. haben / du / Platz

　　8. Jörg / bekommen / Uhr

　　9. Frau Werner / brauchen / Telefon

　10. suchen / ihr / Schule

Plural Forms of Nouns and Definite Article (Nominative and Accusative)

For singular nouns you must know the gender, that is to say, you must know whether the noun is a *der, die,* or *das*-word. In the plural, however, all nouns, regardless of their gender, are *die* in the nominative and the accusative.

As you can see from the list below, most nouns undergo certain changes from the singular to the plural. There is no definite rule for the formation of plural nouns. You must learn each plural form when you learn a new noun. For simplification, all important nouns that you have learned up to this lesson, have been placed into groups whenever the change from the singular to the plural follows certain patterns.

	Singular			Plural
	masculine	*feminine*	*neuter*	
nominative	der	die	das	die
accusative	den	die	das	die

Plural of Nouns

no change

der Computer	die Computer
der Einwohner	die Einwohner
das Fräulein	die Fräulein
der Kilometer	die Kilometer
der Koffer	die Koffer
das Mädchen	die Mädchen
der Schalter	die Schalter
der Schüler	die Schüler

add -*n*, -*en* or -*nen*

die Aufgabe	die Aufgaben
die Eisdiele	die Eisdielen
die Fahrkarte	die Fahrkarten
die Fläche	die Flächen
die Formel	die Formeln
die Fremdsprache	die Fremdsprachen
die Haltestelle	die Haltestellen
die Idee	die Ideen
der Junge	die Jungen
die Kassette	die Kassetten
die Klasse	die Klassen
die Minute	die Minuten
der Name	die Namen
die Note	die Noten
die Reise	die Reisen
die Schule	die Schulen
die Seite	die Seiten
die Sekunde	die Sekunden
die Straße	die Straßen
die Tasche	die Taschen
die Vokabel	die Vokabeln
die Arbeit	die Arbeiten
der Automat	die Automaten

die Bedeutung	die Bedeutungen
die Beschreibung	die Beschreibungen
die Entfernung	die Entfernungen
der Herr	die Herren
die S-Bahn	die S-Bahnen
der Staat	die Staaten
die Straßenbahn	die Straßenbahnen
der Student	die Studenten
die Tür	die Türen
die Übung	die Übungen
die Uhr	die Uhren
die Universität	die Universitäten
die Wohnung	die Wohnungen
die Freundin	die Freundinnen

add -e or ⸚e

der Bus	die Busse
der Freund	die Freunde
das Gleis	die Gleise
das Jahr	die Jahre
der Kiosk	die Kioske
das Regal	die Regale
der Tag	die Tage
das Telefon	die Telefone
der Vorort	die Vororte
der Weg	die Wege
der Ausdruck	die Ausdrücke
die Bank	die Bänke
der Fahrplan	die Fahrpläne
der Fuß	die Füße
der Platz	die Plätze
der Schlaukopf	die Schlauköpfe
die Stadt	die Städte
der Vorschlag	die Vorschläge

add ⸚er

das Buch	die Bücher
das Fach	die Fächer
das Haus	die Häuser
das Land	die Länder
das Wort	die Wörter*

add -s

das Büro	die Büros
die Cola	die Colas
der Kuli	die Kulis
das Sprachlabor	die Sprachlabors

*The word "**das Wort**" has two different plural forms depending on the meaning. **Das Wort (die Wörter)** means "the word" (several words in a sentence) but **das Wort (die Worte)** means "the word" (saying or quotation). The first form (**das Wort/die Wörter**) is used more frequently and will be stressed throughout this book.

Folgt den Beispielen!

8. Die Aufgabe steht da.   Die Aufgaben stehen da.
   der Zug
   die Beschreibung
   der Automat
   das Mädchen
   die S-Bahn

9. Versteht ihr das Buch?   Versteht ihr die Bücher?
   die Vokabel
   der Schüler
   der Beamte
   die Frau
   die Formel
   der Vorschlag

10. Sie suchen die Kassette.   Sie suchen die Kassetten.
    der Ausdruck
    das Wörterbuch
    das Büro
    die Schule
    der Bahnhof
    die Aufgabe
    das Regal

11. Change the following sentences from the singular to the plural.

> **Beispiel:** *Ich trage die Tasche.*
> *Wir tragen die Taschen.*

1. Der Junge versteht die Aufgabe.
2. Der Vorschlag ist nicht praktisch.
3. Wo liegt die Stadt?
4. Fragst du den Beamten?
5. Findet das Mädchen das Haus?
6. Ich schreibe die Übung.
7. Der Schüler lernt das Wort.
8. Wie heißt der Monat?

12. Provide the plural form as indicated.

1. ein Tag: zwei _____
2. ein Telefon: drei _____

3. eine Freundin: beide _____

4. eine Uhr: viele _____

5. ein Koffer: ein paar _____

6. ein Platz: zehn _____

7. ein Nachbarland: fünf _____

8. eine Straßenbahn: nicht viele _____

9. ein Herr: ein paar _____

10. ein Fahrplan: so viele _____

Negation

The word *kein* means "no" and negates nouns.

Examples: *Ich habe kein Geld.* (I have no money.)
Sie hat keine Fahrkarte. (She has no ticket.)

The endings of *kein* are identical to those of the *ein*-words.

Examples: *Er kauft ein Buch. Er kauft kein Buch.*
Ich suche einen Platz. Ich suche keinen Platz.

The word *nicht* means "not" and negates verbs, adjectives and adverbs.

Examples: *Ich komme nicht.* (I am not coming.)
Er schwimmt nicht gut. (He isn't swimming well.)

With a few exceptions, *nicht* appears after the subject, verb and object, whichever comes last in the sentence.

Examples: *Wir fragen nicht.* (We aren't asking.)
Wir fragen den Jungen nicht. (We aren't asking the boy.)

Folgt den Beispielen!

13. Gibt es da ein Sprachlabor?   Nein, da gibt es kein Sprachlabor.
    Gibt es da ein Büro?
    Gibt es da eine Uni?
    Gibt es da eine Eisdiele?
    Gibt es da einen Bahnhof?
    Gibt es da ein Haus?

14. Sagst du ein Wort?   Nein, ich sage kein Wort.
    Hast du eine Kassette?
    Brauchst du einen Vorschlag?
    Suchst du einen Beamten?
    Findest du eine Straße?
    Lernst du eine Aufgabe?
    Kaufst du einen Computer?

15. Verstehst du das?   Nein, ich verstehe das nicht.
    Ist die Schule weit von hier?
    Bist du sauer?

Geht Andreas nach Hause?

Suchst du es?

Wohnt Kerstin in Hamburg?

Kommt er pünktlich?

Steht der Zug da drüben?

16. Sabine kommt aus Deutschland.   Sabine kommt nicht aus Deutschland.

Frau Müller geht in die Stadt.

Wir sprechen schnell.

Findet Jürgen die Kassette?

Übt Ursula viel?

Der Beamte weiß es.

Bist du zu Hause?

17. Restate these sentences in the negative.

> **Beispiele:** *Der Schüler fragt. Der Schüler fragt nicht.*
> *Brauchst du einen Koffer? Brauchst du keinen Koffer?*

1. Haben Sie einen Computer?
2. Wir kaufen eine Cola.
3. Sie sprechen schnell.
4. Kommt ihr aus der Schule?
5. Heute abend gehen sie in die Stadt.
6. Warum schreibt er eine Arbeit?
7. Hast du Geld?
8. Der Student geht nach Hause.
9. Bekommen Sie eine Karte?
10. Oliver weiß das.

18. Answer the following questions in the negative.

1. Gehst du pünktlich in die Schule?
2. Bist du sauer?
3. Lernst du die Beschreibung auswendig?
4. Weißt du die Bedeutung?
5. Glaubst du das?
6. Hast du viel Zeit?
7. Kommt die S-Bahn in fünf Minuten?

The Command Form

Familiar Command

To form commands in English, the speaker simply takes the infinitive without "to," e.g., "go," "run" or "write." In German, the familiar command form in the singular is constructed by eliminating the "*en*" from the infinitive, i.e., by maintaining the stem.

Examples: *Geh! geh(en)* Go!
Schreib! schreib(en) Write!
Frag! frag(en) Ask!

NOTE: Frequently an "e" is added to the stem so that it would also be correct to say "*Schreibe!*, *Gehe!*, *Frage!*" However, an "e" *must* be added if the stem ends in *-d*, *-t* and *-ig*.

Examples: *Warte!* Wait!

When you address more than one person, the familiar (plural) form is as follows:

    Geht! Schreibt! Fragt!

It is helpful to remember that the familiar plural command is the same as the second person plural without "*ihr.*"

NOTE: The ending "et" instead of just "t" is added to a verb stem that ends with *-d* or *-t*. *Wartet hier! Findet das!*

Formal Command

The singular and the plural formal command are formed by inverting subject and verb.

    Gehen Sie! Schreiben Sie! Fragen Sie!

You will notice right away that this formation is identical to the construction of a question. There is, however, a distinct difference in the intonation of a question and a formal command.

Command Forms of *haben* and *sein*

The following are the command forms for *haben* and *sein*:

Hab keine Angst!	*Sei pünktlich!*
Habt keine Angst!	*Seid pünktlich!*
Haben Sie keine Angst!	*Seien Sie pünktlich!*

The *wir*-Command Form *(Let's…)*

The *wir*-command form is used when asking for some action in the sense of *Let's* (do something)…!

Examples: *Gehen wir!* Let's go!
             Fragen wir den Beamten! Let's ask the official!

Folgt den Beispielen!

19. Du bleibst nicht lange.   Bleib nicht lange!
    Du kaufst die Fahrkarte.
    Du sagst das Wort.
    Du lernst fleißig.
    Du kommst bald.
    Du gehst in die Stadt.
    Du wartest dort.

20. Sie sprechen Deutsch.   Sprechen Sie Deutsch!
    Sie fragen den Herrn.
    Sie suchen die Straße.
    Sie lösen die Aufgabe.
    Sie lesen das Buch.
    Sie gebrauchen die Formel.
    Sie fahren zur Uni.

21. Ihr habt keine Angst.   Habt keine Angst!
    Ihr schreibt die Arbeit.
    Ihr hört die Beschreibung.
    Ihr glaubt das nicht.
    Ihr lernt es auswendig.
    Ihr besprecht die Übung.
    Ihr seht den Computer.

22. Schreibst du das Wort?   Schreib das Wort!
    Warten Sie dort?
    Lernt ihr die Aufgabe?
    Suchen Sie die Kassette?
    Gehst du zu Fuß?
    Kommt ihr bald nach Hause?
    Hast du keine Angst?

23. Ihr seid pünktlich.   Seid pünktlich!
    Du bist froh.
    Sie sind fleißig.
    Ihr seid schnell da.
    Du bist nicht ungeduldig!
    Sie sind um drei Uhr hier.

24. **Convert these sentences into commands.**

> **Beispiel:** *Du sitzt hier.*
> *Sitz hier!*

1. Du lernst den Ausdruck auswendig.
2. Sie schreiben nicht.
3. Ihr fragt den Studenten.
4. Sie gehen zu Fuß.
5. Ihr kommt pünktlich.
6. Du bist nicht so langweilig.
7. Sie haben keine Angst.
8. Du kaufst die Bücher.

Wo, wohin and *woher*

Wo (where) is a question word asking about a location, whereas *wohin* (where to) and *woher* (where from) are question words asking about direction.

Examples: *Wo wohnst du?* Where are you living?
Wohin gehst du? Where are you going (to)?
Woher kommst du? Where are you coming from?

Folgt dem Beispiel!

25. Klaus geht *in die Stadt.*　　　　　Wohin geht Klaus?
Heike wohnt *in München.*
Die Jungen kommen *aus der Schule.*
Die Haltestelle ist *da drüben.*
Die Studenten fahren *nach Deutschland.*
Das Mädchen kommt *aus Hamburg.*

26. *Wo? Wohin?* Use one of the two question words to form questions.

1. Herr und Frau Meister fahren *nach Dortmund.*
2. Jürgen wohnt *in Würzburg.*
3. Monika bleibt heute *zu Hause.*
4. Die Studenten gehen *zur Uni.*
5. Die Straßenbahn steht *an der Haltestelle.*
6. Mein Freund geht *nach Hause.*

gern

The word *gern* used with a verb indicates liking something or someone.

Examples:　*Ich lese gern.* I like to read.
　　　　　Gehst du gern zu Fuß? Do you like to walk?
　　　　　Hat er das Mädchen gern? Does he like the girl?

Folgt dem Beispiel!

27. Was machst du gern?　　　　　Ich lese gern Bücher.
Bücher lesen
in die Stadt fahren
die Aufgaben lösen
die Kassette hören
den Beamten fragen
den Vorschlag machen
Deutsch sprechen

28. Answer these questions by using *gern* in your answers.

1. Was machst du gern?
2. Wohin gehst du gern?

3. Was schreibst du gern?
4. Wen fragst du gern?
5. Wer lernt die Aufgaben gern?
6. Wo sitzt sie gern?

Omission of Article

The article is omitted whenever there is a reference to an occupation or a nationality.

Examples: *Jürgen ist Student.*
Herr Schulz ist Beamter.
Herr und Frau Lehmann sind Amerikaner.

Lesestück 1

Auf dem Weg zur Uni

Jürgen ist Student an der Universität Würzburg. Er wohnt in einer Wohnung° in der Nähe von der Universität. Auf dem Weg zur Uni wohnt auch Ursula, seine Freundin. Jürgen geht oft zu Ursula, klingelt an der Tür und wartet, bis sie aus dem Haus kommt. Das dauert auch nicht lange. Ursula begrüßt Jürgen. Dann gehen beide zu Fuß weiter.

apartment

Jürgen und Ursula sind Studenten.

Sie sprechen gern Englisch.

Jürgen und Ursula gehen nicht gern auf der Straße°. Dort ist immer zu viel Verkehr°. Sie gehen lieber auf einem Feldweg° zur Uni. Dort ist es sehr ruhig°, und auch der Blick auf die Stadt Würzburg ist besonders schön. Natürlich° sprechen Jürgen and Ursula oft über ihr Studium. Beide studieren Fremdsprachen°. Sie sprechen besonders gern Englisch. Jürgen hat Lust im nächsten Jahr nach England zu fahren. Ursula hat auch Lust, aber eine Reise° nach England kostet sehr viel, und sie hat dafür° zu wenig Geld.

An der Haltestelle sehen sie auf den Fahrplan. Da steht, um wieviel Uhr der Bus kommt. Nach der Uni fahren sie vielleicht° in die Stadt. Heute haben sie viel Zeit. Manchmal° sitzen sie auf einer Bank und besprechen ein Buch auf Englisch. Ursula kennt viele Vokabeln. Sie lernt die neuen Wörter° immer auswendig. Englisch ist für Jürgen manchmal etwas schwer. Es gibt immer so viele neue Wörter. Ursula hat ein Wörterbuch°. Jürgen findet dort schnell die Bedeutung° für die Wörter und Ausdrücke.

street
traffic/field path
quiet

of course
foreign languages

trip
for that

perhaps
sometimes

new words

dictionary
meaning

Um wieviel Uhr kommt der Bus?

Jürgen sucht eine Kassette.

Was machen sie im Sprachlabor?

72

Um halb zwei gehen Jürgen und Ursula zum Sprachlabor°.
Ursula bekommt eine Kassette in einem Büro°. Jürgen sucht° eine
andere Kassette auf einem Regal°. Er findet sie auch gleich. Dann
gehen sie ins Sprachlabor und üben Englisch — hören°, sprechen
und verstehen°.

language lab
office/looks for
shelf
listening
understanding

Fragen über das Lesestück

1. Wo ist Jürgen Student?
2. Wohnt er weit von der Uni?
3. Fahren Jürgen und Ursula zur Uni?
4. Warum gehen Jürgen und Ursula nicht gern auf der Straße?
5. Was studieren beide?
6. Was kostet viel?
7. Warum sehen beide auf den Fahrplan?
8. Warum fahren Jürgen und Ursula vielleicht später in die Stadt?
9. Was tun sie manchmal?
10. Was ist für Jürgen etwas schwer?
11. Was bekommt Ursula in einem Büro?
12. Wohin gehen sie dann? Was machen sie dort?

Erweiterung

29. Match each word from the list with the most appropriate word on the left.

1. Koffer - _____	Land Bahnhof
2. Buch - _____	Stadt Geld
3. Gymnasium - _____	Schule Seite
4. Englisch - _____	Jahreszeit Uhr
5. Bremen - _____	Oktober Gepäck
6. Gleis - _____	Fach Mittwoch
7. Mark - _____	
8. Monat - _____	
9. DDR - _____	
10. Tag - _____	
11. Herbst - _____	
12. Zeit - _____	

30. Wie heißt das auf deutsch?

1. Memorize the description!
2. The exercise is on page 36.
3. I don't understand the suggestion.

4. They like to speak English.

5. Are you discussing the book, Elke and Sabine?

6. They prefer to read.

7. Are you always so impatient, Peter?

8. I'm 18 years old.

31. **Complete each word by adding another noun of one or more syllables.**

     Beispiel: *Physik* _____
                  Physikaufgabe

1. Halte_____
2. Eis_____
3. Nachbar_____
4. Feld_____
5. Straßen_____
6. Bundes_____

7. Schlau_____
8. Fahr_____
9. Haupt_____
10. Jahres_____
11. Fremd_____
12. Sprach_____

32. **Beantwortet die Fragen!**

Wie alt bist du?

Was verstehst du nicht?

Was brauchst du?

Wohin gehst du?

Was machst du besonders gern?

Was kostet viel?

Was für Fächer hast du?

Was machst du heute nachmittag?

Verstehst du die Lektion?

Rückblick

I. Provide the proper verb form.

1. (kaufen) _____ ihr die Kassetten?
2. (lesen) Die Studenten _____ die Bücher.
3. (wissen) Das _____ ich nicht.
4. (fragen) _____ doch die Frau, Andreas!
5. (sein) _____ Sie verärgert, Herr Lehmann?
6. (üben) Wir _____ die Wörter.
7. (haben) _____ keine Angst, Susanne und Monika!
8. (lernen) Die Schüler _____ es auswendig.
9. (brauchen) Ich _____ kein Geld.
10. (suchen) Was _____ du denn, Sabine?
11. (finden) Jürgen _____ Englisch etwas schwer.
12. (verstehen) _____ ihr die Beschreibung?

II. Form questions from these statements.

1. Ursula geht nicht zur Uni.
2. Die Eisdiele ist gleich um die Ecke.
3. Die Schule beginnt um acht Uhr.
4. Peter hat eine Freundin.
5. Die Studenten fahren nach Deutschland.
6. Ihr versteht die Vokabeln.
7. Er weiß die Bedeutung.
8. Hamburg liegt im Norden.
9. Hessen grenzt an die DDR.
10. Wir bekommen etwas Geld.

III. Form questions by asking for the italicized words. Use these question words: *was, wer, wen, wo, woher, wohin.*

1. Die Eisdiele ist *in der Nähe.*
2. *Herr Meister* wartet auf dem Bahnhof.
3. Beide fahren *nach Hause.*
4. Um ein Uhr kommen sie *aus der Schule.*
5. Wir fragen *einen Beamten.*
6. Die Schüler lernen *die Bedeutung.*
7. Ich kenne *Katrin* nicht.
8. Die Mädchen haben *fünfzig Mark.*
9. Die S-Bahn steht *dort drüben.*
10. Die Studenten gehen *zur Uni.*

IV. Complete the following sentences.

1. Wir gehen gern _____.
2. Sie hat zu wenig _____.
3. Die Schüler besprechen _____.
4. Eine Reise nach Deutschland _____.
5. Ich habe Lust, aber _____.
6. Heute nachmittag fahren sie _____.
7. Er wohnt _____.
8. Ich kaufe _____.

V. Complete these sentences by using either *viel* or *viele.*

1. München hat _____ Einwohner.
2. Ich habe nicht _____ Geld.
3. Wie _____ Kassetten braucht ihr?
4. Lernt ihr _____ Wörter auswendig?
5. Haben Sie _____ Zeit?
6. Wir haben _____ zu tun.
7. In Nordrhein-Westfalen gibt es _____ Städte.
8. _____ Studenten gehen zur Universität in Würzburg.

Lesestück 2

Die BRD — Länder und Hauptstädte

Die Nationalfahne° der BRD ist schwarz-rot-gold°. Bonn, die Hauptstadt, liegt am Rhein im Westen der BRD. Die Bundesrepublik besteht aus° zehn Ländern.*

Im Norden liegt *Schleswig-Holstein*. Dieses Land grenzt an° Dänemark und die DDR. Kiel ist die Hauptstadt von Schleswig-Holstein. Das Land und die Stadt *Hamburg* liegen auch im Norden. Hamburg ist die größte° Stadt in der Bundesrepublik. Das kleinste° Land ist *Bremen*. Es liegt nur ungefähr 90 Kilometer von Hamburg entfernt°. *Niedersachsen*, ein anderes° Land im Norden der BRD, grenzt im Westen an die Niederlande und im Osten an die DDR. Die Hauptstadt von Niedersachsen heißt Hannover.

*national flag/
black-red-gold*

consists of

borders on

largest/smallest

away/another

* *Berlin (West) is also considered a* **Land** *but does not have the same voting power in the congressional houses in Bonn as the ten* **Länder** *located in the Federal Republic.*

München ist die Hauptstadt von Bayern.

Mainz ist die Hauptstadt von Rheinland-Pfalz.

Düsseldorf liegt in
Nordrhein-Westfalen.

Hannover liegt
im Norden der BRD.

Die meisten Einwohner hat das Land *Nordrhein-Westfalen*. Dieses Land grenzt an die Niederlande und Belgien. Düsseldorf ist die Hauptstadt von Nordrhein-Westfalen. In der Mitte° der Bundesrepublik liegt *Hessen*. Hessen grenzt an die DDR. Die Hauptstadt heißt Wiesbaden. Ein anderes Land ist *Rheinland-Pfalz*. Es grenzt an Belgien, Luxemburg und Frankreich. Die Hauptstadt von Rheinland-Pfalz ist Mainz. Genauso wie° Bonn liegt auch diese Stadt am Rhein. Das *Saarland* grenzt an Luxemburg und Frankreich. Saarbrücken ist die Hauptstadt vom Saarland.**

      °middle

      °just like

Das Land *Baden-Württemberg* liegt im Südwesten der Bundesrepublik und grenzt an Frankreich und die Schweiz. Die Hauptstadt von Baden-Württemberg ist Stuttgart. Das größte Land in der Bundesrepublik ist *Bayern*. Bayern liegt im Süden und grenzt an die Schweiz, Österreich, die Tschechoslowakei und die DDR. München ist die Hauptstadt von Bayern.

Es gibt eigentlich noch ein anderes Land — *West-Berlin*. West-Berlin liegt in der DDR und hat einen besonderen° Status.

      °special

***The definite article is used before the name* **Saarland** *(das Saarland),* **Schweiz** *(die Schweiz) and* **Tschechoslowakei** *(die Tschechoslowakei).*

Fragen über das Lesestück

1. Wie viele Länder gibt es in der Bundesrepublik?
2. Wie heißt die Hauptstadt von Schleswig-Holstein?
3. Wie heißt die größte Stadt in der BRD?
4. Wo liegt Bremen?
5. Welches Land hat die meisten Einwohner?
6. Welches Land liegt in der Mitte der BRD?
7. An welche Länder grenzt Rheinland-Pfalz?
8. Wo liegt Baden-Württemberg?
9. Wie heißt das größte Land?
10. Wo liegt West-Berlin?

Sprachspiegel

I. Pretend you are a teacher talking to your students. Use the command form where appropriate. *Wie heißt das auf deutsch?*

1. Write the descriptions.
2. Memorize the formulas.
3. Where are the books? The problem is on page 56.
4. Read page 56.
5. Don't be so impatient.
6. I don't understand what you are saying.
7. The expression is quite simple.
8. Read it carefully.
9. Practice the words.
10. Go to the language lab.

II. *Auf dem Weg zur Schule.* **Describe (in narrative style) the following sequence, using the cues merely as a guideline.**

You're walking to school…picking up your friend on the way…waiting several minutes before s/he comes out of the house…taking the streetcar at the stop nearby…talking about several items concerning school…getting off…checking the schedule at the stop…indicating a desire to go to the ice cream parlor after school…showing your dictionary to your friend…finding a word/vocabulary item…hurrying to school because the first class begins soon.

Wie sagt man's?

Woher kommst du?
Aus Bremen.
Wohnst du schon lange hier?
Seit März.

Wie alt bist du?
Siebzehn. Und du?
Schon neunzehn.

Verstehen Sie Deutsch?
Ein wenig.
Prima. Sprechen wir etwas!

Wie lange bleibst du noch?
Bis fünf Uhr.
Gut, ich brauche deine Hilfe.

Was lernst du denn so fleißig?
Die Deutschaufgaben.
Sind sie schwer?
Nein, ganz einfach.

Warum bist du denn so ungeduldig?
Die Kassette ist so lang.
Übe den Dialog doch später!
Ja, du hast recht.

Bist du sauer?
Ich brauche eine Tasche.
Hier ist meine.
Habe ich aber Glück!

Was suchst du denn?
Das Sprachlabor.
Es ist gleich um die Ecke.
Danke.

Zungenbrecher

Brauchbare Bierbrauerburschen brauen brausendes Braunbier.
(Useful beer brewery fellows are brewing foaming brown beer.)

Kulturecke 1

School Life in the *BRD*

School life in the Federal Republic of Germany is considerably different from our own. There is practically no social life at a German school. Although schools offer physical education classes — and many have modern facilities — students wishing to participate in various sports activities usually join local sports clubs.

In the first four grades, ages 6 to 10, all children must attend the elementary school (*Grundschule*). These younger children usually carry briefcases or satchels strapped to their backs. During their years in the *Grundschule*, children are accustomed already to a sizeable stack of homework.

At the age of 10, or after fourth grade, most children and their parents face the difficult decision of which of three different schools to attend. Most students go to the *Hauptschule* where they receive a basic education for the next five years. The second choice is the *Realschule*. Here the students will remain for the next six years and receive training for higher level but non-academic occupations of all kinds. Finally, study at the *Gymnasium*, grades 5 to 13, leads to the *Abitur*, the final certificate that is a prerequisite for attending a university. Students going to the *Gymnasium* have a very concentrated curriculum. It is not uncommon for these students to take as many as ten or more different subjects a week. A typical schedule readily shows the emphasis on academic subjects.

In recent years, the *Gesamtschule* has become the answer for many children whose parents and teachers cannot make the proper choice of which school to attend after fourth grade. The *Gesamtschule* is an orientation for the two years following the *Grundschule*. It gives students an opportunity to switch, based on their ability, to any of the other three schools after the sixth grade.

Many students carry briefcases.

Was für ein Fach haben diese Schüler?

Students use bulletin boards to make announcements.

Students put their belongings
on hooks in the hall.

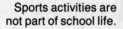

Sports activities are
not part of school life.

A special problem has been created by the numerous children of foreign workers (*Gast-arbeiter*) living in Germany. These children have to become immersed in the German language and culture at a rapid pace. Many schools offer special classes for these children before they can be integrated into the German educational system.

How do students get to school? In recent years, school buses have become a more and more popular way to get to school, although many students walk to school. Others take public transportation or ride their bikes. Some of the older students ride their mopeds, which are usually parked in a specially designated area in the parking lot. There are also a few cars in the parking lot that students over 18 years of age have been allowed to drive.

Most school buildings were built during the past twenty years. There are differences from American schools. Upon entering a *Gymnasium* in the area of Köln, for example, it becomes immediately apparent that students do not have any lockers. This is true in most German schools. Students put their belongings, such as coats and motorcycle helmets, on hooks in the hall. In the main hallway are bulletin boards that are used by the students and administrators to make various announcements. This school, as in most other German schools, offers no warm meals. Students can bring their own bag lunches or purchase various snacks and cold beverages at a counter and from several automats. However, the lunch counter is open only during recess (*Große Pause*).

At the *Gymnasium,* students must prove themselves. Only 15% of all students receive their *Abitur.* Teachers do not have a classroom of their own. For most subjects, students stay with the same classmates in the same room. The earlier grades at the *Gymnasium* offer rather general subjects, while upper grades introduce such subjects as English literature and philosophy.

German students generally spend fewer hours at school than American students, staying only until noon or 1:00 to 2:00 P.M. However, many of them have school on Saturday as well. And, of course, after school, students must spend considerable time doing their homework.

Kulturecke 2

School Life in the *DDR*

Education in the German Democratic Republic starts with pre-school care, which is provided for children whose parents work. Parents can take their children from the age of five months to three years to day nurseries, called *Kinderkrippen*. The *Kindergarten* is responsible for the education of children between the ages of three and six. The attendance of children at both *Kinderkrippen* and *Kindergarten* is free of charge, except for a very nominal amount that is paid for meals.

The backbone of the educational system is the ten-year general polytechnical school, called *Oberschule*. It has been a tradition to welcome first-graders with *Schultüten*, huge cones filled with candies and cookies. These cones are displayed in many stores before the start of the school year.

Let's visit the *Johannes R. Becher Oberschule* in Leipzig, a typical school located in a newer community. Immediately at the entrance of the school is a picture of Johannes R. Becher with an inscription intended to inspire the students of this school. The main objective of the school is shown on a bulletin board nearby. The statistics of the best athletes in the school are displayed here. Along the hallway are many colorful displays that further demonstrate the importance of working together with people in the DDR and those of other countries.

Looking down the hallway, one immediately notices that there are no lockers for students. This is true for most schools in the German Democratic Republic. Students have specified areas outside the classrooms for hanging up their jackets or coats and leaving their briefcases or other items.

From the first grade on, youngsters receive a general education that will prepare them for their later life in the socialist society of the German Democratic Republic. In the third grade, students continue with their basic studies in reading, writing and mathematics, but they are also given some insight into the world of work and the community around them. Over two-thirds of all first through fourth graders stay after school at the *Schulhort*, which has been established so students can take part in sports, games or hobbies while their parents are at work.

At the sixth grade, the spectrum of subjects taught widens considerably. Students begin their second year of study of Russian, their first foreign language. Furthermore, sixth graders are required to expand their knowledge in natural and social sciences as well as mathematics. Before entering a seventh grade classroom, one immediately recognizes the emphasis placed on technology and the natural sciences by examining the colorfully decorated classroom door. In this classroom, seventh grade students are studying physics. After the teacher has introduced a specific topic, students work out problems in their textbooks. Next door is an eighth grade chemistry class attentively listening to the lesson presented. Students are encouraged to assist the teacher in the chemistry experiments.

A glance at a tenth grade schedule reveals the general character of instruction at that level. Besides Russian, another foreign language, English, has been added to the schedule. Advanced mathematics and science, as well as courses on civic and polytechnic instruction, have also been included. The latter course is an introduction to socialist production where students are asked to donate their time to working in factories or on farms.

It is quite common for tenth graders to be asked to clean the school building thoroughly during the last two or three weeks of their school year. While some clean the building, others take care of the shrubs and trees around the school or even paint benches in the school yard. At the end of tenth grade, students complete their required schooling with a final examination and receive the so-called *Abschlußzeugnis* (final grade report). Students may continue for another

First graders are welcomed
with *Schultüten*.

Third grade students continue
their basic studies.

Some tenth grade students
clean the building.

Students paint benches
in the school yard.

Lektion 4

Most students can eat
a warm meal at school.

School meals cost 55 pfennigs.

two years (*Erweiterte Oberschule*) after which they will receive their *Abitur* and become eligible to attend the university.

Between 10:00 A.M. and 11:00 A.M. students usually have a recess (*Große Pause*) of about 15 to 20 minutes. During this time all students go to the school yard to play, talk to their friends or eat a snack. Over 70 percent of all students eat a warm meal at school. The school cafeteria serves warm meals between 11:30 A.M. to 1:00 P.M. for a cost of 55 pfennigs. Each class is assigned a specific block of time to eat. It is customary for the teacher to eat with the students.

Many youngsters belong to the Ernst Thälmann Pioneer organization (*Junge Pioniere*), recognized by their white blouses or shirts, and the Free German Youth (*Freie Deutsche Jugend* or *FDJ*), who wear blue blouses or shirts. The *Junge Pioniere* are 6 to 14 years of age; they can join the *FDJ* youth group at 14. These youth groups have a direct influence in school affairs through their elected committees. In particular, the older group, the *FDJ,* has strong communication ties with the parent-teacher association of the school.

Vokabeln

alt old
der **April** April
die **Aufgabe, -n** problem, exercise
der **August** August
der **Ausdruck,** ̈**e** expression
    ausreichend sufficient
    auswendig lernen to memorize,
      learn by heart
die **Bank,** ̈**e** bench
die **Bedeutung,-en** meaning, significance

    befriedigend satisfactory
die **Beschreibung, -en** description
    besonders especially
    besprechen to discuss
die **Biologie** biology
der **Blick** view
das **Buch,** ̈**er** book
das **Büro,-s** office
der **Bus,-se** bus
die **Chemie** chemistry
    dein your

das **Deutsch** German (language, subject in school)
der **Dezember** December
eben just
England England
das **Englisch** English (language, subject in school)
englisch English
die **Erdkunde** geography
das **Fach,-̈er** (school) subject
der **Februar** February
der **Feldweg,-e** field path
finden to find
fleißig hard-working, industrious
die **Formel,-n** formula
die **Fremdsprache,-n** foreign language
der **Frühling,-e** spring
gar nicht not at all
geben to give
    es gibt there is (are)
gebrauchen to use, apply
gern gladly, with pleasure
    gern gehen like (enjoy) to walk
die **Geschichte** history
gründlich thorough, careful
der **Herbst,-e** fall, autumn
die **Hilfe** help, assistance
hören to listen, hear
ihr their
im (or: **in dem**) in the
ins (or: **in das**) in(to) the
die **Jahreszeit,-en** season
der **Januar** January
der **Juli** July
der **Juni** June
die **Kassette,-n** cassette
klingeln to ring
    an der Tür klingeln to ring the doorbell
kosten to cost
die **Kunst** art
das **Land,-̈er** "state" in the **BRD**
lernen to learn
    auswendig lernen to memorize, learn by heart
lesen to read
lösen to solve
der **Mai** May
manchmal sometimes
mangelhaft inadequate
der **März** March
die **Mathematik** (or: **Mathe**) mathematics
die **Musik** music
nächst next
natürlich of course, natural(ly)
neu new
die **Note,-n** (school) grade, mark
der **November** November

der **Oktober** October
die **Physik** physics
die **Physikaufgabe,-n** physics problem
praktisch practical
das **Regal,-e** shelf
die **Reise,-n** trip
ruhig quiet, peaceful
sauer angry, annoyed
der **Schlaukopf,-̈e** genius, smartie
schön beautiful
der **Schüler,-** pupil, student (at elementary and secondary school)
die **Seite,-n** page
der **September** September
sitzen to sit
der **Sommer,-** summer
der **Sport** sport
das **Sprachlabor,-s** language lab
der **Status** status
stehen to stand, be located
die **Straße,-n** street
der **Student,-en** student (at university)
studieren to study (at university)
das **Studium,-dien** studies
suchen to look for, search
die **Tür,-en** door
üben to practice
die **Übung,-en** exercise, practice
    Übung macht den Meister! Practice makes perfect.
ungeduldig impatient
ungenügend unsatisfactory
die **Uni** the 'U' (abbreviation for **Universität**), university
die **Universität,-en** university
der **Verkehr** traffic
verlieren to lose
    Verlier keine Worte! Don't waste any words!
verstehen to understand
viele many
vielleicht perhaps
die **Vokabel,-n** (vocabulary) word
der **Vorschlag,-̈e** suggestion
was für what kind of
weiter further
    Sie gehen weiter. They keep going.
wenig little
der **Winter,-** winter
wirklich really
woher where from
wohin where to
die **Wohnung,-en** apartment
das **Wort,-e** word (saying, quotation)
    Verlier keine Worte! Don't waste any words!
das **Wort,-̈er** word
das **Wörterbuch,-̈er** dictionary

Dialog

Gehen wir ins Kino!

ANGELIKA:	Grüß Gott!
DIANA:	Grüß Gott, Angelika!
ANGELIKA:	Möchtest du ins Kino gehen?
DIANA:	Ja, das ist eine prima Idee.
ANGELIKA:	Dieser Film soll ganz toll sein.
DIANA:	Die Vorstellung beginnt schon um drei.
ANGELIKA:	Ich rufe noch schnell Rainer und Gerd an. Vielleicht kommen sie mit.
DIANA:	Wo bleiben die beiden denn?
ANGELIKA:	Sie sind wie immer unpünktlich.
DIANA:	Na, endlich seid ihr da. Wir warten schon lange.
RAINER:	Das ist nicht unsere Schuld.
GERD:	Warum ruft ihr uns so spät an?
RAINER:	Jetzt bin ich aber gespannt. Welcher Film läuft denn hier?
ANGELIKA:	*Conan der Barbar,* ein Film aus Amerika.
DIANA:	Und er beginnt gleich. Los, kommt!
ANGELIKA:	Vier Karten zu acht Mark, bitte.
VERKÄUFERIN:	Das macht 32 Mark.
ANGELIKA:	Danke schön.
DIANA:	Das Kino ist ja ganz leer.
PLATZANWEISER:	Ihr könnt hier sitzen.
GERD:	Der Film ist wirklich klasse.
DIANA:	Du hast recht.
RAINER:	Angelika will ihn sogar noch einmal sehen.
ANGELIKA:	Ja! Vielleicht nächste Woche.

Fragen über den Dialog

1. Was ist eine prima Idee?
2. Wann beginnt der Film?
3. Wen ruft Angelika an?
4. Kommen Rainer und Gerd pünktlich?
5. Warum ist es nicht Rainers und Gerds Schuld?
6. Welcher Film läuft heute?
7. Wieviel kostet eine Karte?
8. Ist das Kino schon voll?
9. Was möchte Angelika nächste Woche tun?

Let's Go to the Movie Theater!

ANGELIKA:	Hello!
DIANA:	Hello, Angelika!
ANGELIKA:	Would you like to go to a movie?
DIANA:	That's a great idea.
ANGELIKA:	This movie is supposed to be fantastic.
DIANA:	The show will be starting already at three.
ANGELIKA:	I'll call up Rainer and Gerd right now. Perhaps they'll come along.
DIANA:	Where are those two?
ANGELIKA:	As usual, they're not on time.
DIANA:	Well, finally you're here. We've already been waiting a long time.
RAINER:	That's not our fault.
GERD:	Why do you call us so late?
RAINER:	I'm really wondering now. Which movie is playing here?
ANGELIKA:	*Conan, the Barbarian,* a movie from America.
DIANA:	And it starts right away. Come on, let's go!
ANGELIKA:	Four tickets at eight marks, please.
SALES CLERK:	That's 32 marks.
ANGELIKA:	Thank you.
DIANA:	The movie theater is quite empty.
USHER:	You can sit here.
GERD:	The movie is really great.
DIANA:	You're right.
RAINER:	Angelika even wants to see it again.
ANGELIKA:	Yes, perhaps next week already.

Nützliche Ausdrücke

Möchtest du…?	Would you like…?
Das ist eine prima Idee.	That's a great idea.
Der Film soll toll sein.	The movie is supposed to be fantastic.
Endlich seid ihr da.	Finally you're here.
Das ist unsere Schuld.	That's our fault.
Ich bin gespannt.	I'm wondering. I'm anxious.
Welcher Film läuft heute?	Which movie is playing today?
Los, kommt!	Come on, let's go!
Der Film ist klasse.	The movie is great.
Ich wohne erst einen Monat hier.	I've been living here only a month.
Er arbeitet in der Stadt.	He works downtown.
Sein Auto steht vor dem Haus.	His car is in front of the house.
Er sitzt am Tisch.	He is sitting at the table.
Sie geht einkaufen.	She goes shopping.
Er macht seine Hausaufgaben.	He does his homework.
Er spielt mit seinen Freunden.	He plays with his friends.
Der Pullover soll bald fertig sein.	The pullover is supposed to be finished soon.
Er geht spät zu Bett.	He goes to bed late.
Sie sehen fern.	They watch TV.

Sie gehen einkaufen. (Wiesbaden)

Sie sitzen am Tisch.

Ergänzung

1. Welche Zimmer gibt es in einer Wohnung?

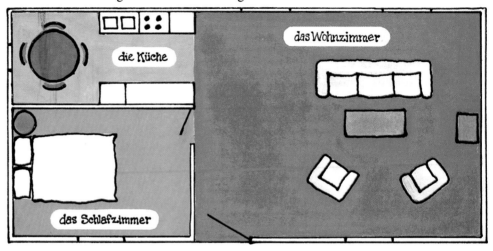

2. Welcher Tag ist heute? Heute ist Montag, der 2. (zweite) Februar.
   Wann hast du Geburtstag? Ich habe am 19. (neunzehnten) Juli Geburtstag.
   Welches Datum haben wir heute? Heute haben wir den 25. (fünfundzwanzigsten)
   September.

3. Herr Uwe Schmidt ist Ralfs und Julias Vater.
Frau Renate Schmidt ist Ralfs und Julias Mutter.
Herr und Frau Schmidt sind Ralfs und Julias Eltern.
Ralf ist Julias Bruder.
Julia ist Ralfs Schwester.
Ralf und Julia sind Geschwister.

Ralf ist der Sohn von Herrn und Frau Schmidt.
Julia ist die Tochter von Herrn und Frau Schmidt.
Ralf ist der Enkel von Herrn und Frau Neumann.
Julia ist die Enkelin von Herrn und Frau Neumann.

Herr Walter Neumann ist Ralfs und Julias Großvater.
Frau Gerda Neumann ist Ralfs und Julias Großmutter.
Herr und Frau Neumann sind Ralfs und Julias Großeltern.

Der Bruder von Herrn Uwe Schmidt ist Ralfs und Julias Onkel.
Die Schwester von Frau Renate Schmidt ist Ralfs und Julias Tante.

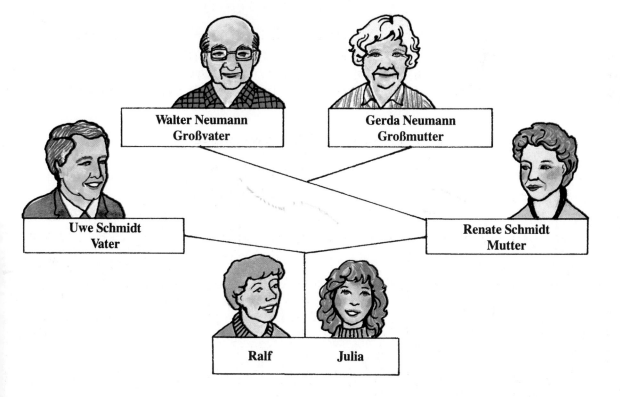

4. 1 DM (Deutsche Mark) hat 100 Pfennige.
1 km (Kilometer) ist ungefähr 0,6 Meilen.
1 Kilometer (km) hat 1 000 Meter (m).

Aussprach
übung

short / u /	long / u /
und	du
um	gut
muß	ruft
Lust	sucht
Mutter	Zug
uns	nur
zum	Juni
durch	Uhr
Musik	klug
short / e /	**long / e /**
essen	lest
denn	der
Westen	sehr
Ecke	seht
gern	leer
sechs	Idee
Bett	mehr
Berg	Weg
fertig	gebt

Übungen

The Modal Auxiliaries: *dürfen, können, mögen*, müssen, sollen, wollen*

Modal auxiliaries (sometimes called helping verbs) help to set the mood of the particular sentence in which they occur. Let's take one sentence in English and change the modal auxiliary.

He **is allowed to** go to the movie.	*Er darf ins Kino gehen.*
He **can (is able to)** go to the movie.	*Er kann ins Kino gehen.*
He **likes to** go to the movie.	*Er mag ins Kino gehen.*
He **must (has to)** go to the movie.	*Er muß ins Kino gehen.*
He **is supposed to** go to the movie.	*Er soll ins Kino gehen.*
He **wants to** go to the movie.	*Er will ins Kino gehen.*

As you can see, the meaning or "mood" in each of these sentences is different. The same is true in German. You will notice, however, that the word order remains constant in these sentences.

---

*Mögen is used most commonly to express liking or preference in the sense of *gern haben* (like to have), *gern essen* or *trinken* (like to eat or drink). Today it is quite frequently used in the negative, often without the main verb. *Er mag das Buch nicht.* (He doesn't like the book). A more common form derived from *mögen* is *möchten* (would like to). *Er möchte nach Deutschland fahren.* (He would like to go to Germany).

It is very important to remember that the infinitive is placed at the end of the sentence. The modal auxiliary appears in the position normally held by the verb when it is a single word.

Example:

		modal auxiliary		infinitive
statement	Paul	will	in die Stadt	gehen.
question		Will	Paul in die Stadt	gehen?

If a modal auxiliary is used with a verb containing a separable prefix, the prefix is not separated from the verb.

Examples: *Wir wollen Christine heute abend anrufen.*

Except for *sollen*, all other modal auxiliaries show a vowel change from the singular to the plural.

	dürfen may, be permitted to	**können** can, to be able to	**mögen** to like	**müssen** must, to have to	**sollen** to be supposed to	**wollen** to want to
ich	darf	kann	mag	muß	soll	will
du	darfst	kannst	magst	mußt	sollst	willst
er **sie** **es**	darf	kann	mag	muß	soll	will
wir	dürfen	können	mögen	müssen	sollen	wollen
ihr	dürft	könnt	mögt	müßt	sollt	wollt
sie	dürfen	können	mögen	müssen	sollen	wollen
Sie	dürfen	können	mögen	müssen	sollen	wollen

NOTE: A frequently used form of „*mögen*" is „*möchten*" (would like to). The verb forms are as follows: *ich, er, sie, es möchte; du möchtest; wir, sie* (pl.), *Sie möchten; ihr möchtet.*

Folgt den Beispielen!

1. Rainer will das nicht wissen.   Rainer will das nicht wissen.
   wir   Wir wollen das nicht wissen.
   ich
   die Studenten
   der Herr
   du

2. Kannst du das Buch lesen?   Kannst du das Buch lesen?
   wir / die Zeitung
   die Schüler / die Wörter
   ihr / die Ausdrücke
   Angelika / die Karte
   der Beamte / den Fahrplan

3. Ich muß die Verkäuferin fragen.   Ich muß die Verkäuferin fragen.
   die Mädchen   Die Mädchen müssen die Verkäuferin
                  fragen.

   Gerd
   ihr
   du
   der Student

4. Was soll ich denn tun?   Was soll ich denn tun?
   die Schüler / fragen
   der Junge / schreiben
   du / sagen
   wir / verstehen
   ihr / kaufen
   die Frau / wissen

5. Sie dürfen in die Stadt gehen.   Sie dürfen in die Stadt gehen.
   Diana und Angelika   Diana und Angelika dürfen in die Stadt
                         gehen.

   Peter
   ich
   Frau Müller
   du

6. Mögt ihr das nicht?   Mögt ihr das nicht?
   du   Magst du das nicht?
   Kerstin
   der Student
   die Jungen
   die Verkäuferin

7. Wir möchten ins Kino gehen.   Wir möchten ins Kino gehen.
   Frau Schulz / das Buch lesen
   ich / die Musik hören
   Angelika / die Karten kaufen
   die Schüler / den Film sehen
   du / nach Hause gehen
   der Student / die Aufgaben lösen

8. Willst du Rainer anrufen? (können)   Kannst du Rainer anrufen?
   Er muß bald im Büro sein. (sollen)

Möchten Sie ins Kino gehen? (wollen)

Könnt ihr das Buch kaufen? (dürfen)

Sollen wir hier sitzen? (müssen)

Ich will das nicht. (mögen)

9. **Supply the proper form of the modal auxiliaries as indicated in parentheses. Use these modal auxiliaries:** *wollen, sollen, können, dürfen, mögen, müssen.*

   1. Wann (want to) _____ du Ursula anrufen?
   2. Die Studenten (supposed to) _____ ein paar Bücher lesen.
   3. (would like to) _____ Sie den Film aus Deutschland sehen?
   4. Wir (can) _____ schon um vier ins Kino gehen.
   5. Ich (permitted to) _____ heute abend in die Stadt fahren.
   6. Stefan (like) _____ das gar nicht.
   7. (have to) _____ du eine Arbeit schreiben?

10. **Beantwortet die Fragen!**

   1. Was willst du heute nachmittag machen?
   2. Möchtest du ins Kino fahren?
   3. Kannst du den Koffer tragen?
   4. Darfst du zum Sprachlabor gehen?
   5. Sollst du schon um neun nach Hause kommen?
   6. Mußt du die Ausdrücke lernen?

11. **In the following sentences, provide the proper form of the modal auxiliaries as well as the main verb of the sentence.**

   1. _____ ihr die Musik _____ ? (want to hear)
   2. Herr Meier _____ bald in der Stadt _____ . (have to be)
   3. Wann _____ die Vorstellung _____ ? (supposed to begin)
   4. Ich _____ das Auto _____ . (would like to buy)
   5. Wir _____ die Fremdsprache _____ . (have to learn)
   6. _____ Diana die Tasche _____ ? (supposed to look for)
   7. Was _____ du auf der Uni _____ ? (want to study)
   8. Er _____ schon um neun Uhr _____ . (can come)
   9. Du _____ das nicht _____. (permitted to do)
   10. _____ Sie den Studenten _____ ? (can ask)

12. **Construct meaningful sentences using the information given.**

   1. Was / sollen / wir / heute nachmittag / tun
   2. Student / können / Bedeutung / nicht / verstehen
   3. Zug / sollen / halb zwei / kommen
   4. Mutter / müssen / in die Stadt fahren

5. Warum / wollen / du / nicht / Beamter / fragen
6. Ich / möchten / Wörterbuch / kaufen
7. Werden / ihr / zu Hause bleiben
8. Dürfen / du / Formel / gebrauchen

Future Tense

In trying to express events that will take place any time from the present, we may use the future tense.

Examples: I will read a book.
   Ich werde ein Buch lesen.

Similar to the modal auxiliaries, *werden* takes on the same word order.

	werden	
ich	werde	I will
du	wirst	you will
er **sie** **es**	wird	he will she will it will
wir	werden	we will
ihr	werdet	you will
sie	werden	they will
Sie	werden	you will

NOTE: If the sentence contains a reference to the future, e.g. ,,*morgen*" or ,,*nächstes Jahr,*" the present tense is used most of the time.

Folgt den Beispielen!

13. Sie werden nach Deutschland fahren.
      ich
      wir
      der Junge
      die Mädchen
      du

      Sie werden nach Deutschland fahren.
      Ich werde nach Deutschland fahren.

14. Wirst du die Verkäuferin fragen?
      er / die Wörter schreiben
      ich / den Ausdruck lernen
      wir / eine Karte kaufen
      Diana / Angelika anrufen
      die Schüler / die Bücher lesen

      Wirst du die Verkäuferin fragen?
      Wird er die Wörter schreiben?

15. Der Film beginnt um acht.   Der Film wird um acht beginnen.
    Jürgen klingelt an der Tür
    Dort ist immer viel Verkehr.
    Die Busse kommen bald.
    Ich verstehe die Beschreibung.
    Gehen Sie zu Fuß?
    Lernt ihr Deutsch?
    Wir üben die Wörter.

16. Change the following sentences from the present to the future tense.

   1. Wann arbeitest du heute?
   2. Die Jungen hören Musik.
   3. Jürgen sucht eine Kassette.
   4. Was zeigt der Computer?
   5. Ich verliere keine Worte.
   6. Dein Vorschlag ist ganz praktisch.
   7. Wir brauchen deine Hilfe.
   8. Oliver weiß sehr viel.

17. Answer each question by using the future tense.

   Beispiel: *Brauchst du eine Tasche? Ja, ich…*
                 Ja, ich werde eine Tasche brauchen.

   1. Hast du Angst? Nein, ich…
   2. Lernt Stefan die Vokabeln auswendig? Ja, Stefan…
   3. Kommt die Straßenbahn pünktlich? Ja, sie…
   4. Kauft ihr diese Karten? Nein, wir…
   5. Bist du gespannt? Ja, ich…
   6. Steht sein Auto vor dem Haus? Nein, es…
   7. Beginnt die Vorstellung um acht? Ja, sie…
   8. Verstehst du die Verkäuferin? Nein, ich…
   9. Gehen die Mädchen zu Fuß? Ja, sie…
   10. Wohnt Herr Braun in einem Mietshaus? Ja, er…

Personal Pronouns

Nominative (Third Person Singular)
In German, as you have learned in previous units, there are three personal pronouns *er, sie,* and *es,* which can be replaced with *der, die* and *das* respectively.

Der Junge ist hier.   *Er* ist hier. (he)
Der Zug ist hier.   *Er* ist hier. (it)

Die Frau ist dort.   *Sie* ist dort. (she)
Die Karte ist dort.   *Sie* ist dort. (it)

Das Mädchen ist da drüben.   *Es* ist da drüben. *(it/she)*
Das Kino ist da drüben.   *Es* ist da drüben. *(it)*

Accusative (Third Person Singular)

The accusative case for the pronouns *er, sie, es* is *ihn, sie, es*. Notice that only the masculine pronoun, i.e., *er*, changes to *ihn*. The other two pronouns *sie* and *es* have the same forms in the nominative as well as in the accusative case.

Er sucht **den Jungen.**
Er sucht **den Ball.**   *Er sucht* **ihn.**
Er sucht **einen Ball.**

Ich sehe **die Frau.**
Ich sehe **die Karte.**   *Ich sehe* **sie.**
Ich sehe **eine Karte.**

Wir finden **das Mädchen.**
Wir finden **das Buch.**   *Wir finden* **es.**
Wir finden **ein Buch.**

	masculine	feminine	neuter
nominative	er	sie	es
accusative	ihn	sie	es

Additional Personal Pronouns

In addition to the third person singular, of course, there are other personal pronouns. These, as well as the previously mentioned pronouns, are all included in the table below.

Singular		Plural	
nominative	*accusative*	*nominative*	*accusative*
ich	mich (me)	wir	uns (us)
du	dich (you)	ihr	euch (you)
er sie es	ihn (him, it) sie (her, it) es (it)	sie	sie (them)
		Sie (sg. & pl.)	Sie (you)

Folgt den Beispielen!

18. Sie suchen die Zeitung.   Sie suchen sie.
    Sie lesen das Buch.
    Sie schreiben den Ausdruck.
    Sie kaufen die Kassette.
    Sie brauchen das Telefon.
    Sie lernen die Aufgabe.
    Sie sehen den Bahnhof.

19. Brauchst du den Fahrplan?   Ja, ich brauche ihn.
   Verstehst du die Formel?
   Kaufst du den Koffer?
   Suchst du die Straße?
   Kennst du das Haus?
   Fragst du den Studenten?
   Lernst du die Seite auswendig?

20. Ich kaufe eine Karte.   Ich kaufe sie.
   Auto
   Pullover
   Buch
   Zeitung
   Fahrplan
   Cola

21. Er fragt _____ . (ich)   Er fragt mich.
   Suchst du _____ ? (er)
   Ihr schreibt _____ . (es)
   Wir verstehen _____ . (sie-pl.)
   Ich suche _____ . (du)
   Susanne kennt _____ . (sie-sg.)
   Er findet _____ . (ihr)

22. **Provide the pronouns for the nouns indicated in parentheses.**

   Beispiel: *(Karte) Er kauft _____ .*
       Er kauft sie.

  1. (Bahnhof) Suchen Sie _____?
  2. (Arbeit) Wir verstehen _____ .
  3. (Platzanweiser) Frag _____ doch!
  4. (Aufgabe) Schreibt ihr _____?
  5. (Mark) Brauchst du _____?
  6. (Junge) Ich mag _____ nicht.
  7. (Schlaukopf) Wir kennen _____ .
  8. (Buch) Kauft ihr _____?
  9. (Film) Werden Sie _____ sehen?
  10. (Café) Die Touristen wollen _____ finden.

23. **Supply the proper personal pronouns in German for those in parentheses.**

  1. Kann ich (you) _____ etwas fragen, Herr Peters?
  2. Wir werden (her) _____ morgen anrufen.
  3. Braucht ihr (him) _____ nicht.
  4. Sie werden (me) _____ nicht verstehen?

5. Sag (us) _____ das bitte!
6. Ich werde (you) _____ schon finden, Jörg.
7. Wir brauchen (you) _____, Petra und Andrea.

Verbs with Separable Prefixes

You can combine verbs with prefixes and thus change their meaning. In most cases such prefixes are prepositions, just as in English (to take — to undertake).

Examples: *(einsteigen) Sie steigt ein.* She gets in.
(aussteigen) Sie steigt aus. She gets out.

These prefixes, which you can add or eliminate, are called *separable*. The prefixes are separated from their verbs and placed at the end of the sentence.

Examples: *(anrufen) Angelika **ruft** um vier Uhr **an.***
*(fernsehen) Wir **sehen** heute abend **fern.***
*(mitkommen) Warum **kommt** ihr nicht ins Kino **mit**?*
*(einkaufen) Frau Müller **kauft** gern am Freitag **ein**.*

Folgt dem Beispiel!

24. Die Jungen kommen mit.
    fernsehen
    einkaufen
    anrufen
    einsteigen

Die Jungen kommen mit.

25. Complete each sentence by filling in the appropriate verb with its separable prefix.

1. (to call up) Warum _____ er nicht _____?
2. (to watch TV) Ich _____ gern _____.
3. (to get in) _____ Sie schnell in die S-Bahn _____!
4. (to come along) Wir möchten nicht _____.
5. (to shop) Was _____ du heute _____?

Er steigt in die Straßenbahn ein.

Lesestück 1

Bei Familie Höhne

Familie Höhne wohnt in Marzahn, einem Vorort von Ost-Berlin. Die Mietshäuser° in dieser Gegend° sind ganz neu. Herr und Frau Höhne und ihr Sohn Klaus wohnen erst ein Jahr hier in einem Mietshaus. *apartment buildings/area*

Jeden Tag muß Herr Höhne schon um sieben Uhr zur Arbeit gehen. Er arbeitet in einem Büro in der Stadt. Sein Auto steht vor dem Haus. Es dauert ungefähr fünfzehn Minuten bis Herr Höhne im Büro ist.

Klaus sitzt um halb acht am Tisch und frühstückt°. Ein paar Minuten später sagt er „Tschüs!" zu seiner Mutter und geht aus dem Haus. Die Schule ist nicht weit und er kann zu Fuß dorthin gehen. *has breakfast*

Frau Höhne arbeitet jeden Tag ein paar Stunden. Sie arbeitet in einem Café gleich um die Ecke. Nach der Arbeit geht sie oft einkaufen. Eine HO-Kaufhalle° ist in der Nähe. Dort kann sie kaufen, was sie für die Familie braucht. *supermarket*

Um ein Uhr kommt Klaus aus der Schule. Zuerst° muß er seine Hausaufgaben machen. Das dauert meistens° eine Stunde. Dann spielt er oft mit seinen Freunden oder auch gern mit seinen Autos. *first* / *mostly*

Was macht Klaus?

Klaus und sein Vater spielen ein Spiel.

Frau Höhne häkelt.

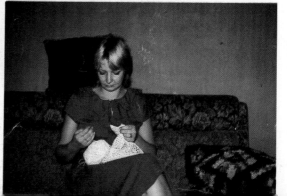

Herr Höhne kommt um fünf Uhr nach Hause. Dann möchte er immer zuerst die Zeitung° lesen. Eine Stunde später sitzen alle drei am Tisch und essen Abendbrot°. Meistens gibt es Kalte Platte°. Nach dem Abendbrot arbeitet Frau Höhne eine Weile in der Küche. Dort ist immer viel zu tun. Nach der Arbeit sitzt Frau Höhne gern im Wohnzimmer und häkelt°. Sie häkelt einen Pullover. Er soll in zwei Wochen fertig sein.

newspaper

eat supper/ cold cuts

crochets

Klaus und sein Vater spielen unterdessen° ein Spiel. Wer wird gewinnen°? Herr Höhne gewinnt meistens, aber manchmal hat auch Klaus Glück. Um neun Uhr muß Klaus ins Bett. Herr und Frau Höhne sitzen dann oft in Wohnzimmer und sehen fern.

meanwhile

win

Fragen über das Lesestück

1. Wie lange wohnt Familie Höhne schon in dem Mietshaus?
2. Um wieviel Uhr geht Herr Höhne zur Arbeit?
3. Wo arbeitet er?
4. Muß Klaus weit zur Schule gehen?
5. Wo arbeitet Frau Höhne?
6. Wo geht sie einkaufen?
7. Was macht Klaus nach der Schule?
8. Wann kommt Herr Höhne nach Hause?
9. Was macht er zuerst?
10. Was essen Höhnes heute?
11. Was machen Klaus und sein Vater später? Und Frau Höhne?
12. Was tun Herr und Frau Höhne nach neun Uhr?

Erweiterung

26. Wie heißt das auf deutsch?

1. Would you like to go to Germany?
2. The performance is very popular.
3. Can we sit here?
4. The newspaper is supposed to be well-known.
5. Is Mrs. Schmidt going shopping tomorrow?
6. I'm watching TV.
7. My birthday is…(Give your birthday.)
8. Today is…(Give today's date.)
9. I'm working downtown.
10. We eat supper at 7:30.

27. Welcher Tag ist heute? Heute ist der...

1. ninth of November
2. thirtieth of August
3. fifteenth of January
4. first of March
5. eleventh of June

28. Give the male or female counterpart including the appropriate article.

1. die Mutter - _____
2. der Sohn - _____
3. der Junge - _____
4. die Freundin - _____
5. der Großvater - _____
6. die Tante - _____
7. der Bruder - _____
8. die Enkelin - _____

29. Beantwortet die Fragen!

Welcher Film läuft heute?

Wie soll der Film sein?

Was machst du heute abend?

Welches Datum haben wir heute?

Hast du Brüder? Wie viele?

Hast du Schwestern? Wie viele?

Wohnst du in der Stadt oder in einem Vorort?

Wohnst du in einem Mietshaus oder in einem Haus?

Wo gehst du manchmal einkaufen?

Rückblick

I. Provide the article for each noun and then give the plural form.

Beispiel: _____ *Junge:* _____
der Junge: die Jungen

1. _____ Freundin: _____
2. _____ Kino: _____
3. _____ Tisch: _____
4. _____ Zimmer: _____
5. _____ Vater: _____
6. _____ Mutter: _____
7. _____ Büro: _____
8. _____ Kassette: _____
9. _____ Haus: _____
10. _____ Stadt: _____
11. _____ Sohn: _____
12. _____ Ecke: _____
13. _____ Bett: _____
14. _____ Land: _____
15. _____ Verkäuferin: _____
16. _____ Vorstellung: _____
17. _____ Film: _____
18. _____ Auto: _____
19. _____ Bruder: _____
20. _____ Buch: _____

II. Convert these sentences into commands.

Beispiel: *Sie sehen den Film.*
Sehen Sie den Film!

1. Ihr schreibt die Arbeit.
2. Du sitzt am Tisch.
3. Sie sind pünktlich.
4. Du hast keine Angst.
5. Ihr fragt den Platzanweiser.
6. Sie suchen den Platz.
7. Du verlierst keine Worte.
8. Du bist bald da.
9. Ihr kauft die Karten.
10. Sie kommen heute abend.

III. Restate these sentences in the negative.

1. Die Reise dauert sehr lange.
2. Die Vorstellung beginnt um sechs Uhr.
3. Ich brauche eine Kassette.
4. Sven ist Student.
5. Herr Höhne arbeitet in München.
6. Die Jungen spielen zu Hause.
7. Hast du Angst?
8. Sie geht heute nachmittag einkaufen.
9. Haben Sie ein Auto?
10. Verstehst du die Aufgabe?

IV. Match the last part (right side) with the first part (left side) to form a new meaningful noun. Also provide the article and the meaning of this noun.

1. _____ Nachbar _____	-brot
2. _____ Miets _____	-stelle
3. _____ Fremd _____	-sprache
4. _____ Schlau _____	-fest
5. _____ Geburts _____	-land
6. _____ Musik _____	-diele
7. _____ Sprach _____	-aufgabe
8. _____ Eis _____	-sportler
9. _____ Wohn _____	-tag
10. _____ Haus _____	-weg
11. _____ Groß _____	-vater
12. _____ Fahr _____	-kopf
13. _____ Abend _____	-stadt
14. _____ Halte _____	-haus
15. _____ Winter _____	-labor
16. _____ Feld _____	-zimmer
17. _____ Haupt _____	-plan

V. **Supply the missing months. Keep the proper sequence.**

Januar, _____, März, April, _____, _____, Juli, August, _____, _____, November, _____

VI. **Wie heißen die vier Jahreszeiten?**

Lesestück 2

Österreich

Österreich ist eine Republik. Das Land liegt in der Mitte von Europa. Österreich ist ungefähr so groß wie der Staat Maine. Es hat mehr als sieben Millionen Einwohner. Fast° 99% sprechen Deutsch als Muttersprache°. Sieben Länder grenzen an Österreich — die Schweiz, Liechtenstein, Italien, Jugoslawien, Ungarn, die Tschechoslowakei und die Bundesrepublik Deutschland. Österreich hat neun Bundesländer. Die Nationalfahne ist rot-weiß-rot.

almost

mother tongue

Österreich ist im Winter sehr beliebt.

In Österreich gibt es viele Berge.

Graz liegt im Süden Österreichs.

Lektion 5

Das Land liegt zum größten Teil° in den Alpen. Die Berge° *mostly/mountains*
verlaufen° von Westen nach Osten. Der höchste° Berg in Österreich *runs/highest*
ist der Großglockner. Er ist 3 798 m (Meter) hoch. Die Donau ist
der längste Fluß°. Sie fließt° von Westen nach Osten und hat in *longest river/flows*
Österreich eine Länge° von 347 Kilometern. *length*

Die Hauptstadt von Österreich ist Wien. Mehr als 20% der
Österreicher wohnen in der Hauptstadt. Wien liegt im Osten Öster-
reichs. Dort ist das Land flach°. Die Donau fließt durch° Wien. Im *flat/through*
Süden liegt Graz, eine andere große Stadt. Linz liegt im Nordosten.
Die Donau fließt auch durch Linz. Nach Wien, Graz und Linz
kommt Salzburg im Nordwesten. Salzburg ist eine beliebte° Stadt. *popular*
Viele Touristen kommen jedes Jahr im Sommer zum Musikfest° *music festival*
nach Salzburg. Innsbruck ist die fünftgrößte Stadt in Österreich.
Diese Stadt liegt im Westen und ist während° jeder Jahreszeit be- *during*
liebt. Besonders schön ist es dort im Winter. Viele Wintersportler
besuchen° dann Innsbruck und Umgebung°. *visit/area*

Der größte See° ist der Neusiedlersee. Er liegt im Osten. Es *lake*
gibt viele Seen in Österreich. Ein anderer bekannter° See ist der *well-known*
Mondsee. Er liegt im Nordwesten von Österreich. Im Winter wie
auch im Sommer ist Österreich ein beliebtes Ferienland°. *vacation country*

Fragen über das Lesestück

1. Wie groß ist Österreich?
2. Wie heißen die Nachbarländer von Österreich?
3. Wie viele Bundesländer hat Österreich?
4. Wie heißt der höchste Berg? Wie hoch ist er?
5. Fließt die Donau von Norden nach Süden?
6. Wo liegt Wien?
7. Wie heißen die drei größten Städte in Österreich?
8. Warum ist Salzburg so beliebt?
9. Wo liegt Innsbruck?
10. Ist Österreich nur im Sommer beliebt?

Sprachspiegel

I. Develop your own dialog using the information given strictly as a guideline. Be as creative as possible!

You suggest to your two friends that you go to a movie. Friend A wants to see a movie from France, but Friend B prefers one from Germany. Friend B wins this argument, especially since the tickets are cheaper. You inquire about the movie schedule. Friend B suggests that you go in the afternoon. The tickets will not be very expensive at that time. Friend A mentions that you should ask Friend C to come along. You talk to him/her over the phone, but s/he tells you that s/he has too much homework and won't be able to join you. Friend A indicates that you should take the streetcar, because otherwise you'll miss the early show. All of you agree and go to the next streetcar stop.

II. Describe what you do during a typical day. The description doesn't need to be long. Use the vocabulary and structure that you have learned so far. Your description should include the following information:

1. where you live (city/suburb, house/apartment)
2. time you go to school and how far you have to go
3. how you get there (car, walk, etc.)
4. how long you are at school and time you come home
5. what you do after school
6. time you eat supper and with whom
7. what you do after supper
8. when you go to bed

Wie sagt man's?

Wie alt bist du, bitte?
Fünfzehn.
Dann kannst du diesen Film sehen.

Ihre Karte, bitte.
Bitte sehr.
Sie können hier sitzen.
Vielen Dank.

Der nächste Film beginnt um sieben.
Warten wir doch hier!
Wir haben noch so viel Zeit.
Dann gehen wir jetzt ins Café.

Tschüs!
Wohin gehst du denn?
In die Kaufhalle.
Warte, ich komme mit.

Du hast immer Glück.
Beim Spiel schon.
Da hast du recht, aber nicht in der Schule.

Der Film soll klasse sein.
Das weiß ich. Da werde ich wenig verstehen.
Etwas Englisch verstehst du vielleicht.

Das ist meine Familie.
Sie ist sehr groß.
Das können Sie wohl sagen.

Der Film soll klasse sein.

Und wer ist das?
Mein Freund Herbert. Er kommt aus Wiesbaden.
Meine Eltern wohnen auch in Wiesbaden.
Wie interessant.

Was für ein Film ist es?
Aus Frankreich. Er spielt schon fünf Wochen hier.
Dann muß er ja ganz toll sein.
Das glaube ich auch.

Gehst du gern ins Kino?
Ja, besonders am Sonntag nachmittag.
Warum gerade sonntags?
Dann kosten die Karten nur fünf Mark.

Zungenbrecher

In Ulm und um Ulm und um Ulm herum.
(In Ulm and around Ulm and all around Ulm.)

Kulturecke

Entertainment and Leisure-Time Activities

Germans love to be entertained. This is obvious to the visitor who sees numerous posters announcing the various events taking place, particularly in the bigger cities. Besides these billboards, big, round columns (*Litfaßsäulen*) covered with posters can be seen in the streets.

The larger cities provide the most opportunities for different types of entertainment. Neighborhood movie theaters feature both German and foreign films. American movies are particularly popular. There are more than 185 theaters that receive subsidies from state and local governments. Many of the major theaters today, as in Düsseldorf, for example, have been built in striking contemporary styles. These major theaters offer a fantastic selection of performances that will suit almost everyone. Most Germans buy their theater tickets well in advance. Besides the indoor theaters, there are numerous outdoor theaters presenting plays during the summer months for local audiences, tourists and vacationers. Small-time entertainment is provided by young adults, particularly students, who play their musical instruments in major shopping areas.

Every large city has a zoo, and there are a number of American and European troupes touring the country every year. As in the U.S., German cities hold fairs at least once or twice a year offering carnival attractions of many types and the traditional rides for thrill-seekers.

There are numerous festivals in Germany throughout the year. These festivals always include a parade with local bands. Dressed in their folk costumes, these groups provide color and entertainment for the townspeople and visitors. The largest bands and crowds can be seen at the annual *Oktoberfest* in München, where over a million people congregate in an atmosphere that the Germans call *Gemütlichkeit*. The *Oktoberfest* takes place from late September to early October, but the famous *Karneval* in Köln is usually held during the month of February. Hundreds of thousands of people line the streets to witness the parade.

The German people enjoy many leisure-time activities. From September through May, millions of German fans watch the major and minor soccer matches throughout the country every week. During the summer, many Germans head for the water for swimming, sailing or fishing. Some rent boats of various types and explore the rivers and lakes on their own. Every city has one or more outdoor swimming pools that are modern and offer many facilities to the public. Germans also enjoy going to indoor swimming pools, especially during the colder season. The winter months offer other entertainment opportunities. Ice-skating, for example, has become very popular in recent years, particularly among the young. Furthermore, Germans head south to the mountainous area and go skiing — downhill or cross-country.

Every eighth German is a hiker. Major parks and forests have numerous hiking paths that are usually outlined on large boards right at the entrance of the path. Picnic facilities are also available along these hiking trails and are welcomed by those who spend several hours hiking. Bicycling has always been a favorite diversion among all age groups. There are many well-marked bicycle paths in the cities and towns and throughout the countryside. Some people enjoy horseback riding in the city parks and in the country.

People who don't care to exert themselves in active sports can stroll around in the beautifully landscaped parks scattered throughout Germany. After a long walk, it is no problem to find a place to sit down. Benches have been provided for people to relax and watch the world go by. Ice cream stands add further delight for people of all ages.

Outdoor cafés have long been traditional German gathering places. Here, people can order a cup of coffee or cola and sit for an hour or two without an obligation to order anything else. Outdoor chess games have become quite popular. Chess figures two or three feet high are moved on one-foot squares. Minigolf courses have sprung up throughout Germany. Unusual to Americans will be the concrete putting area. Most Germans consider yard work a leisure-time activity. Those who are not fortunate to have their own yard may have a *Kleingarten* on the edge of town. On this rented plot, they can spend hours and hours tending flowers, trees, fruits and vegetables.

Germans enjoy reading. There are newspaper stands all over. Many Germans, regardless of age, can be seen reading outdoors, particularly as they relax on public benches. As soon as the working parent comes home from work, it is quite customary to read the local paper.

The most common leisure-time activity in Germany is watching television. Although most Germans have a wide range of interests, more than one-fourth consider television viewing as their only pastime. Similar to American teenagers, many young people in Germany enjoy listening to popular music. Others learn and practice their own instruments, and a few play along with recorded music instruction. In all German communities, it is traditional for men to meet frequently at the local tavern to play cards.

Bicycling is a favorite German pastime.

Germans enjoy the rivers.

Germans head south to go skiing. (Alpen)

Some people enjoy horseback riding.

An outdoor swimming pool. (Kochel)

A map of the hiking paths. (Frankfurt)

You can camp all over Germany.

Vokabeln

das **Abendbrot** supper
die **Alpen** Alps
Amerika America
anrufen to call up
arbeiten to work
außerhalb outside
das **Auto,-s** car
bei at
das **Bett,-en** bed
    Er muß ins Bett. He has to go
    to bed.
der **Bruder,-** brother
das **Bundesland,-er** Federal District
das **Café,-s** café, coffee shop
das **Datum, Daten** date (calendar)
die **Donau** Danube
dorthin (to) there
dürfen to be permitted to, may
einkaufen to shop
    einkaufen gehen to go shopping
die **Eltern** (pl.) parents
der **Enkel,-** grandson
die **Enkelin,-nen** granddaughter
erst only, first
essen to eat
Europa Europe
die **Familie,-n** family
fernsehen to watch TV
fertig ready, done, finished
der **Film,-e** movie, film
frühstücken to have breakfast
der **Geburtstag,-e** birthday
die **Gegend,-en** area
die **Geschwister** (pl.) siblings
gespannt sein to wonder, be curious
gewinnen to win
der **Großvater,-** grandfather
die **Großmutter,-** grandmother
die **Großeltern** (pl.) grandparents
Grüß Gott! Hello!
häkeln to crochet
die **Hausaufgabe,-n** homework
    die Hausaufgaben machen
    to do homework
die **HO-Kaufhalle,-n** (government-owned)
   supermarket
hoch high
ihn it, him
Italien Italy
Jugoslawien Yugoslavia
die **Karte,-n** ticket
das **Kino,-s** movie theater
klasse sein to be great
können to be able to, can

die **Küche,-n** kitchen
laufen to run
leer empty
lieber rather
Liechtenstein Liechtenstein
Los! Come on!
    Los, kommt! Come on, let's go!
mehr als more than
meistens mostly, most of the time
das **Mietshaus,-er** apartment building
mitkommen to come along
möchten to would like to
mögen to like
müssen must, to have to
die **Mutter,-** mother
nochmal once more
oder or
der **Onkel,-** uncle
der **Platzanweiser,-** usher
der **Pullover,-** pullover
die **Republik,-en** republic
das **Schlafzimmer,-** bedroom
die **Schuld** fault
die **Schwester,-** sister
sein his
der **Sohn,-** son
sollen to be supposed to, should
das **Spiel,-e** game
spielen to play
die **Tante,-n** aunt
der **Tisch,-e** table
die **Tochter,-** daughter
toll fantastic, wild, terrific
der **Tourist,-en** tourist
Ungarn Hungary
unpünktlich late, not on time
uns us
unsere (form of *unser*) our
unterdessen meanwhile, in the
    meantime
der **Vater,-** father
die **Verkäuferin,-nen** sales clerk (female)
vor in front of, before
die **Vorstellung,-en** performance, show
weiß white
der **Wintersportler,-** winter sportsman
das **Wohnzimmer,-** living room
wollen to want to
die **Zeitung,-en** newspaper
zuerst first
zum (or: **zu dem**) to the

Lesestück

Ein Tag bei Grubers

Familie Gruber wohnt in Mülheim, einem Vorort von Köln. Sind Grubers eine typische deutsche Familie? Vielleicht. Herr Gruber steht schon um sechs Uhr auf°. Eine halbe Stunde später sitzt er in der Küche. Da kann er die Zeitung ruhig lesen. Frau Gruber deckt den Tisch°, kocht° Kaffee und wartet auf Heike und Kerstin, ihre beiden Töchter.

steht...auf gets up

sets the table/cooks

Heike, 16 Jahre alt, kommt zuerst in die Küche. Sie ist noch etwas müde°. Dann kommt Kerstin. Sie ist 13 Jahre alt. Kerstin ist auch noch nicht munter°. Um sieben Uhr frühstückt die Familie. Was gibt's heute? Brot° mit Butter, Marmelade, Milch und Kaffee.

tired

awake

bread

Um halb acht geht Herr Gruber zur Arbeit. Er muß nur zehn Minuten zu Fuß gehen. Etwas später verlassen° Heike und Kerstin das Haus. Heike besucht ein Gymnasium und Kerstin geht auf eine Realschule. Heikes Schule ist gleich um die Ecke. Kerstin muß mit der Straßenbahn fahren.

leave

Um halb ein Uhr macht Frau Gruber das Mittagessen°. Heike und Kerstin kommen kurz° nach eins aus der Schule. Das Mittagessen ist dann immer fertig. Heike und Kerstin sind sehr hungrig°. Sie sitzen in der Küche am Tisch und warten auf das Essen°. Frau Gruber bringt es auch bald. Heute essen sie Beefsteak mit Soße°, Kartoffeln°, Karotten, Erbsen°, und zum Nachtisch° Apfelmus°.

lunch

shortly

hungry

meal

gravy/potatoes
peas/for dessert/
apple sauce

Nach dem Essen macht Kerstin ihre° Hausaufgaben. Sie hat heute viel zu tun. Sie muß einen Aufsatz° schreiben. Das ist nicht so leicht. Später ruft sie Marion, ihre Freundin, an. Marion hat aber heute keine Zeit. Sie kann Kerstin nicht besuchen. Kerstin hat viele Kassetten. Sie hört gern Musik.

her

essay

Heike sitzt in ihrem Zimmer. Sie muß ein Buch lesen und dann viele Fragen beantworten°. Die Fragen sind sehr schwer. Heike ist erst um vier mit den Hausaufgaben fertig. Dann spielt sie gern Gitarre°.

answer questions

guitar

Um sechs Uhr steht das Abendbrot auf dem Tisch. Meistens essen Grubers Kalte Platte — Brot mit Butter, Schinken°, Wurst°, Käse° und Tomaten. Dazu° trinken sie Tee. Frau Gruber stellt° alles auf den Tisch.

ham/sausage
cheese/with it/
puts

Am Abend sitzen alle im Wohnzimmer. Was gibt's denn heute im Fernsehen°? Herr Gruber möchte die Nachrichten° im Ersten Programm sehen. Das interessiert Frau Gruber und Kerstin nicht. Heike zeigt auch wenig Interesse. Sie strickt° einen Pullover und wartet gespannt auf das nächste Programm — einen Spielfilm° aus Amerika.

on TV/news

knits

feature film

Fragen über das Lesestück

1. Wo liegt Mülheim?
2. Um wieviel Uhr sitzt Herr Gruber in der Küche?
3. Was macht Herr Gruber zuerst? Und Frau Gruber?
4. Wie alt sind die beiden Töchter?
5. Was essen sie alle heute morgen?
6. Muß Herr Gruber zur Arbeit fahren?
7. Wie weit ist Heikes Schule entfernt?
8. Um wieviel Uhr kommen Kerstin und Heike aus der Schule?
9. Was gibt es heute zum Mittagessen?
10. Was muß Kerstin nach dem Essen machen?
11. Warum kann Marion Kerstin heute nicht besuchen?
12. Was hört Kerstin gern?
13. Was muß Heike heute nachmittag tun?
14. Was spielt sie später?
15. Was essen Grubers zum Abendbrot?
16. Wo sitzen alle am Abend?
17. Was möchte Herr Gruber sehen?
18. Was macht Heike?

Übungen

I. Select the proper question word *(wo, wohin, wie, was, woher).*

1. _____ ist eine Eisdiele?
2. _____ kommen Sie, Herr Hoffmann?
3. _____ heißt das Mädchen da?
4. _____ wollt ihr später gehen?
5. _____ macht die Familie später?
6. _____ wirst du denn dort kaufen?
7. _____ fahren die Studenten?
8. _____ wartet Kerstin?

II. Beantwortet diese Fragen!

1. Wohin willst du später gehen?
2. Was möchtest du heute abend essen?
3. Wo kannst du eine Kassette kaufen?
4. Was sollst du lesen?
5. Was mußt du jetzt tun?
6. Wohin darfst du denn fahren?

III. Change the following sentences from the singular to the plural.

Beispiel: *Ich brauche den Fahrplan.*
            Wir brauchen die Fahrpläne.

1. Der Junge fragt den Beamten.
2. Suchst du die Kassette?
3. Der Student schreibt die Arbeit.
4. Wird er die Tante besuchen?
5. Das Mädchen spielt die Gitarre.
6. Der Tag ist sehr schön.
7. Kennt die Schwester den Onkel?
8. Die Vorstellung beginnt bald.
9. Der Film kommt aus Amerika.
10. Ich lerne die Vokabel.

IV. Provide the proper answer by selecting from the information listed below.

1. _____ ist ein Fluß in der BRD und fließt von Süden nach Norden.
2. _____ liegt in der DDR.
3. _____ ist die Hauptstadt von Österreich.
4. _____ liegt im Norden von Deutschland.
5. _____ ist eine Stadt und liegt in der Nähe von Wiesbaden.
6. _____ ist die Hauptstadt von Bayern.
7. _____ grenzt an die Schweiz.
8. _____ fließt durch Linz.
9. _____ ist die Hauptstadt der Bundesrepublik.
10. _____ ist ein Berg in Österreich.

Berlin	Bonn
Österreich	die Donau
Mainz	München
Wien	der Rhein
der Großglockner	Dänemark

St. Pölten, eine Stadt in Österreich

Was bedeutet dieses Schild?

Wo ist die Autobahn nach Kassel? (Würzburg)

V. Supply the correct form of the definite or indefinte article, where necessary.

1. Fragen Sie d_____ Platzanweiser!
2. Hast du ein_____ Idee?
3. D_____ Auto kostet viel Geld.
4. Wann kommt d_____ Straßenbahn?
5. Möchtest du ein_____ Buch kaufen?
6. Kann ich d_____ Fahrplan sehen?
7. Wo steht d_____ Computer?
8. Wir wollen ein_____ Film aus Deutschland sehen.
9. Der Schüler kann d_____ Aufgabe gut verstehen.
10. Herr Höhne wird ein_____ Zeitung lesen.
11. Kennen Sie d_____ Familie?
12. Sie häkelt ein_____ Pullover.

VI. Form questions by asking for the italicized words. Use the question words *wer, wen, was, wo* or *wohin.*

1. Wir verstehen *die Wörter* nicht.
2. Die Schüler warten *in der Schule.*
3. Stuttgart liegt *in Baden-Württemberg.*
4. *Herr Gruber* arbeitet in Köln.
5. Ich werde *den Beamten* fragen.
6. *Viele Touristen* kommen zum Musikfest nach Salzburg.
7. Wir fahren vielleicht später *in die Stadt.*
8. Andreas braucht *das Geld* nicht.
9. Angelika und Diana gehen heute *ins Kino.*
10. Er ruft *Jürgen* zu Hause an.

VII. Complete each sentence.

1. Dieser Film _____.
2. Verstehst du _____?

3. Er geht _____.

4. Um wieviel Uhr _____?

5. Jeden Tag muß ich _____.

6. Nach der Schule will ich _____.

7. Was machst du _____?

8. Wirst du später _____?

VIII. Situation A

Beckers möchten nach Deutschland fahren. Herr Becker will gern nach München in Bayern fahren, aber Frau Becker will lieber nach Köln am Rhein fahren. Herr Becker macht den Vorschlag: ,,Warum fahren wir nicht zuerst nach Köln und dann nach München?" Frau Becker ist das recht. Zwei Monate später kommen sie nach Hamburg. Von dort fahren sie über Hannover weiter nach Köln. Sie bleiben drei Tage in Köln und fahren dann über Stuttgart nach München.

Fragen

1. Wohin möchte Frau Becker fahren?

2. Wo liegt Köln?

3. Wohin kommen sie zuerst?

4. Wie viele Tage bleiben sie in Köln?

5. Wohin fahren sie zuletzt?

Situation B

Herr Wenzel arbeitet schon zehn Jahre in einem Büro in der Stadt. Jeden Morgen muß er schon um sieben Uhr sein Haus verlassen. Bis in die Stadt sind es nur fünfzehn Minuten. Er geht meistens zu Fuß. Es ist zu viel Verkehr in der Stadt und für sein Auto gibt es dort keinen Parkplatz. Er ist immer der erste im Büro. Herr Wenzel geht um vier Uhr wieder nach Hause.

Fragen

1. Wo arbeitet Herr Wenzel?

2. Um wieviel Uhr geht er zur Arbeit?

3. Wie kommt er in die Stadt?

4. Hat Herr Wenzel ein Auto?

5. Was macht er um vier Uhr?

IX. Substitute an appropriate pronoun for the italicized words.

Beispiel: *Der Zug* kommt in fünf Minuten.
Er kommt in fünf Minuten.

1. Wo ist *die Haltestelle?*

2. Kennen Sie *Herrn Fellner?*

3. *Das Kino* ist gleich um die Ecke.

4. Fragen Sie *die Verkäuferin!*

5. *Die Zeitung* kostet 80 Pfennig.
6. *Frau Höhne* arbeitet heute nicht.
7. *Der Student* studiert Mathematik.
8. Wir brauchen *den Koffer-Kuli.*
9. Verstehst du *die Frau?*
10. Ich lese *das Buch* gern.

Nützliche Ausdrücke

Here is a summary of some phrases that you may find useful to know when starting a conversation in German:

Sprechen Sie Englisch?	Do you speak English?
Verstehen Sie mich?	Do you understand me?
Ich spreche nur wenig Deutsch.	I speak only a little German.
Bitte, sprechen Sie etwas langsamer.	Please, speak a little more slowly.
Wiederholen Sie bitte!	Please repeat.
Ich verstehe Sie sehr gut.	I understand you very well.
Ich bin Amerikaner.	I am an American (male).
Ich bin Amerikanerin.	I am an American (female).
Woher kommen Sie?	Where are you from?
Ich komme aus...	I come from...
Ich bin seit zwei Wochen in Deutschland	I have been in Germany for two weeks.
Mein Name ist...(Ich heiße...)	My name is...

Ich komme aus Leipzig.

Cultural Notes

Greetings

Guten Tag! (Hello!)	is the most commonly used greeting throughout the day. *Tag!* is more commonly heard in conversations.
Grüß Gott! (Hello!)	is used by people in Southern Germany when greeting each other.
Grüß dich! (Hello!)	is frequently heard among young adults in Southern Germany.
Servus! (Hello!)	is used occasionally by young people in Southern Germany and Austria. Sometimes *"Servus!"* is used to say "Hello!" and "Good-bye!"
Grüzü! (Hello!)	is heard primarily in the northern part of Switzerland. It means the same as *"Grüß dich!"*
Guten Morgen! (Good morning!)	is used during the morning hours. *Morgen!* is more casual and heard quite frequently.
Guten Abend! (Good evening!)	is used during the evening hours until midnight. Many Germans, however, will simply say *'n Abend!*
Auf Wiedersehen! (Good-bye!)	is the most commonly used good-bye phrase. In conversation, Germans will simply say *Wiedersehen!*
Auf Wiederhören! (Good-bye!)	is used when ending a telephone conversation. It means "hope to hear you again." More casually, a person will say *Wiederhören!*
Tschüs! (Good-bye!)	is the most common good-bye phrase in Northern Germany. It is very casual, however, and only used among good friends and relatives. *Tschüs* originated from the French *adieu*.
Pfüat di! (Good-bye!)	is used mostly in Austria and means *"Behüt dich Gott!"*

Telephone

When answering the phone, whether at home or in the office, it is customary in Germany to give one's family name. *(Weber!* or *Hier Weber!)* Young people usually answer the phone with their first and last name.

When calling someone you know, you would say, *Hier ist...* If you don't know the person, you should start out with, *Mein Name ist...*

Asking to be transfered to someone else, the caller may say, for instance, *Guten Tag, hier ist Weber, ich möchte Herrn Müller sprechen, bitte!* or *Könnte ich bitte Herrn Müller sprechen?* or *Bitte verbinden Sie mich mit Herrn Müller.*

Company operators often answer calls with an additional *Guten Tag* or *Grüß Gott.* When transferring a call they will say, *Moment (Augenblick), bitte* or *ich verbinde* (I'll connect you).

The official word for telephone is *Fernsprecher,* but everyone says *Telefon.* The word for phone booth is *die Telefonzelle.* These public phone booths are easily recognized by their bright yellow color. There are always public phones in local post offices and railroad stations.

Most phones have dialing instructions clearly posted. In calling you should follow these steps:

1. Lift the receiver.
2. Put your coins in the slot (two 10 pfennig coins for local calls).
3. Wait for the dial tone.
4. Dial the number.

Long distance calls to other German cities or foreign countries can be made from any phone booth marked *Ausland*. Of course, these calls can be made from any post office, hotel or private phones. If you place a long distance call, you should know the *Vorwahl* or *Vorwahlnummer* (area code). In case you don't know this number, you can either look it up in a telephone directory or call the *Auskunft* (information). The number for the *Auskunft* is: 118.

Long distance calls are measured by units *(1 Einheit = 23 Pfennig)*. For instance, a person from Munich may call his/her friend in Hamburg for 1 mark but only be able to talk to him/her for a very short time. The caller must feed the coin-operated phone with additional coins, whenever there is little money left as indicated by lit-up numbers; otherwise s/he will be disconnected immediately.

ein
Fernsprecher

eine
Telefonzelle

Money

There are eight different coins in German money (BRD).

    1 Pfennig
    2 Pfennig
    5 Pfennig
  10 Pfennig (called *ein Groschen*)
  50 Pfennig
    1 Mark (100 Pfennig)
    2 Mark
    5 Mark

Deutsche Mark

There are seven different banknotes (BRD).

     5 DM (Deutsche Mark)
   10 DM
   20 DM
   50 DM
  100 DM
  500 DM
1 000 DM

Train Stations

In German train stations you will find two large schedules prominently posted. One is marked *Ankunft* (arrival), the other *Abfahrt* departure). There are several columns on the *Ankunft* schedule with the following heading: *Zeit* (time), *Zug Nr.* (train number), *aus Richtung* (from) and *Gleis* (track). The *Abfahrt* schedule indicates the same type of information for departing trains.

Tickets are bought at the window marked *Fahrkarten* (tickets). In case you have any questions you would simply inquire at the office marked *Information* or *Auskunft* (information). You could also ask the official *(Beamte)* in the blue uniform wearing a cap with a yellow band inscribed with the word *Information*.

der Hauptbahnhof in München

der Beamte

Streetcars and Subways

In most cities tickets for streetcars must be bought in advance. You can buy your ticket from an automat, which is usually right at the streetcar stop.

There are several German cities with subway systems (Berlin, Hamburg, Munich, Frankfurt). Some Germans buy their tickets from an automat if they travel by subway infrequently. Others have *Zeitkarten* (season or subscription tickets valid for a week or a month) which are used by daily commuters. In Hamburg and Munich, a practical system has been introduced; the same ticket is valid for all means of transportation — the subway *(U-Bahn)*, city train *(S-Bahn)*, streetcars *(Straßenbahnen)*, buses *(Busse)* and in Hamburg even river boats and ferries.

Purchase tickets at an automat.

eine Straßenbahn in Freiburg

Dialog

In der Bank

1. ANGESTELLTER:	Guten Tag!
DAME:	Guten Tag! Ich möchte Reiseschecks einlösen.
1. ANGESTELLTER:	Für welchen Betrag?
DAME:	100 Dollar, bitte.
1. ANGESTELLTER:	Kann ich bitte Ihren Paß sehen?
DAME:	Bitte schön.
1. ANGESTELLTER:	Vielen Dank.
DAME:	Wie steht der Kurs heute?
1. ANGESTELLTER:	Der Dollar steht bei 2 Mark 62. Gehen Sie mit dem Abschnitt an die Kasse, bitte.
DAME:	Hier ist mein Abschnitt.
2. ANGESTELLTER:	Wie möchten Sie das Geld haben?
DAME:	In Fünfzigern und Zwanzigern.
2. ANGESTELLTER:	50... 100... 150... 200... 220... 240... 260. Die Gebühr ist 2 Mark.
DAME:	So, jetzt kann ich wenigstens einkaufen gehen.
2. ANGESTELLTER:	Ja, mit dem Geld können Sie schon etwas kaufen.
DAME:	Das hoffe ich auch.
2. ANGESTELLTER:	Viel Spaß!

Fragen über den Dialog

1. Was will die Dame in der Bank tun?
2. Wie viele Dollar möchte sie einlösen?
3. Was will der Angestellte sehen?
4. Wohin soll die Dame mit dem Abschnitt gehen?
5. Wie viele Mark bekommt sie?
6. Was will die Dame mit dem Geld machen?

At the Bank

EMPLOYEE 1:   Hello!

LADY: Hello! I would like to cash traveler's checks

EMPLOYEE 1:   For what amount?

LADY: 100 dollars, please.

EMPLOYEE 1:   Can I see your passport, please?

LADY: Here you are.

EMPLOYEE 1:   Thank you very much.

LADY: What's the exchange rate today?

EMPLOYEE 1:   The dollar is at 2 marks 62. Go to the cashier with the slip, please.

LADY: Here is my slip.

EMPLOYEE 2:   How would you like to have the money?

LADY: In fifties and twenties.

EMPLOYEE 2:   50… 100… 150… 200… 220… 240… 260. The fee is 2 marks.

LADY: So, at least I can go shopping now.

EMPLOYEE 2:   Yes, with the money you can buy something all right.

LADY: I hope so, too.

EMPLOYEE 2:   Have fun!

Nützliche Ausdrücke

Wie steht der Kurs heute?	What's the exchange rate today?
Der Dollar steht bei…	The dollar is at…
Gehen Sie an die Kasse, bitte.	Go to the cashier, please.
Das hoffe ich auch.	I hope so, too.
Viel Spaß!	Have fun!
Er hat viel vor.	He is planning a lot.
Ich parke bei der Parkuhr.	I'm parking at the parking meter.
Wie ist die Auswahl?	How is the selection?
Sie begutachten die Waren.	They are looking the goods over.
Die Hose gefällt Heike.	Heike likes the pants.
Die Hose steht Heike gut.	The pants look good on Heike.
Ich bin an der Reihe.	It's my turn.

Sie begutachtet die Waren.

Ergänzung

1. Kleidungsstücke

Was hat er an?
Er hat einen Pullover an.
Was hat sie an?
Sie hat einen Rock an.

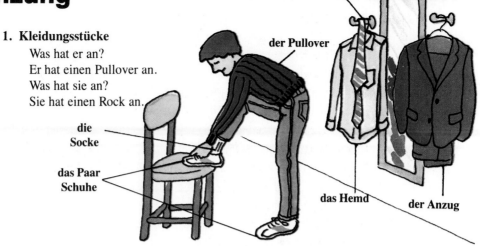

die Krawatte

der Pullover

die
Socke

das Paar
Schuhe

das Hemd

der Anzug

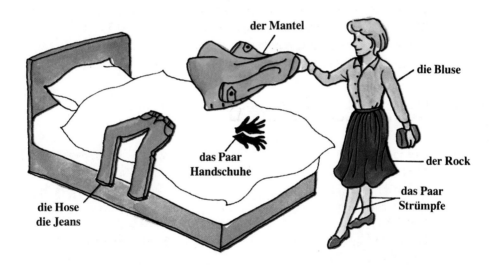

der Mantel

die Bluse

das Paar
Handschuhe

der Rock

die Hose
die Jeans

das Paar
Strümpfe

2. Farben

Welche Farbe hat die Hose?
Sie ist schwarz.

schwarz	grau
weiß	gelb
blau	grün
braun	rosa
rot	orange

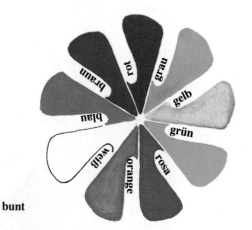

rot
grau
braun
gelb
blau
grün
weiß
rosa
orange

bunt

Ausspracheübung

/sch/		
schon	sprechen	Stadt
schnell	Spaß	Straße
schade	Sprache	Stunde
schwarz	später	Strumpf
schreiben	Spiel	stellen
Geschichte	Sport	Studium
Geschwister	gespannt	bestimmt
Vorschlag	besprechen	bestehen

Übungen

Dative

Indirect object

In the sentence *Ich kaufe ein Buch*, you know that *Ich* is the subject, *kaufe* is the verb, and *ein Buch* is the direct object or accusative. Now consider this sentence: *Ich kaufe dem Freund eine Karte*.

In this sentence *dem Freund* is called the indirect object or dative. Whereas *eine Karte* is directly connected with the action of the verb, *dem Freund* is indirectly connected with the verb and therefore called the indirect object. The easiest way to identify the indirect object is to determine if "to" or "for" can be put before the noun. In the above example, it would be "I am buying a ticket *for* the friend." (or: "I am buying the friend a ticket.")

	Singular			Plural
	masculine	*feminine*	*neuter*	
nominative	der	die	das	die
	ein	eine	ein	
accusative	den	die	das	die
	einen	eine	ein	
dative	dem	der	dem	den
	einem	einer	einem	

To form the dative plural noun an -*n* or -*en* is added to the plural, unless the plural noun already ends in -*n* or -*s*. The dative plural article is always *den*, regardless of the gender of the noun.

Folgt den Beispielen!

1. Ich zeige der Dame den Paß.
   Herr
   Mädchen
   Beamter
   Angestellter
   Verkäuferin
   Onkel

   Ich zeige der Dame den Paß.
   Ich zeige dem Herrn den Paß.

2. Geben Sie dem Bruder die Karte!
   Schwester
   Junge
   Platzanweiser
   Mädchen
   Dame
   Verkäuferin

   Geben Sie dem Bruder die Karte!
   Geben Sie der Schwester die Karte!

3. Wir zeigen dem Herrn die Stadt.
   Besucher
   Dame
   Tourist
   Student
   Frau
   Mädchen

   Wir zeigen den Herren die Stadt.

4. Gebt doch den Besuchern einen Fahrplan!
   Amerikaner

   Student
   Tourist
   Junge
   Dame

   Gebt doch den Besuchern einen Fahrplan!
   Gebt doch den Amerikanern einen
     Fahrplan!

Verbs Followed by the Dative Case

There are a number of verbs in German that require the dative case. Some of these verbs are *antworten* (to answer), *geben* (to give), *glauben* (to believe), *gefallen* (to like, please), *passen* (to fit, suit).

Examples: *Antworten Sie dem Herrn!*
               Er glaubt der Verkäuferin.

Folgt den Beispielen!

5. Glaubst du dem Jungen nicht?
   Amerikanerin
   Tourist
   Mädchen
   Schüler
   Frau
   Verkäuferin

   Glaubst du dem Jungen nicht?
   Glaubst du der Amerikanerin nicht?

6. Er antwortet dem Touristen.
   Student
   Freund
   Dame
   Verkäuferin
   Mädchen

   Er antwortet dem Touristen.
   Er antwortet dem Studenten.

7. Die Jeans gefallen dem Mädchen.
   Schüler
   Amerikanerin
   Verkäuferin
   Dame
   Tourist
   Besucher

   Die Jeans gefallen den Mädchen.

8. Construct meaningful sentences using the cue words given.

1. Ich / glauben / Dame / kein / Wort
2. Student / zeigen / Tourist / Stadt
3. Kaufen / du / Mädchen / Paar Handschuhe
4. Warum / antworten / Sie / Beamter / nicht
5. Wir / geben / Angestellter / Geld
6. Können / du / Herr / Zeit / sagen
7. Hose / passen / Junge / sehr gut
8. Stehen / Tante / Kleid

The Question Word: *Wem?*

You are already familiar with the question word *wer?* (who), which refers to the subject (person), and the question word *wen?* (whom), which refers to the direct object (person). The question word *wem?* (to whom or for whom) refers to the dative case (person).

Examples: *Sie glauben **dem** Mädchen. **Wem** glauben sie?*
*Wir kaufen **der** Tante eine Bluse. **Wem** kaufen wir eine Bluse?*

Folgt dem Beispiel!

9. Wem wirst du es zeigen?   Der Dame.
    (Dame)

   Wem wirst du es bringen?
    (Freund)

   Wem wirst du es sagen?
    (Verkäuferin)

   Wem wirst du es glauben?
    (Freundin)

   Wem wirst du es bringen?
    (Vater)

   Wem wirst du es zeigen?
    (Schwester)

Dative Prepositions

The dative case always follows these prepositions:

aus	out of, from
außer	besides, except
bei	with, near, at
mit	with
nach	after, to
seit	since
von	from, of
zu	to, at

Examples: *Er kommt aus der Schule.*
          Ich habe außer einem Bruder auch eine Schwester.
          Herr Schulz wohnt beim See.
          Kommst du mit einer Freundin?
          Wohin gehen wir nach dem Film?
          Seit einem Jahr wohne ich hier.
          Ich komme vom Kino.
          Sie fahren zum Bahnhof.

Contractions

These dative prepositions and articles are contracted as long as there is no special emphasis on the article.

bei	+	dem	=	beim
von	+	dem	=	vom
zu	+	dem	=	zum
zu	+	der	=	zur

Folgt den Beispielen!

10. Sie wartet beim Eingang.
    Kino
    Uni
    Kasse
    Bank
    Schule
    Haus

    Sie wartet beim Eingang.
    Sie wartet beim Kino.

11. Wohin gehst du? (Bahnhof)
    Wohin gehst du? (Bank)
    Wohin gehst du? (Haus)
    Wohin gehst du? (Schule)
    Wohin gehst du? (Universität)
    Wohin gehst du? (Eingang)

    Ich gehe zum Bahnhof.

12. Was kaufst du außer einem Anzug?
    Mantel
    Hose
    Buch
    Krawatte
    Hemd

    Was kaufst du außer einem Anzug?
    Was kaufst du außer einem Mantel?

13. Woher kommst du? (Haus)
    Woher kommst du? (Kino)
    Woher kommst du? (Schule)
    Woher kommst du? (Stadt)
    Woher kommst du? (Büro)
    Woher kommst du? (Bank)

    Aus dem Haus.

14. Was machen wir nach der Klasse?
    Film
    Vorstellung
    Schule
    Reise
    Kino

    Was machen wir nach der Klasse?
    Was machen wir nach dem Film?

15. Komm doch mit dem Freund!
    Komm doch mit dem Mädchen!
    Komm doch mit dem Jungen!
    Komm doch mit der Freundin!
    Komm doch mit dem Besucher!
    Komm doch mit dem Angestellten!

    Komm doch mit den Freunden!

16. Provide the proper preposition and the correct form of the definite article. Use these prepositions: *aus, außer, bei, mit, nach, seit, von, zu.*

1. Wir kommen _____ Geschäft.
2. Wohnst du weit _____ Bahnhof?
3. Ich bin _____ Monat Juni nicht mehr zu Hause.
4. Sie stehen direkt _____ Eingang.
5. Ursula geht _____ Freundin ins Kino.
6. Ich werde eine Karte _____ Herrn bekommen.
7. _____ Uni fahren wir _____ Eisdiele.
8. Parken Sie Ihren Wagen _____ Parkuhr!
9. _____ Geld kannst du bestimmt etwas kaufen.
10. Warum kommt ihr so spät _____ Schule?

17. Complete the following sentences.

1. Wir fahren mit _____.
2. Er kommt aus _____.
3. Antworte _____.
4. Kannst du _____ sagen?
5. Die Schüler gehen nach _____ zur _____.
6. Sie werden beim _____ warten.
7. Ich sage _____ auf deutsch.
8. Die Schuhe gefallen _____.

18. Beantwortet diese Fragen!

1. Mit wem kommst du?
2. Von wem wirst du etwas hören?
3. Wem paßt die Hose?
4. Wem zeigst du die Stadt?
5. Bei wem wohnst du?
6. Wem möchtest du die Karten kaufen?

19. Change the following sentences from the singular to the plural.

Beispiel: *Sie kommt aus dem Kino.*
  Sie kommen aus den Kinos.

1. Ich wohne beim Fluß.
2. Der Tourist kommt von der Stadt.
3. Glaubst du dem Mädchen nicht?
4. Das Kleid steht der Amerikanerin gut.
5. Der Beamte antwortet dem Besucher.
6. Er parkt das Auto bei der Parkuhr.
7. Der Schüler geht zum Zug.

20. **Supply the definite article for the dative or accusative. Contract the preposition and the article wherever possible.**

1. Geben Sie _____ Verkäuferin _____ Geld!
2. Sie kommen aus _____ Geschäft.
3. Die Studenten gehen mit _____ Kassetten zu _____ Sprachlabor.
4. Können Sie _____ Buch lesen?
5. Wir sagen es _____ Platzanweiser.
6. Sprechen Sie doch mit _____ Angestellten!
7. Kannst du _____ Schüler _____ Computer zeigen?
8. Die Touristen fahren zu _____ Bergen.
9. Was kaufst du außer _____ Bluse?
10. Bei _____ Besuchern gibt es immer viel Spaß.
11. Mußt du heute nicht zu _____ Uni gehen?
12. Und was macht ihr nach _____ Vorstellung?

Expression of Quantity: *Wieviel?* (How much?) — *Wie viele?* (How many?)

Generally speaking, *wieviel?* is used when expressing a mass or a sum.

Examples: *Wieviel Uhr ist es?*
Wieviel kostet der Pullover?

On the other hand, *wie viele?* is used when referring to items that can be counted.

Examples: *Wie viele Karten brauchen wir?*
Wie viele Freunde hast du?

NOTE: The words *ein paar* (a few) and *ein Paar* (a pair) also express quantity. Note that the "*P*" in "ein *Paar*" (meaning "a matching pair") is always capitalized.

Folgt dem Beispiel!

21. Wir kaufen *vier* Karten.   Wie viele Karten kaufen wir?
    Ich habe *etwas* Geld.
    Die Dame kauft *zwei* Kleider.
    Die Klasse beginnt um *elf* Uhr.
    Zehn Touristen fahren nach
       Deutschland.
    Drei plus fünf ist *acht*.
    Er braucht fünf Reiseschecks.

22. *Wieviel?* oder *Wie viele?*

1. _____ Zeit hast du morgen?
2. _____ Geld brauchen wir denn?

3. _____ Tage bleiben Sie in Europa?
4. _____ Studenten studieren in Würzburg?
5. _____ Reiseschecks wollen Sie einlösen?
6. _____ Krawatten wirst du kaufen?
7. _____ ist neun und acht?
8. _____ kostet diese Reise?

Compound Nouns

The article of a compound noun is determined by the article of the last word in the compound.

Examples: *der Nachbar, das Land = das Nachbarland*
die Reise, der Scheck = der Reisescheck
das Haus, die Aufgabe = die Hausaufgabe

23. **Match the words on the right with those on the left to determine the proper compound noun. Also provide the article and the meaning of each compound noun.**

1. die Straße		die Sprache
2. der Winter		der Anweiser
3. die Kleidung		der Sportler
4. der Platz		die Abteilung
5. die Dame		der Scheck
6. die Geburt		der Tag
7. die Mutter		der Schuh
8. die Reise		die Aufgabe
9. die Bank		das Stück
10. das Haus		die Bahn
11. die Hand		der Angestellte
12. der Abend		das Brot

Die Schweiz ist ein Nachbarland der BRD.

Lesestück 1

Heike und Birgit gehen einkaufen

Heike und Birgit gehen gern zusammen einkaufen. Zur Innenstadt° ist es zu Fuß zu weit. Deshalb° sprechen sie mit Heikes Vater. Herr Gruber hat heute sowieso° vor, in die Stadt zu fahren. Manchmal ist es nicht leicht im Zentrum einen Parkplatz zu finden. Heute hat Herr Gruber aber Glück. Er parkt den Wagen° direkt an einer Parkuhr.

Birgit möchte lieber im Kaufhof° einkaufen. Da ist die Auswahl immer groß. Herr Gruber will auch etwas kaufen. Er sagt den Mädchen, sie sollen in einer halben Stunde beim Eingang° warten.

Im Schaufenster° begutachten Birgit und Heike die vielen Waren. Birgit gefällt besonders eine Handtasche°. Vielleicht wird sie diese kaufen. In der Damenabteilung° findet Heike eine Hose. Sie ist rot und gefällt Heike gut. Birgit glaubt auch, daß die Hose Heike gut steht. Soll sie die Hose anprobieren°? Birgit zeigt auf den Preis. Die Hose ist sehr preiswert°. Heike zieht die Hose in einer Umkleidekabine° an°. Birgit muß zugeben°, daß Heike die Hose gut paßt.

Birgit möchte ein Paar Socken kaufen. Die Socken sind weiß. Sie sind auch nicht teuer°. Heike und Birgit gehen an die Kasse. Dort bezahlen° sie für die Hose und die Socken.

Herr Gruber hat vor, in drei Wochen mit der Familie in den Schwarzwald° zu fahren. Deshalb sucht er in der Bücherabteilung eine Karte von Süddeutschland. Er findet sie auch sofort° und wartet an der Kasse, bis er an der Reihe ist. Die Karte ist nicht sehr preiswert, aber auf der Reise kann er sie bestimmt° gut gebrauchen. Später kommen Herr Gruber, Heike und Birgit wieder aus dem Geschäft° und gehen zum Auto zurück°.

downtown

therefore

anyhow

car

name of department store

entrance

display window

purse

ladies' department

try on

reasonable/zieht… *an put on*/ *fitting room*/*admit*

expensive

pay

Black Forest

right away

undoubtedly

store/gehen… zurück *go back*

Soll Heike die Hose anprobieren?

Fragen über das Lesestück

1. Warum wollen Heike und Birgit mit dem Auto in die Stadt fahren?
2. Wo parkt Herr Gruber das Auto?
3. Warum kauft Birgit gern im Kaufhof ein?
4. Wie lange werden Heike und Birgit einkaufen gehen?
5. Was möchte Birgit vielleicht kaufen?
6. Was probiert Heike an?
7. Was muß Birgit zugeben?
8. Sind die Socken preiswert?
9. Was kauft Birgit? Und Heike?
10. Wohin werden Grubers fahren?
11. Was kauft Herr Gruber?
12. Warum muß Herr Gruber warten?

Erweiterung

24. Which word from the list best describes each statement?

1. Dort studieren die Studenten.
2. Ich muß da bezahlen.
3. Ein Zug kommt dort pünktlich an.
4. Wir probieren die Jeans dort an.
5. Dort werde ich Reiseschecks einlösen.
6. Ich brauche es. Dann kann ich einen Mantel kaufen.
7. Dort kann man Kleidungsstücke kaufen.
8. Mein Wagen steht dort.
9. Die Schüler lernen dort.
10. Viele wohnen da.
11. Die Straßenbahn steht da.
12. Dort gibt es viel Verkehr.

Bank
Geld
Innenstadt
Mietshaus
Universität
Umkleidekabine
Gymnasium
Haltestelle
Bahnhof
Geschäft
Kasse
Parkplatz

25. Write a sentence in German defining the following words.

Beispiel: *Kino*
> *Dort läuft ein Film.*

1. Büro
2. Fluß
3. Land
4. Kleidungsstück
5. Buch

6. Familie
7. Haus
8. Sprache
9. Koffer
10. Schule

26. Beantwortet die folgenden Fragen!

Beispiel: *Ist das Hemd weiß? Nein,...*
Nein, das Hemd ist nicht weiß. Es ist blau.

1. Ist die Krawatte bunt? Ja,...
2. Ist der Pullover grün? Nein,...
3. Sind die Handschuhe preiswert? Nein,...
4. Sind die Socken schwarz? Ja,...
5. Ist der Mantel teuer? Nein,...
6. Ist die Bluse braun? Nein...

27. Wie heißt das auf deutsch?

1. Go to the cashier's counter!
2. I would like to see your passport.
3. Do you have a slip (of paper)?
4. I'm wearing a suit.
5. Does she wear a blouse?
6. They would rather listen to music.
7. Wait at the entrance, please.
8. I have to admit that it fits well.
9. It's his turn.
10. We hope that, too.

28. Beantwortet die Fragen!

Wie steht der Dollar heute?

Was sollst du mit dem Abschnitt machen?

Wem mußt du das sagen?

Was hast du heute an?

Was möchtest du kaufen?

Um wieviel Uhr kommst du aus der Schule?

Was machst du dann?

Was ist sehr preiswert?

Und was ist teuer?

Rückblick

I. Form questions asking for the italicized words. Use the question words *wer, wen, wem* or *was*.

1. Wir zeigen *den Besuchern* den Computer.
2. *Der Zug* steht schon da.
3. *Wir* haben Lust, heute abend ins Kino zu gehen.
4. Du sollst *der Tante* das Wörterbuch geben.
5. Ich kann *die Bedeutung* nicht verstehen.
6. Peter wird *mit den Studenten* sprechen.
7. Marion und Angelika kaufen *eine Gitarre*.

8. Du mußt *dem Beamten* glauben.
9. Die Geschwister werden *beim Onkel* wohnen.
10. *Die Verkäuferinnen* gehen um fünf nach Hause.
11. Die Mädchen besuchen *Heike.*
12. Ich kann *Jürgen* kein Wort sagen.

II. Change the following sentences from the present to the future tense.

1. Der Film aus Amerika läuft lange.
2. Ist das der Dame recht?
3. Wir gehen heute nachmittag zur Bank.
4. Gewinnen Sie das Spiel?
5. Ich löse ein paar Reiseschecks ein.
6. Birgit und Heike geben zu, daß die Hose gut paßt.
7. Hast du keine Zeit?
8. Warum fahren wir nicht nach Deutschland?

III. Complete the sentences using the modal auxiliary given plus a verb form of your choice where needed.

Beispiel: (*wollen*) _____ *du ein Hemd* _____?
Willst du ein Hemd kaufen?

1. (sollen) Susanne _____ bis morgen das Buch _____.
2. (mögen) _____ ihr die Kalte Platte nicht?
3. (werden) Uwe _____ die Kassette _____.
4. (können) _____ Sie die Reiseschecks _____?
5. (wollen) Wir _____ kein Englisch _____.
6. (dürfen) Ich _____ um drei in die Stadt _____.
7. (müssen) _____ ihr schon so bald _____?

IV. Complete each sentence with the proper form of one of these modal auxiliaries: *dürfen, können, müssen, sollen, wollen.*

1. Könnt ihr heute nachmittag ins Kino gehen? Wir haben Lust, aber wir _____ die Hausaufgaben machen.
2. Zuerst muß ich das Buch lesen, dann _____ ich zur Eisdiele mitkommen.
3. Frau Müller, ich habe keine Zeit. Ich _____ nicht mit Gabriele in die Stadt fahren.
4. _____ du nach Deutschland fahren? Ja, aber eine Reise ist sehr teuer.
5. Dein Vater sagt, du _____ um zehn Uhr zu Hause sein.

V. Select the proper verb form from the list on the next page and complete each sentence. Be sure to separate the prefix, where appropriate.

1. Was _____ ihr heute nachmittag _____? Das wissen wir noch nicht.
2. _____ Sie doch _____ in die Stadt, Herr Schmidt! Wir werden ein paar Kleidungsstücke kaufen.
3. Ich muß _____, die Physikaufgaben sind sehr leicht.
4. Um sieben Uhr _____ ich _____. Der Spielfilm soll sehr interessant sein.
5. Paßt die Hose? Ich weiß nicht. Ich _____ sie lieber erst _____.
6. Der Zug steht schon da. _____ Sie bald _____!

7. Wo ist das Telefon? Ich will Werner sofort _____.

8. Ich _____ nur einen Reisescheck _____. Ich brauche nicht viel Geld.

9. Wo ist die Universität? Ich komme direkt aus der Stadt. Schade. _____ Sie _____! Die Uni ist nur einen Kilometer von hier.

10. _____ du lieber im Zentrum _____? Ja, die Auswahl ist dort viel größer.

anprobieren	einsteigen
einkaufen	anrufen
fernsehen	vorhaben
zugeben	zurückgehen
einlösen	mitkommen

VI. Supply the proper form of *kennen* or *wissen*.

1. Ich _____ nicht, wo sie wohnt.

2. _____ Sie die Amerikanerin?

3. Wie heißt das auf deutsch? _____ du das?

4. Wir _____ Würzburg sehr gut.

5. _____ ihr, wie das Mädchen heißt?

6. Willst du mit Ursula ins Kino gehen? Aber ich _____ sie doch gar nicht.

7. Jörg _____ nicht, was er jetzt machen soll.

Lesestück 2

Die Schweiz

Die Schweiz ist ein sehr beliebtes Land. Jedes Jahr kommen viele Besucher° in die Schweiz. Dieses kleine Land paßt ungefähr 190 mal in die Vereinigten Staaten (ohne Alaska und Hawaii). Die Schweiz ist halb so groß wie der Staat South Carolina. — *visitors*

Die Schweiz hat fünf Nachbarländer: Frankreich, Italien, Österreich, Liechtenstein und die Bundesrepublik Deutschland. Mehr als sechs Millionen Menschen° wohnen in diesem Land. 65% sprechen Deutsch, 18% Französisch, 12% Italienisch und 5% andere Sprachen°. Die Nationalfahne ist rot und hat ein weißes Kreuz° in der Mitte. — *people / languages / cross*

Der größte Teil der Schweiz liegt in den Bergen. Die Alpen erreichen° eine Höhe° von über 4 600 m (Monte Rosa). Der Rhein ist der längste Fluß in der Schweiz. Er fließt 376 Kilometer durch das Land und dann weiter durch die Bundesrepublik Deutschland und die Niederlande zur Nordsee°. — *reach/height / North Sea*

Die größte Stadt der Schweiz ist Zürich. Diese Stadt liegt am Zürichsee. Die zweitgrößte Stadt ist Basel. Wie Zürich liegt auch Basel im Norden der Schweiz. Der Rhein fließt durch Basel. Genf ist eine weitere Großstadt. Diese Stadt liegt im Süden am Genfer See, direkt an der Grenze° zu Frankreich. Bern, die Hauptstadt der Schweiz, ist die viertgrößte Stadt und liegt im Westen. Eine andere — *border*

Bern ist Hauptstadt der Schweiz.

Viele Besucher kommen im Winter in die Schweiz.

Basel liegt im
Norden der Schweiz.

große und beliebte Stadt ist Luzern. Diese Stadt liegt in der Mitte
der Schweiz.

Während der Sommermonate besuchen viele Touristen die
Schweiz sehr gern. Hier können sie viel in den Bergen wandern°.   *hike*
Besonders im Winter zeigen Besucher viel Interesse in die Schweiz
zu kommen. Während der Wintermonate ist die Schweiz ein Paradies für Wintersportler.

Fragen über das Lesestück

1. Besuchen viele Touristen die Schweiz?
2. Wie groß ist die Schweiz?
3. Wie heißen die Nachbarländer der Schweiz?
4. Wie viele Einwohner hat die Schweiz?
5. Sprechen alle Deutsch?
6. Ist das Land in der Schweiz flach?
7. Wohin fließt der Rhein von der Schweiz aus weiter?
8. Wie heißen die drei größten Städte in der Schweiz? Wo liegen sie?
9. Wie heißt die Hauptstadt der Schweiz?
10. Wo liegt Luzern?
11. Kommen Besucher nur im Sommer in die Schweiz?

Sprachspiegel

I. Write one or two paragraphs describing the following sequence of events:

You're driving to the center of the city to look for a bank. There is a lot of traffic, but finally you find a parking meter close to the bank. You go into the bank where you wait at a counter. Finally, it's your turn. You inquire about today's currency exchange rate and decide how many traveler's checks you wish to change. The clerk asks for your passport. S/he tells you that you speak German very well. S/he gives you a slip of paper and asks you to go to another counter. There you tell another clerk the denominations in which you would like to receive your money. S/he complies with your request and you thank him or her. Then you leave the bank and decide to do some shopping.

II. Answer the following questions with as much detail as possible.

1. Du hast 200 Mark. Was möchtest du kaufen?
2. Was hast du heute an? Welche Farben haben die Kleidungsstücke?
3. Wo gehst du gern einkaufen? Warum?
4. Probierst du gern Kleidungsstücke an? Warum? Warum nicht?

Die Mädchen gehen gern einkaufen.

Welche Farben haben die Blusen? (Bonn)

Wie sagt man's?

Ich möchte einen Reisescheck einlösen.
Darf ich Ihren Paß sehen?
Ja, hier bitte.

Der Kurs ist heute zwei Mark siebzig.
Gut. Dann löse ich 50 Dollar ein.
Bitte sehr. Zwei Fünfziger, ein Zwanziger und das Kleingeld.

Gibt es eine Bank in der Nähe?
Ja, direkt am Bahnhof.
Und wo ist der?
Gehen Sie Richtung Stadtmitte. Dann fragen Sie noch einmal.

Ich suche etwas als Geschenk für meinen Bruder.
Wir haben diese Krawatten. Gar nicht teuer.
Ja, sie sind sehr preiswert.
Möchten Sie die blaue hier?
Nein, geben Sie mir lieber die bunte.

Wo kann ich hier Bücher kaufen?
Suchen Sie etwas besonderes?
Ja, ein Wörterbuch.

Wie gefällt Ihnen diese Bluse?
Ganz gut. Sie ist aber nicht sehr preiswert.
Kommen Sie nächste Woche. Dann kostet sie nur 50 Mark.

Zeigen Sie mir bitte Kassetten!
Besondere Musik?
Moderne Musik aus Amerika.
Kommen Sie bitte hierher!

Wo bekomme ich einen Anzug?
In der Herrenabteilung.
Und eine Landkarte?
In der Bücherabteilung dort drüben.

Willst du die Hose anprobieren?
Sie ist viel zu teuer.
Aber sie steht dir gut.
Ich glaube auch.

KASSE

Ich möchte einen Reisescheck einlösen.

Zungenbrecher

Sieben Schneeschaufler schaufeln sieben Schaufeln Schnee.
(Seven snow shovelers shovel seven shovels snow.)

Kulturecke

Shopping

Americans planning to shop in Germany should become familiar with the German monetary system. There are six different bills: 500 marks, 100 marks, 50 marks, 20 marks, 10 marks and 5 marks, which is not much in circulation any longer. The denominations are easily recognized — the larger the size of the bill, the greater the value. There are eight different coins: 5 marks, 2 marks, 1 mark, 50 pfennigs, 10 pfennigs, 5 pfennigs, 2 pfennigs and 1 pfennig.

German shops are not open as many hours as American stores. Although stores are open Monday through Friday from about 8:00 or 9:00 A.M. until about 6:00 P.M., they close on Saturday at 2:00 P.M., except on the the first Saturday of each month and the four Saturdays before Christmas. Banks and small stores usually close for a two-hour break at noon.

Most Germans go shopping several times a week to take care of their daily needs. Signs posted outside the shops indicate what kind of commodity is being sold. Germans usually buy their breads and rolls fresh at the local bakery (*Bäckerei*). There are some 200 different kinds of bread (*Brot*), 30 kinds of rolls (*Brötchen oder Semmeln*) and no less than 1,200 different kinds of pastries. Wherever there is a bakery, the butcher shop (*Metzgerei*) is not far away. There are many different types of butcher shops, most of which highlight their own homemade sausages. There are more than 1,500 different kinds of German sausages — raw, boiled, smoked, seasoned in various ways and shaped in all kinds of forms.

Two thirds of all Germans like to do some of their shopping at the local market (*Markt*), which is usually in the vicinity of the main shopping area of the town or city. Market day (*Markttag*) is held once or twice a week. Germans prefer to buy their fresh vegetables and fruits at the market. And they love flowers. Therefore, it is not surprising to see colorful flower stands at every market.

Most of the shopping, however, is done in the supermarkets (*Supermarkt*) found throughout the country. At these chain-operated stores, the shopper can purchase all items necessary for daily living. The big, American-style department store (*Kaufhaus*) also plays an important role, particularly in the larger towns and cities. As a matter of fact, American influence is readily noticed in stores throughout much of Germany.

There are still differences, however. A *Drogerie* is not the same as an American drugstore. A *Drogerie* will sell toilet articles, household cleaners, baby food, camera supplies, wallpapers, paints and even seeds. It does not fill prescriptions, though, and you will not find a lunch counter or soda fountain either. An *Apotheke* (pharmacy) sells both prescription and non-prescription medicines.

To buy clothes and shoes, an American should study the German measurement system carefully. The measurements are considerably different and can easily create problems, unless there is some reference to the American system. In cities, you will find a great variety of shoe stores (*Schuhgeschäfte*) and clothing stores (*Kleidergeschäfte*). American-made jeans have been popular among Germans for many years. Every average-sized town and city has specialty jeans shops. The American influence on dry-cleaning stores becomes quite apparent. More and more Germans take their clothes to a dry-cleaner (*Reinigung*).

Germans enjoy more leisure time than ever before. Therefore, it is not surprising to find numerous stores catering to leisure-time activities. A store marked *Spiel und Freizeit* attracts that group of people. German parents buy many toys for their children. Numerous toy stores (*Spielwaren*) attest to that fact. Reading is an important pastime. There are many newspaper stands where local, national and sometimes international newspapers and magazines, as well as postcards and stamps are sold. Many bookstores (*Buchhandlungen*) display their books outside of the shop so that people can browse and decide which book they want to buy.

ein Kaufhaus (Heidelberg)

Die meisten Deutschen gehen ein paar
Mal die Woche einkaufen. (Freiburg)

eine Bäckerei (Essen)

Heute ist Markttag. (Freiburg)

Was kauft
diese Dame?

For the camera buff, German cameras have long been known for their superior quality. Camera equipment and film can be bought at camera shops (*Fotogeschäfte*) found all over. American music has always been popular with Germans. Record shops (*Schallplattengeschäfte*) sell many recordings of current American hits. These stores, of course, also sell audio cassettes and have added video cassettes in recent years. As a matter of fact, there are now specialty stores in Germany that rent video cassettes to the home market.

Every week millions of Germans participate in the various national lotteries ranging from the number lottery (*Lotto*) to the soccer lottery (*Toto*). They buy their lottery tickets in a *Lotteriegeschäft*. During the summer months, the highways are overcrowded because many Germans go on vacation trips. The travel business is brisk, and numerous travel bureaus (*Reisebüros*) offer specialty rates.

As a traveler, you will be impressed with the abundance of specialty shops. For example, candy stores offer a huge selection of sweets, both typical and exotic, to whet your appetite. You might come by a shop that sells only different kinds of teas (*Teeladen*) or a store that offers a variety of different kinds of fruits (*Früchtehaus*). And, finally, you may be in the heart of the Black Forest and stand in front of a clock shop (*Uhrengeschäft*) where the whole store front has been turned into one gigantic cuckoo clock.

ein Schallplattengeschäft (Neuß)

ein Lotteriegeschäft (Darmstadt)

Was kann man in diesem Geschäft kaufen? (Wiesbaden)

Vokabeln

der **Abschnitt,-e** slip (of paper)
der **Angestellte,-n** employee (male)
anhaben to have on
anprobieren to try on
anziehen to put on (clothes)
der **Anzug,-̈e** suit
außer besides, except
die **Auswahl** selection, choice
die **Bank,-en** bank
begutachten to look over, evaluate
bestimmt undoubtedly, certainly
der **Betrag,-̈e** amount
bezahlen to pay
bitte please
blau blue
die **Bluse,-n** blouse
braun brown
die **Bücherabteilung,-en** book department
bunt colorful
die **Dame,-n** lady
die **Damenabteilung,-en**
     ladies' department
daß that
deshalb therefore
direkt direct, immediate, straight
der **Dollar,-s** dollar
der **Eingang,-̈e** entrance
einlösen to cash (in)
die **Farbe,-n** color
Französisch French (language)
die **Gebühr,-en** fee
gefallen to like
     Es gefällt mir. I like it.
gelb yellow
das **Geschäft,-e** store
grau gray
grün green
der **Handschuh,-e** glove
die **Handtasche,-n** purse
das **Hemd,-en** shirt
hoffen to hope
die **Hose,-n** pants, slacks
Ihr your (formal)
die **Innenstadt,-̈e** downtown, center of city
Italienisch Italian (language)
die **Jeans** (pl.) jeans
die **Kalte Platte** cold-cut platter
die **Karte,-n** map
die **Kasse,-n** cashier's counter
der **Kaufhof** name of department store
das **Kleid,-er** dress
das **Kleidungsstück,-e** article of clothing
die **Krawatte,-n** tie
der **Kurs,-e** exchange

der **Mantel,-̈** coat
orange orange
das **Paar,-e** pair
das **Paradies,-e** paradise
parken to park
der **Parkplatz,-̈e** parking space, parking lot
die **Parkuhr,-en** parking meter
der **Paß,-̈sse** passport
der **Preis,-e** price
preiswert reasonable
die **Reihe,-n** row
     Er ist an der Reihe. It's his turn.
der **Reisescheck,-s** traveler's check
der **Rock,-̈e** skirt
rosa pink
das **Schaufenster,-** display window
der **Schuh,-e** shoe
der **Schwarzwald** Black Forest
die **Socke,-n** sock
sofort right away, immediately
der **Sommermonat,-e** summer month
sowieso anyhow, anyway
der **Spaß** fun
     Viel Spaß! Have fun!
der **Strumpf,-̈e** stocking
teuer expensive
die **Umkleidekabine,-n** fitting room
vorhaben to plan, intend
der **Wagen,-** car
die **Ware,-n** product, goods
wenigstens at least
der **Wintermonat,-e** winter month
zeigen auf to point to
das **Zentrum,-tren** center
zugeben to admit
zurückgehen to go back

Dialog

Im Hotel

FRAU BINDER:	Endlich sind wir da!
HERR BINDER:	Ich kann gleich hier beim Eingang parken.
FRAU BINDER:	Hast du das Gepäck?
HERR BINDER:	Was heißt Gepäck? Wir haben nur einen Koffer. Ich bringe ihn gleich mit.
FRAU BINDER:	Das stimmt. Wir bleiben ja nur zwei Tage hier.
JAN BINDER:	Das Hotel ist aber toll! Ganz elegant!
HERR BINDER:	Kommt! Gehen wir hinein!
HERR BINDER:	Haben Sie noch Zimmer frei? Wir sind drei Personen.
ANGESTELLTE:	Für drei Personen? Ja, das geht. Bitte füllen Sie das Anmeldeformular aus.
FRAU BINDER:	Du meine Güte! Was Sie alles wissen wollen!
ANGESTELLTE:	So, hier ist Ihr Zimmerschlüssel. Sie haben Zimmer 28. Fahren Sie am besten mit dem Fahrstuhl. Oder warten Sie! Ich komme mit und zeige Ihnen das Zimmer.
ANGESTELLTE:	Zimmer 28, bitte schön.
FRAU BINDER:	Es sieht ja ganz gemütlich aus.
JAN BINDER:	Aber das Beste ist doch der Fernsehapparat.

Fragen über den Dialog

1. Wo parkt Herr Binder?
2. Wie viele Koffer haben Binders?
3. Wie viele Tage wollen sie im Hotel bleiben?
4. Was muß Herr Binder ausfüllen?
5. Wie kommen Binders zum Zimmer 28?
6. Wer zeigt Binders das Zimmer?
7. Wie sieht das Zimmer aus?
8. Was gefällt Jan?

In the Hotel

MRS. BINDER: We are finally here.

MR. BINDER: I can park right here at the entrance.

MRS. BINDER: Do you have the luggage?

MR. BINDER: What do you mean by luggage? We only have one suitcase. I'll bring it along right away.

MRS. BINDER: That's true. We'll stay here for only two days.

JAN BINDER: Wow, the hotel is great. Very elegant.

MR. BINDER: Come on. Let's go inside.

MR. BINDER: Do you still have rooms? There are three of us.

CLERK: For three persons? Yes, that's possible. Please fill out the registration form.

MRS. BINDER: My goodness! All the details you want to know.

CLERK: So, here is your room key. You have Room 28. It's best that you take the elevator. Or wait! I'll come along and show you the room.

CLERK: Here you are, Room 28.

MRS. BINDER: It looks quite pleasant.

JAN BINDER: But the best is still the TV set.

Nützliche Ausdrücke

Das stimmt.	That's true. That's right.
Gehen wir hinein!	Let's go inside.
Das geht.	That's possible.
Füllen Sie das Formular aus!	Fill out the form!
Du meine Güte!	My goodness!
Gehen Sie am besten…	It's best that you go…
Es sieht ganz gemütlich aus.	It looks quite pleasant.
Er stempelt den Ausweis.	He stamps the identification card.
Sie bereiten das Essen zu.	They prepare the meal.
Sie essen dasselbe.	They eat the same.
Wir machen einen Klassenausflug.	We are going on a class trip.
Ich habe Hunger.	I'm hungry.
Räumt das Geschirr ab!	Clear the dishes!
Macht die Tische sauber!	Clean the tables!

Sie macht den Tisch sauber.

Ergänzung

1. Wie ist das Wetter heute?

Es ist kalt. (kühl, warm, heiß)
Es ist schön. (schlecht)
Die Sonne scheint. (Es regnet. Es schneit.)

Es ist kalt.

Es ist heiß.

2. Verkehrsmittel

das Schiff

das Flugzeug

die Straßenbahn

der Bus

der Zug

das Fahrrad

das Boot

das Motorrad

das Auto

149

Aussprecheübung

short / ü /	long / ü /
Glück	drüben
müssen	Übung
fünf	kühl
Flüsse	Brüder
pünktlich	Schüler
dürft	Süden
gründlich	Züge
Jürgen	für
Küche	Bücher
Würste	Frühling
zurück	Güte
Günter	Tür

Übungen

Dative (Indirect Object) — Personal Pronouns

As you have already seen in the previous unit, the direct object (accusative) is the result of the action (verb) of the sentence, whereas the indirect object receives the action indirectly through the direct object.

Examples:

	dir. obj.	
Ich kaufe	eine Karte	

	indir. obj.	dir. obj.
Ich kaufe	dem Freund	eine Karte

Now substitute a personal pronoun for the indirect object in the last sentence.

	indir. obj	dir. obj.
Ich kaufe	ihm	eine Karte

Notice that there is no change in word order but simply a substitution of an indirect (dative) object pronoun. For review, the pronouns you have already learned are *also* included in the table following.

150

	Singular			Plural	
nominative	accusative	dative	nominative	accusative	dative
ich	mich	mir	wir	uns	uns
du	dich	dir	ihr	euch	euch
er sie es	ihn sie es	ihm ihr ihm	sie Sie(sg. & pl.)	sie Sie	ihnen Ihnen

Folgt den Beispielen!

1. Bringst du dem Touristen das Gepäck?   Ja, ich bringe ihm das Gepäck.
   Bringst du der Verkäuferin das Geld?
   Bringst du der Mutter die Zeitung?
   Bringst du der Freundin die
       Reiseschecks?
   Bringst du dem Bruder den Anzug?

2. Zeig dem Schüler doch das Wörterbuch!   Zeig ihm doch das Wörterbuch!
   Zeig dem Besucher doch den Fahrplan!
   Zeig der Angestellten doch die Hose!
   Zeig dem Lehrer doch die Aufgabe!
   Zeig dem Studenten doch die Kassette!
   Zeig der Dame doch die Straße!

3. Kauft er mir ein Hemd?   Kauft er mir ein Hemd?
       ihr   Kauft er euch ein Hemd?
       Sie (form.)
       sie (sg.)
       du
       wir

4. Geben sie uns etwas Zeit?   Geben sie uns etwas Zeit?
       ich   Geben sie mir etwas Zeit?
       ihr
       Sie (form.)
       er
       sie (sg.)

5. Es geht ihm gut.   Es geht ihm gut.
       wir   Es geht uns gut.
       du

ihr
Sie (form.)
sie (sg.)

6. Die Hose steht dir gut.   Die Hose steht dir gut.
   das Kleid / sie (sg.)   Das Kleid steht ihr gut.
   der Mantel / ich
   das Hemd / er
   die Bluse / Sie (form.)
   der Rock / du

7. Sprechen Sie mit der Dame!   Sprechen Sie mit ihr!
   Sprechen Sie mit dem Herrn!
   Sprechen Sie mit dem Angestellten!
   Sprechen Sie mit dem Studenten!
   Sprechen Sie mit der Verkäuferin!
   Sprechen Sie mit der Schwester!

8. Wohnt der Amerikaner bei Ihnen?   Wohnt der Amerikaner bei Ihnen?
   er   Wohnt der Amerikaner bei ihm?
   wir
   ihr
   sie (sg.)

9. Er kauft die Gitarre von mir.   Er kauft die Gitarre von mir.
   die Karte / wir   Er kauft die Karte von uns.
   das Fahrrad / du
   das Buch / ihr
   der Pullover / Sie (form.)
   die Bluse / sie (sg.)

10. Sollen wir mit dem Jungen spielen?   Sollen wir mit ihm spielen?
    Darf ich bei der Tante wohnen?
    Wollt ihr zu der Dame kommen?
    Werden Sie bei den Freunden bleiben?
    Möchtest du zu der Großmutter fahren?
    Wird er mit dem Lehrer sprechen?

11. Change the italicized nouns with their corresponding articles into pronouns.

      Beispiel: *Ich zeige **dem Touristen** die Stadt.*
                   *Ich zeige **ihm** die Stadt.*

1. Petra kauft *der Freundin* eine Bluse.
2. Ich glaube *dem Herrn* nicht.
3. Kannst du *der Dame* die Zeitung bringen?
4. Wie oft kommt ihr zu *der Tante?*

5. Herr Hoffmann wohnt schon zwei Wochen bei *dem Amerikaner.*
6. Antworte *dem Lehrer* doch!
7. Er wird *der Dame* die Tasche bringen.
8. Die Kleidungsstücke gefallen *den Besuchern.*
9. Wir gehen mit *dem Onkel* ins Kino.
10. Außer *den Jungen* kommen noch viele Mädchen.

12. Supply the appropriate missing pronoun.

1. Geben Sie (me) _____ fünf Mark bitte!
2. Ich zeige (you) _____ den Weg, Herr Schulz.
3. Glaubst du (her) _____ nicht, Angelika?
4. Der Lehrer wird mit (you) _____ sprechen, Jan und Heiko.
5. Sie wohnen bei (us) _____.
6. Wir möchten es (them) _____ sagen.
7. Er kann (you) _____ das nicht kaufen, Ursula.
8. Die Schüler antworten (him) _____ nicht.

13. Answer the following questions. Use a personal pronoun in your answer.

1. Gehst du mit dem Freund in die Stadt?
2. Kaufst du der Schwester eine Tasche?
3. Zeigst du dem Studenten das Gebäude?
4. Antwortest du dem Beamten?
5. Glaubst du der Verkäuferin?
6. Gefallen den Amerikanern die Berge?
7. Fahrt ihr zu der Tante?
8. Wer kommt außer dir noch mit?

Verbs with Stem Vowel Change

A number of verbs in German do not follow the regular pattern of conjugation but undergo a change in the second and third person singular. You will become familiar with two such groups of verbs, one changing from *a* to *ä*, the other one from *e* to *i* (or *ie*).

Stem vowel change *a* to *ä*
Here are the verbs with vowel changes that you already know.

	du	er, sie, es
fahren	fährst	fährt
tragen	trägst	trägt
verlassen	verläßt	verläßt

NOTE: When forming command forms, the familiar singular command form does not have a vowel change. For example, *Fahr nach Hause! Trag den Koffer!*

Stem vowel change *e* to *i* and *e* to *ie*

Here are the verbs with vowel changes that you already know.

	du	er, sie, es
essen	ißt	ißt
geben	gibst	gibt
sprechen	sprichst	spricht
lesen	liest	liest
sehen	siehst	sieht

Only the basic verbs (without prefixes) are listed. Verbs with separable or inseparable prefixes such as *fernsehen* or *zugeben* have the same forms as *sehen* or *geben* plus their respective prefix.

Folgt den Beispielen!

14. Wohin fährst du?   Wohin fährst du?
    Peter   Wohin fährt Peter?
    ihr
    der Zug
    wir
    die S-Bahn

15. Ich trage den Koffer.   Ich trage den Koffer.
    er   Er trägt den Koffer.
    wir
    der Tourist
    ihr
    du

16. Er verläßt bald das Haus.   Er verläßt bald das Haus.
    die Mutter   Die Mutter verläßt bald das Haus.
    ich
    der Lehrer
    wir
    der Student

17. Wir sprechen Deutsch.   Wir sprechen Deutsch.
    der Herr   Der Herr spricht Deutsch.
    ihr
    die Amerikanerin
    du
    ich

18. Ich sehe gern fern.   Ich sehe gern fern.
    Jürgen   Jürgen sieht gern fern.
    wir
    die Familie

ihr
das Mädchen

19. Um wieviel Uhr essen wir?   Um wieviel Uhr essen wir?
    die Jugendlichen   Um wieviel Uhr essen die Jugendlichen?
    ihr
    du
    Herr und Frau Binder
    er

20. Was lesen Sie denn?   Was lesen Sie denn?
    die Schüler   Was lesen die Schüler denn?
    du
    der Student
    ihr
    die Dame

21. Complete each sentence by providing the appropriate verb form as indicated in parentheses.

  1. Die Angestellte (to speak) _____ Englisch.
  2. Herr Binder (to eat) _____ schon um fünf Abendbrot.
  3. (to give) _____ mir bitte etwas Geld, Susanne.
  4. Die Studenten (to read) _____ das Buch sehr gern.
  5. Der Junge (to admit) _____ es nicht _____.
  6. Um wieviel Uhr willst du (to watch TV) _____?
  7. Was (to carry) _____ du denn?
  8. Die Kleidungsstücke (to like) _____ mir sehr.
  9. (to see) _____ Sie die Straßenbahn?
10. Frau Reuter (to leave) _____ am Dienstag das Hotel.

Was ißt die Familie zum Abendbrot?

Lesestück 1

In der Jugendherberge

Es gibt mehr als 600 Jugendherbergen in der Bundesrepublik. Alle diese Jugendherbergen stehen in dem Buch „Deutsches Jugendherbergsverzeichnis"°. In den meisten Städten sieht man Schilder° mit dem Wort „Jugendherberge". Man braucht nur diesen Schildern zu folgen°, um eine Jugendherberge zu finden.

Register of German youth hostels/signs

follow

Viele Jugendliche° kommen mit dem Bus, mit dem Zug oder mit dem Auto. Nur wenige° kommen heute noch mit Motorrädern oder mit Fahrrädern. Für die Übernachtung° muß man einen Jugendherbergsausweis° haben. Der Herbergsvater° stempelt den Ausweis gleich nach der Ankunft° und zeigt den Jugendlichen die Zimmer, wo sie übernachten°. Viele Zimmer haben vier bis acht Betten.

young people
a few
accomodation
youth hostel ID/ hostel director/ arrival
stay overnight

Man kann in einer Jugendherberge auch essen. Man bereitet das Essen in der Küche zu. Die Übernachtung und das Essen sind in einer Jugendherberge sehr preiswert. Die Jugendlichen essen in einem Speisesaal°. Natürlich gibt es keine Auswahl. Alle essen dasselbe. Viele Schüler machen Klassenausflüge zu den Jugendherbergen. Da kommen immer Lehrer° mit. Manchmal haben die Jugendlichen noch Hunger. Dann gehen sie zur Essenausgabe°. Dort bekommen sie noch etwas.

dining hall

teachers
serving counter

Die Jugendlichen essen in einem Speisesaal.

Eine Jugendherberge in Bonn

Viele Zimmer haben vier bis acht Betten.

156

Nach dem Essen räumen ein paar Jugendliche das Geschirr ab und bringen es in die Küche. Andere machen die Tische sauber. In einer Jugendherberge gibt es vieles°, was die Jugendlichen tun können. Einige° spielen immer wieder an den Automaten. Sie sind besonders beliebt. Andere spielen Schach°. Bei diesem Spiel muß man sehr viel denken°. Manche Jugendliche gehen lieber ins Freie°. Dort spielen sie Tischtennis° oder Fußball°.

many things
several
chess
think
outside/
table tennis/soccer

In einer Jugendherberge gibt es auch einen Briefkasten°, einen Briefmarkenautomaten°, Automaten für Getränke° und Süßigkeiten° und eine Telefonzelle°.

mailbox
stamp automat/
beverages
sweets/phone booth

Fragen über das Lesestück

1. Wie kann man eine Jugendherberge in einer Stadt finden?
2. Wie kommen die Jugendlichen zu den Jugendherbergen?
3. Was braucht man für eine Übernachtung?
4. Wie wissen die Jugendlichen, wo sie in der Jugendherberge übernachten?
5. Ist das Essen in der Jugendherberge teuer?
6. Wer kommt bei den Klassenausflügen mit?
7. Wo bekommen die Jugendlichen das Essen?
8. Wohin bringen die Jugendlichen das Geschirr?
9. Was können die Jugendlichen alles in einer Jugendherberge tun?
10. Was gibt es in einer Jugendherberge für die Briefe?

Erweiterung

22. *Wie ist das Wetter heute?* Provide the answers in German as indicated.

1. It's raining.
2. It's hot.
3. It's beautiful.
4. The sun is shining.
5. It's cold.
6. It's snowing.

23. Wie heißt das auf deutsch?

1. Fill out the form please.
2. Show me your passport.
3. The room looks quite pleasant.
4. I'm preparing supper.
5. Are you hungry?
6. Clean the room!

7. It's best that you go to the bank.

8. Why are you stamping the passport?

24. Form complete sentences by using the cues given.

1. Fahren / Sie / mit / Fahrstuhl
2. Ich / können / bei / Eingang / parken
3. Lehrer / zeigen / ich / Computer
4. Jungen / kaufen / Mädchen / Kassette
5. Kleid / gut stehen / Dame
6. Angestellten / sprechen / mit / wir

25. Complete the following sentences.

1. _____ mit dem Auto?
2. _____ Bücher.
3. Um wieviel Uhr _____ Mittagessen?
4. _____ das Gepäck?
5. _____ oft Deutsch, Martin?
6. Die Touristen _____ die Berge.

26. Wie heißt das auf deutsch?

Beispiel: It's best that you go home.
Geh am besten nach Hause!

1. It's best that you go downtown.
2. It's best that you drive to Munich.
3. It's best that you see the movie.
4. It's best that you clear the dishes.
5. It's best that you ask him.
6. It's best that you prepare the meal.

27. Beantwortet die Fragen!

Wo mußt du das Auto parken?

Was sollst du ausfüllen?

Wie ist das Wetter heute?

Machst du manchmal einen Klassenausflug?

Um wieviel Uhr ißt du Abendbrot?

Was spielst du gern?

Gehst du gern ins Freie? Was machst du dort?

Was machen die Jugendlichen? (Ulm)

Rückblick

I. Complete the sentences using the information given plus the infinitive form of a verb of your choice where needed.

   Beispiel: *(müssen) _____ du die Reiseschecks _____?*
        Mußt du die Reiseschecks einlösen?

 1. (sollen) Wir _____ das Anmeldeformular _____.

 2. (dürfen) _____ ihr dort _____?

 3. (werden) _____ du nach Hause _____?

 4. (können) Er _____ gut Gitarre _____.

 5. (mögen) _____ du das nicht?

 6. (müssen) Die Schüler _____ die Aufgaben _____.

 7. (wollen) Ich _____ ein Motorrad _____.

II. Complete each sentence by supplying the appropriate form of the article as well as one of these prepositions: *aus, außer, bei, mit, von* or *zu*. Contract preposition and article whenever possible.

 1. Die Studenten kommen _____ Sprachlabor.

 2. Wohnen Sie _____ Hotel?

 3. Wer kommt _____ Lehrer noch mit?

 4. Fahren Sie _____ Zug nach München!

 5. Wir warten _____ Eingang.

 6. Die Touristen machen eine Reise _____ Bergen.

 7. Um wieviel Uhr kommen die Besucher _____ Theater.

 8. Ich muß noch schnell _____ Bank gehen.

 9. Herr Schmidt fährt _____ Jungen und Mädchen _____ Jugendherberge.

 10. Wirst du das Buch _____ Dame bekommen?

III. Complete the following sentences.

 1. Das Auto steht nicht weit von _____.

 2. Außer _____ spielt auch Birgit Musik.

 3. Sie fahren zu _____.

 4. Um wieviel Uhr kommt ihr aus _____?

 5. Wir möchten ein Zimmer mit _____.

 6. Nach _____ können wir zur Eisdiele gehen.

 7. Die Touristen fahren von _____ zu _____.

 8. Wohnt er nicht bei _____?

IV. Put each verb into the present and then into the future tense.

 1. du / fahren

 2. ich / fernsehen

 3. ihr / lesen

 4. der Lehrer / sprechen

 5. die Dame / lesen

1. Fragen Sie *den Beamten* bitte!
2. Ich gehe mit *Hans* zur Schule.
3. Wie viele Monate wohnst du schon bei *der Dame*?
4. Der Amerikaner kann *die Verkäuferin* nicht verstehen.
5. Wir werden *den Jungen* suchen.
6. Was bekommst du von *der Mutter*?
7. Sprechen Sie doch mit *dem Herrn*!
8. Um wieviel Uhr soll ich *Frau Binder* anrufen?

VI. Unscramble each sentence and rewrite it so that each one makes sense.

1. Schule / sein / müssen / Mädchen / um / in / die / der / acht / Uhr
2. Nicht / wir / wissen / kommt / Straßenbahn / wann / die
3. Kino / Lust / ins / wir / gehen / keine / haben / zu
4. Reise / Dieter / ich / möchten / eine / Deutschland / machen / und / nach
5. Zug / Studenten / Hamburg / mit / fahren / die / dem / nach

Lesestück 2A

Bonn — die Hauptstadt der BRD

Bonn, die Hauptstadt der Bundesrepublik Deutschland, liegt links° **left**
vom Rhein. Auf der anderen Seite liegt das Siebengebirge. Die
Bundeshauptstadt hat ungefähr 300 000 Einwohner. Seit 1949 ist
Bonn das Zentrum der politischen Ereignisse° in der BRD. Von **events**
besonderem Interesse für Besucher sind die verschiedenen° Re- **various/government**
gierungsgebäude°. Das Bundeshaus° zum Beispiel ist sehr be- **buildings**
kannt. Hier versammeln sich° oft der Bundestag° und der Bun- **Federal Building**
desrat°. Alle Abgeordneten° haben ihre Büros im Bundeshoch- **meet/House of**
haus. Der Bundespräsident wohnt in der Villa Hammerschmidt. **Representatives/**
Senate/representatives

Bonn ist eine interessante Stadt. In der Innenstadt liegt der
Marktplatz°. Dort ist ein paar Mal in der Woche Markttag. Die **market square**
Leute° kommen dann in die Stadt und gehen auf dem Markt **people**
einkaufen. Am Marktplatz ist auch das Rathaus°. Es ist schon 250 **city hall**
Jahre alt und sieht wie ein Schloß° aus. **castle**

Bonn ist auch eine kulturelle Stadt. Sie ist zum Beispiel die
Geburtsstadt von Beethoven. Viele Touristen besuchen das
Beethovenhaus. Es sieht heute noch so aus wie zu Beethovens Zeit.
Das Städtische Kunstmuseum° hat eine große Sammlung° von **City Art Museum/**
Gemälden° (1945 bis heute). Die Bonner Universität ist schon 200 **collection**
Jahre alt. Sie bietet° den Studenten eine gute Möglichkeit zum Stu- **paintings**
dium. Gleich in der Nähe von der Universität steht das Münster°. **offers**
Es ist schon 900 Jahre alt. Der Turm° in der Mitte ist 92 Meter **cathedral**
hoch. **tower**

die Universität

Das Rathaus ist direkt am Markt.

das Bundeshochhaus

Viele Leute kommen mit dem Schiff nach Bonn. Auf dem Rhein können sie noch viele andere Sehenswürdigkeiten° sehen.   *sights*

Fragen über das Lesestück

1. Wo liegt das Siebengebirge?
2. Wie viele Einwohner hat Bonn?
3. Warum ist das Bundeshaus so bekannt?
4. Welches Gebäude hat viele Büros für Abgeordnete?
5. Warum ist der Marktplatz so interessant?
6. Warum ist Bonn eine kulturelle Stadt? Gib ein paar Beispiele!
7. Wie alt ist das Bonner Münster?
8. Wie kommen viele Leute nach Bonn?

Lesestück 2B

Berlin (Ost) — die Hauptstadt der DDR

Berlin, die größte deutsche Stadt, liegt im Osten der DDR. Berlin hat zwei Teile, Ost und West. Ost-Berlin ist die Hauptstadt der DDR. Das Symbol von Ost-Berlin ist der Fernsehturm°; er ist der zweitgrößte in Europa. Vom Fernsehturm hat man einen guten Blick auf die ganze Stadt. In der Hauptstadt der DDR gibt es viele Regierungsgebäude, wie zum Beispiel das Staatsratsgebäude°. Der „Palast der Republik" ist nicht nur ein politisches, sondern auch° ein kulturelles Zentrum. Hier gibt es ein Theater, Restaurants und sogar „Bowling".

TV Tower

Council of State Building
nicht nur...sondern auch
not only...but also

der Alexanderplatz

Im Palast der Republik gibt es „Bowling".

Man hat viele Gebäude renoviert.

Der Alexanderplatz ist eine andere bekannte Sehenswürdigkeit. Der Mittelpunkt° vom Alexanderplatz ist die Weltzeituhr°. Sie zeigt die genaue° Zeit in den großen Städten der ganzen Welt°. Am Alexanderplatz sieht man viele Restaurants, Cafés und Hotels. Es gibt dort auch historische Gebäude°, wie zum Beispiel das „Rote Rathaus". Auf der anderen Seite steht die Marienkirche, die älteste° Kirche° Berlins; sie ist 700 Jahre alt.

focal point/ World Time Clock exact/world

buildings

oldest/church

Eine große und bekannte Straße heißt „Unter den Linden". In dieser Straße findet man die Deutsche Staatsoper°. Gleich gegenüber° ist die Humboldt-Universität. Dort studieren viele Studenten aus der DDR und aus anderen Ländern. Ein paar hundert Meter weiter steht das Mahnmal für die Opfer des Faschismus°. Jede Stunde kann man hier die Wachablösung° sehen. Das ist sehr interessant.

State Opera
across

Memorial for the Victims of Fascism changing of the guard

Berlin hat viele Seen und Wälder°. Touristen kommen oft zum Müggelsee und fahren mit der „Weißen Flotte"°. Es gibt eine Auswahl von verschiedenen Schiffen. Manche Besucher fahren nur eine oder zwei Stunden, andere fahren sogar den ganzen Tag auf dem See herum.

forests name of group of boats

In Ost-Berlin kann man heute noch einige alte Gebäude sehen. Die meisten Gebäude hat man aber ganz renoviert. Viele Berliner wohnen außerhalb° in neuen Wohnvierteln°.

outside (of city)/ residential areas

Fragen über das Lesestück

1. Was ist das Symbol für Ost-Berlin?
2. Was gibt es alles im „Palast der Republik"?
3. Was ist die Weltzeituhr? Und wo kann man sie finden?
4. Wo steht die Deutsche Staatsoper?
5. Was kann man beim Mahnmal für die Opfer des Faschismus sehen?
6. Wohin fahren die Touristen gern?
7. Wo wohnen viele Berliner heute?

Sprachspiegel

I. Create a dialog. You have been driving for a long time, and you are anxious to find a hotel room. Your conversation is with the hotel clerk. Be as creative as possible.

II. Answer the questions with as much detail as possible.

1. Was hast du in dem Koffer?
2. Was mußt du alles ausfüllen?
3. Gibt es in der Schule eine Essenausgabe?
4. Was spielst du gern?
5. Machst du manchmal einen Ausflug? Wohin?

III. Write or talk about the German *Jugendherberge*.

Wie sagt man's?

Was kostet bei Ihnen ein Einzelzimmer?
80 Mark pro Nacht, mit Bad.
Mit Frühstück?
Ja, natürlich.

Ich brauche ein Doppelzimmer.
Für wie lange?
Für drei Tage.
Einen Moment…Ja, das geht noch.

Füllen Sie bitte dieses Formular aus?
Bitte schön, hier ist es.
Gibt es im Zimmer auch ein Telefon?
Ja, das haben Sie.

Haben Sie noch ein Zimmer frei?
Leider nicht.
Gibt es hier in der Nähe noch ein anderes Hotel?
Ja, fragen Sie mal im Hotel *Schreiber*.

Ich möchte um halb sieben aufstehen.
Gut. Ich rufe Sie um 6 Uhr 30 an.
Vielen Dank.
Gute Nacht, mein Herr.

Spiel nicht immer an den Automaten!
Es macht doch so viel Spaß.
Das schon, aber es kostet auch viel Geld.
Ich bezahle es ja.

Ich muß Sabine sofort anrufen.
Das sollst du gleich tun.
Wo gibt es denn ein Telefon hier?
Da drüben ist eine Telefonzelle.

Wann macht ihr denn einen Klassenausflug?
Am Freitag.
Und wohin werdet ihr fahren?
In die Berge.

Zungenbrecher

Ein krummer Krebs kroch über eine krumme Klammer.
(A crooked crab crawled over a crooked clip.)

Kulturecke 1

Foreign Influence in Germany

An American arriving in Germany might be surprised to see many non-German words on store fronts, billboards and in the media. Foreigners have had a tremendous impact on the German economy since the end of World War II. Americans have had the greatest influence of any foreign group. Fast food operations, for example, have sprung up all over Germany. Hamburgers, which were unknown ten years ago, can be bought in almost all German cities. American-style jeans are sold in numerous jeans shops in every German city. New technology, such as computers, is now in demand by German companies as well as by people for their homes. Other small businesses, such as those that do photocopying, are as popular in Germany as they are in this country.

The French influence has long been evident in the German clothing industry. When it comes to fashion, the Germans look to their neighbor for new styles and trends. Clothing stores with a French touch are usually more fashionable and, of course, more expensive. Germans also have an appetite for foreign foods. Italian cafés and pizzerias have become very popular. Oriental food is making an inroad into the German food business. There is no problem in finding Chinese-style restaurants.

About 5 million of the 62 million people who live in the Federal Republic of Germany are foreigners. The largest groups are the Turks, Yugoslavs, Italians and Greeks. Therefore, many restaurants cater to the demands of these ethnic groups. Most of these foreigners are so-called *Gastarbeiter*, who came to Germany during a time when unemployment was low and the demand for additional work force high.

American influence is seen throughout Germany.

Fast food operations have become quite popular.

As an example, there are more than 1.5 million Turks living in the Federal Republic. It is estimated that Kreuzberg, a district of West-Berlin, is now the third largest Turkish city in the world. The local stores cater to the Turkish population here. The Turks are able to buy the national foods that they are accustomed to. Local banks provide special service for these as well as other foreigners. Since many companies in West-Berlin employ the Turkish *Gastarbeiter*, they have given their Turkish workers an opportunity to voice their opinions on factory committees.

Most of the foreigners who have come to Germany have maintained their national identity. Although family members speak their native language at home, their children are usually assimilated into the social and cultural life of Germany. At various national festivals, these foreign groups present their national dances to the local audience. These festivals further illustrate the tremendous impact of foreigners living in Germany, and the numerous changes that have taken place in the German cultural life.

Italian foods are
particularly in demand.

Foreigners in Germany have
maintained their identity.

There are numerous ethnic restaurants.

Kulturecke 2

German Influence in the United States

The first German settlers came to America over 300 years ago. Ever since their early arrival, Germans have played a significant role in our national life. One of the most famous Germans to play a historic role in America was General von Steuben, who organized the Revolutionary Army under George Washington. A monument in his honor is a Milwaukee landmark. Another well-known German is Carl Schurz, who fled to the United States where he later became a senator from Missouri and then Secretary of the Interior under President Hayes. During the summer various celebrations take place in the Carl Schurz Memorial Park in Nashota, Wisconsin.

German influence is more obvious in the many U.S. cities where streets have been named after German cities and personalities. As they enter the town of Frankenmuth, Michigan, visitors are welcomed immediately with a German *Willkommen* sign. In the center of the city a descriptive marker summarizes the history of German settlers in the early 19th century. As you look around, it may seem as if you're in a small town in Bavaria, Germany. It's no wonder that Frankenmuth has been labeled "Michigan's Little Bavaria."

German immigrants brought along know-how in farming, fine carpentry and cheese-making as well as excellence in the art of sausage-making. Wherever there are Germans, it is safe to say that a local butcher shop — offering home-made German sausage — is not too far away. Breweries, many of which are quite well-known, also show the definite influence of Germans who introduced fine beers from Germany. Similar to other nationalities, urban German settlers generally congregated in one part of a city or town. Today cities like St. Louis and Milwaukee still show evidence of this early pattern.

Frankenmuth, Michigan

German settlers came to Frankenmuth in the 19th century.

A large population of Germans came to this country in the middle of the 19th century. Many of the newcomers looked for areas resembling the terrain of their homeland. The city of Columbus, Ohio, prides itself on a picturesque section called "German Village."

It is generally assumed that Texas reflects only Spanish and Mexican influences. However, visitors to the Texas town of Fredericksburg are surprised when they are greeted in German upon entering the town. Various stores signal the German influence — clothing stores for children called *Das Kinderhaus*, a restaurant specializing in potato pancakes called *Der Kartoffelpuffer* or again the local German butcher store called *Opa's*. Not far away from Fredericksburg is another town of German origin, New Braunfels. This town was founded in 1845 by Prinz Carl von Solms-Braunfels who came from his native town of Braunfels in Hessen, Germany. The visitors are greeted with a huge billboard that reads *In New Braunfels ist das Leben schön.* Right outside the city is *Oma's Sausage Haus & Bier Garten*, which caters strictly to the tourists passing through this German settlement.

St. Louis shows the German influence.

New Braunsfels, Texas

A sign in Fredericksburg, Texas.

Many Germans
settled in Texas.

168

Vokabeln

abräumen to clear
die **Ankunft,-̈e** arrival
das **Anmeldeformular,-e** registraton form
ausfüllen to fill out
aussehen to look, appear
der **Ausweis,-e** identification (card)
das **Beispiel,-e** example
    zum Beispiel for example
best- best
    am besten the best is
das **Bett,-en** bed
das **Boot,-e** boat
der **Briefkasten,-̈** mailbox
der **Briefmarkenautomat,-en** stamp
    automat
dasselbe the same
denken to think
einige a few, several
elegant elegant
die **Essenausgabe,-n** serving counter
das **Fahrrad,-̈er** bicycle
der **Fahrstuhl,-̈e** elevator
der **Fernsehapparat,-e** television set
das **Flugzeug,-e** airplane
folgen to follow
frei free, available
Freie: ins Freie outside
der **Fußball,-̈e** football
ganz quite
die **Geburtsstadt,-̈e** native town,
    city of birth
gemütlich pleasant
das **Geschirr** dishes
das **Getränk,-e** beverage
die **Güte** goodness
    Du meine Güte! My goodness!
heiß hot
der **Herbergsvater,-̈** youth hostel director
herumfahren do drive (ride) around
hineingehen to go inside
historisch historical, historic
das **Hotel,-s** hotel
der **Hunger** hunger
    Hunger haben to be hungry
immer wieder again and again
interessant interesting
jeder each, every
die **Jugendherberge,-n** youth hostel
der **Jugendherbergsausweis,-e** youth
    hostel identification (card)
der **Jugendliche,-n** youngster, teenager,
    youth
kalt cold
der **Klassenausflug,-̈e** class trip

kühl cool
kulturell cultural
der **Lehrer,-** teacher
der **Markt,-̈e** market
der **Markttag,-e** market day
die **meisten** most
mitbringen to bring along
die **Möglichkeit,-en** possibility
das **Motorrad,-̈er** motorcycle
die **Person,-en** person
politisch political
regnen to rain
renovieren to renovate
das **Restaurant,-s** restaurant
saubermachen to clean
das **Schach** chess
scheinen to shine
das **Schiff,-e** ship, boat
das **Schild,-er** sign
schneien to snow
die **Seite,-n** page, side
sogar even
die **Sonne** sun
der **Speisesaal,-säle** dining hall
stempeln to stamp
stimmen to be correct
    Das stimmt. That's right.
    That's true.
die **Süßigkeiten** (pl.) sweeets
das **Symbol,-e** symbol
die **Telefonzelle,-n** telephone booth
das **Theater,-** theater
das **Tischtennis** table tennis
übernachten to stay overnight
die **Übernachtung,-en** (overnight)
    accommodation
um in order to, to
das **Verkehrsmittel,-** means of
    transportation
warm warm
wenige few
das **Wetter** weather
der **Zimmerschlüssel,-** room key
zubereiten to prepare (a meal)

Dialog

Michaels Party

MICHAEL: Tag, Leute! Ich glaube, alle sind schon da.

ALLE: Herzlichen Glückwunsch zum Geburtstag!

MICHAEL: Mann, die vielen Geschenke! . . .Besonders die Bücher . . . Da kann ich viel lesen.

KERSTIN: Aber nicht jetzt. Wir sind nämlich sehr hungrig.

MICHAEL: Ralf, ist das Essen schon fertig?

RALF: Ja, es steht schon alles auf dem Tisch. Siehst du?

MICHAEL: Mmh, der Kartoffelsalat sieht lecker aus.

RALF: Ich mag die Kalte Platte.

MICHAEL: Bring mir bitte noch etwas Schinken und Käse mit.

RALF: Jetzt aber 'ran an die Arbeit!

KERSTIN: Mit achtzehn kannst du jetzt Auto fahren.

MICHAEL: Ja, die Fahrprüfung liegt schon hinter mir. Ich bekomme den Führerschein nächste Woche.

KERSTIN: Da warne ich euch alle. Bleibt lieber zu Hause! Unsere Straßen sind jetzt nicht mehr sicher.

Fragen über den Dialog

1. Warum sind die Jugendlichen bei Michael?
2. Warum soll Michael die Bücher jetzt nicht lesen?
3. Was steht alles auf dem Tisch?
4. Wie alt ist Michael heute?
5. Was bekommt Michael nächste Woche? Und was kann er dann tun?

Michael's Party

MICHAEL:	Hello, guys! I think everyone is here.
EVERYONE:	Happy Birthday!
MICHAEL:	Wow, that many presents . . . Especially the books . . . I can read a lot.
KERSTIN:	But not now. We're really hungry.
MICHAEL:	Ralf, is the food ready yet?
RALF:	Yes, everything is already on the table. Look!
MICHAEL:	Mmh, the potato salad looks delicious.
RALF:	I like the cold cuts.
MICHAEL:	Please bring me some ham and cheese.
RALF:	Let's go to work now.
KERSTIN:	You're eighteen. You can drive now.
MICHAEL:	Yes, the driver's test is already behind me. I'll get the driver's license next week.
KERSTIN:	I'll warn all of you. You'd better stay home. Our streets aren't safe any more.

Nützliche Ausdrücke

Herzlichen Glückwunsch zum Geburtstag!	Happy Birthday!
Es steht schon auf dem Tisch.	It's already on the table.
Es sieht lecker aus.	It looks delicious.
Jetzt aber 'ran an die Arbeit!	Let's go to work now.
Es liegt schon hinter mir.	It's already behind me.
Sie kauft Fahrkarten an einem Automaten.	She buys tickets at an automat.
Ich entwerte die Fahrkarte.	I cancel the ticket.
Bekommst du einen Sitzplatz?	Are you getting a seat?
Mußt du Eintritt bezahlen?	Do you have to pay admission?
Es gibt etwas für jeden Geschmack.	They have something for everyone's taste.
Bei der Hitze . . .	In this heat . . .
Er gibt gerade bekannt, daß . . .	He is just announcing that . . .
Welche Schallplatte legst du auf?	Which record are you putting on?
Ich mache erst einmal eine Pause.	First of all I'm taking a break.
Strengt es an?	Is it strenuous?

172

Ergänzung

1. Was brauchst du für die Schule?
   Eine Schultasche.

ein Buch
ein Heft
ein Kuli
ein Bleistift
ein Radiergummi
Papier
ein Lineal

2. Was für ein Musikinstrument spielst du?
   Ich spiele Gitarre.

die Trompete
das Klavier
die Blockflöte
die Klarinette
die Geige
die Flöte
das Akkordeon
die Gitarre

Ausspracheübung

short / ö /	long / ö /	short / ä /	long / ä /
zwölf	Söhne	Länder	Väter
können	hören	März	Nähe
Töchter	mögen	Plätze	Universität
Röcke	Österreich	Mäntel	spät
Schlösser	schön	Fläche	Fahrpläne
möchte	größte	Geschäft	Fahrräder
Köln	Flöte	gefällt	Käse

Übungen

Possessive Adjectives (Nominative and Accusative)

A possessive adjective is a pronoun that is used as an adjective to indicate who owns the noun that follows it. It replaces the article in front of the noun and takes on the same endings as those of the indefinite article (*ein*-words).

	Nominative Singular			Plural
	masculine	*feminine*	*neuter*	
ich	mein	meine	mein	meine
du	dein	deine	dein	deine
er	sein	seine	sein	seine
sie	ihr	ihre	ihr	ihre
es	sein	seine	sein	seine
wir	unser	unsere*	unser	unsere*
ihr	euer	euere*	euer	euere*
sie	ihr	ihre	ihr	ihre
Sie	Ihr	Ihre	Ihr	Ihre

	Accusative Singular			Plural
	masculine	*feminine*	*neuter*	
ich	meinen	meine	mein	meine
du	deinen	deine	dein	deine
er	seinen	seine	sein	seine
sie	ihren	ihre	ihr	ihre
es	seinen	seine	sein	seine
wir	unseren	unsere*	unser	unsere*
ihr	eueren	euere*	euer	euere*
sie	ihren	ihre	ihr	ihre
Sie	Ihren	Ihre	Ihr	Ihre

*The **e** in front of the **r** in **unser** and **euer** is often omitted if the ending begins with a vowel.

Folgt den Beispielen!

1. Mein Freund ist schon da.
   Freundin
   Tante
   Lehrer
   Schwester
   Onkel

   Mein Freund ist schon da.
   Meine Freundin ist schon da.

2. Wo ist euer Geschenk?
   Mutter
   Kassette
   Mantel
   Schule
   Zimmer

   Wo ist euer Geschenk?
   Wo ist eu(e)re Mutter?

3. Gepäck (er)
   Buch (ich)
   Fahrkarte (Sie - form.)
   Party (wir)
   Freund (sie - sg.)
   Führerschein (du)

   sein Gepäck

4. Hast du dein Fahrrad?
   mein Reisescheck
   seine Aufgabe
   unser Geld
   ihr Koffer
   deine Uhr

   Hast du dein Fahrrad?
   Hast du meinen Reisescheck?

5. Wir besuchen seinen Onkel.
   Schwester / mein
   Freund / unser
   Großmutter / ihr
   Bruder / euer
   Lehrer / dein

   Wir besuchen seinen Onkel.
   Wir besuchen meine Schwester.

6. Brauchst du deinen Führerschein?
   Geld
   Telefon
   Tasche
   Platz
   Tisch
   Fahrkarte

   Brauchst du deinen Führerschein?
   Brauchst du dein Geld?

7. Wo sind deine Socken?
   Handschuhe / euere

   Wo sind deine Socken?
   Wo sind eu(e)re Handschuhe?

Geschenke / seine
Freundinnen / unsere
Zimmer / ihre
Aufgaben / meine

8. Sein Auto fährt schnell. Seine Autos fahren schnell.
   Euere Gitarre ist teuer.
   Dein Zimmer sieht schön aus.
   Ihr Buch ist sehr interessant.
   Unsere Reise kostet nicht viel.
   Mein Bruder kommt nicht mit.

9. Siehst du mein Hemd? Siehst du meine Hemden?
   Ich suche ihren Pullover.
   Wir lösen unseren Reisescheck ein.
   Kennst du seinen Freund?
   Braucht er unsere Zeitung?
   Frag doch deinen Lehrer!

10. Wen möchtest du fragen? Meine Freunde.
    (Freund)
    Wen möchtest du besuchen?
    (Großvater)
    Was wirst du brauchen?
    (Kassette)
    Was willst du lesen?
    (Buch)
    Wen brauchst du?
    (Bruder)
    Was mußt du haben?
    (Paß)

11. Complete each sentence by providing the missing endings where necessary.

1. Wann ist dein _____ Geburtstag?
2. Verstehst du sein _____ Schwester?
3. Ich muß mein _____ Reiseschecks einlösen.
4. Die Jugendlichen bekommen ihr _____ Ausweis.
5. Haben Sie schon Ihr _____ Führerschein, Herr Werner?
6. Wo sind euer _____ Schilder?
7. Wir besuchen unser _____ Tante nächste Woche.
8. Brauchst du mein _____ Computer?
9. Lies doch dein _____ Buch!
10. Siehst du sein _____ Geschenke?

12. **Supply the German equivalent for the words given in parentheses.**

   1. Suchen Sie (our telephone) _____?

   2. Ich möchte (your bicycle) _____ kaufen, Bernd.

   3. Lest ihr (your newspapers) _____?

   4. Wo wohnt (your brother) _____, Herr Mendel?

   5. Warum suchst du (his books) _____?

   6. (My girlfriend) _____ sucht (her cassette) _____.

   7. (His teacher) _____ ist sehr beliebt.

   8. (Our school) _____ ist nicht weit vom Bahnhof.

   9. (Their father) _____ besucht (my uncle) _____.

  10. Ich werde (her guitar) _____ kaufen.

13. **Complete the following sentences, using a possessive adjective and a noun of your choice.**

     Beispiel: *Verstehst du _____?*
                 Verstehst du seinen Freund?

   1. Wir brauchen _____.

   2. Wo sind _____?

   3. Wann bekommen Sie _____?

   4. _____ fährt sehr schnell.

   5. Die Jugendlichen suchen _____.

   6. _____ kostet viel Geld.

   7. Sie müssen _____ lesen.

   8. Kannst du _____ anprobieren?

   9. Möchte er _____ besuchen?

  10. Bring doch _____ mit!

  11. Er stempelt _____.

  12. Ich fülle _____ aus.

14. **Wie heißt das auf deutsch?**

   1. his shirt

   2. their tables

   3. my apartment

   4. her money

   5. our teacher

   6. my bicycles

   7. their mother

Comparison of Adjectives

In adjectives of comparison there are two levels of comparing that are constructed from the basic form of the adjective, i.e., the *comparative* and the *superlative*. The formation from the basic form to the superlative is similar in both languages. For instance, take the word *fast* (schnell). The comparative is *faster* (schneller) and the superlative is *fastest* (schnellst + ending).

Examples: *das schnelle Auto*   the fast car
                das schnellere Auto   the faster car
                das schnellste Auto   the fastest car

These examples are listed here merely to illustrate the comparison of adjectives. These adjectives (because they involve endings) will be treated specifically in later units.

When the adjective is used as part of the verb, follow this example. (Notice that *am* precedes the superlative and *-en* is added.)

Paul ist pünktlich.   Paul is punctual
Maria ist pünktlicher.   Maria is more punctual.
Herbert is am pünktlichsten.   Herbert is most punctual.

Comparison of Adverbs

The comparison of adverbs is similar to the above. Whereas the adjective (see above) modifies the noun, the adverb (see below) modifies the verb.

Examples: *Die Straßenbahn fährt schnell.*   The streetcar goes fast.
                Das Auto fährt schneller.   The car goes faster.
                Der Zug fährt am schnellsten.   The train goes the fastest.

EXCEPTIONS: When the adjectives or adverbs end in *d, t, tz, s, ß, sch, st, x,* or *z,* the ending in the superlative has an additional *e.*

Examples: *(am) interessantesten, heißesten*

Most one-syllable adjectives or adverbs containing an *a, o,* or *u* change to *ä, ö, ü* in the comparative and the superlative.

Examples: *warm — wärmer — am wärmsten*
                groß — größer — am größten
                dumm — dümmer — am dümmsten

A few irregular forms are also listed here:

gut	besser	am besten
viel	mehr	am meisten
hoch	höher	am höchsten
nahe	näher	am nächsten
gern	lieber	am liebsten

When an unequal comparison is made, use the comparative form and the word *als* (meaning "than").

Example: *Er spielt besser als Hans.* He plays better than Hans.

Folgt den Beispielen!

15. Der Abend ist genauso heiß wie   Der Abend ist heißer als der
       der Nachmittag.   Nachmittag.

    Der Schinken ist genauso teuer wie
       der Käse.

    Das Auto fährt genauso schnell wie
       der Zug.

Das Buch ist genauso toll wie der Film.

Kerstin kommt genauso spät wie
　　Michael.

Der Winter ist genauso kalt wie
　　der Herbst.

Jürgen ist genauso pünktlich wie Peter.

16. Die Vorstellung beginnt spät.　　　　　　Der Film beginnt später.
　　(der Film)
　　Am Montag ist es kühl.
　　(Dienstag)
　　Das Fahrrad ist schnell
　　(das Motorrad)
　　Der Vorort ist groß.
　　(die Stadt)
　　Die S-Bahn fährt langsam.
　　(die Straßenbahn)
　　Jörg ist klug. (Monika)
　　Die Schule sieht schön aus.
　　(die Uni)

17. Das Auto fährt schnell.　　　　　　　　Das Auto fährt schnell.
　　die S-Bahn　　　　　　　　　　　　　Die S-Bahn fährt schneller.
　　der Zug　　　　　　　　　　　　　　Der Zug fährt am schnellsten.

　　Köln ist groß.
　　München
　　Berlin

　　Sven ist klug.
　　Petra
　　Heike

　　Herr Gruber kommt spät.
　　Fräulein Hesse
　　Frau Peters

　　Der Watzmann ist hoch.
　　Die Zugspitze
　　Der Großglockner

　　Ich esse Käse gern.
　　Wurst
　　Schinken

18. **Provide the comparative and superlative forms.**
　　1. schön
　　2. klug

3. groß
4. heiß
5. hoch
6. viel
7. alt
8. schlecht
9. gut
10. toll

19. Wie heißt das auf deutsch?

1. The boys are coming later.
2. Austria is not as big as Germany.
3. The spring is warmer than the fall.
4. Which mountain is higher?
5. The dress costs more than the blouse.
6. Hamburg is just as beautiful as München.
7. The cheese is more delicious than the ham.
8. My brother is older than my sister.
9. The bicycle and the motorcycle are going fast. The car is going fastest.
10. Ursula is smarter than Jürgen.

München

Hamburg

Additional *der*-words*

The endings for the *der*-words, i.e. *dieser* (this), *jeder* (every, each), and *welcher* (which), are the same as those of the definite article.

	Singular			**Plural**
	masculine	*feminine*	*neuter*	
nominative	dies*er*	dies*e*	dies*es*	dies*e*
accusative	dies*en*	dies*e*	dies*es*	dies*en*
dative	dies*em*	dies*er*	dies*em*	dies*en*

Since *jeder* does not have a plural form, you may substitute the word *alle* (all).

Der-words are *der, dieser, jeder, welcher*, and some others which you will learn later.

Folgt den Beispielen!

20. Der Film beginnt um acht.   Dieser Film beginnt um acht.
    Die Krawatte ist bunt.
    Das Geschenk ist von Uwe.
    Die Auswahl ist sehr gut.
    Der Tourist kommt aus Europa.
    Der Student fragt oft.

21. Die Verkäuferin ist beliebt.   Welche Verkäuferin ist beliebt?
    Der Computer kostet viel.
    Die Stadt liegt in Bayern.
    Das Auto sieht schön aus.
    Der Schüler liest die Aufgabe.
    Die Zeitung ist ganz politisch.

22. Wir besuchen das Land.   Wir besuchen dieses Land.
    Kaufst du das Geschenk?
    Ich brauche die Kassette.
    Essen Sie den Käse?
    Er probiert die Hose an.
    Kennst du den Angestellten?

23. Er kauft die Zeitung.   Er kauft fast jede Zeitung.
    Ich frage den Jungen.
    Brauchst du den Pfennig?
    Sie kennt die Verkäuferin.
    Verstehen Sie die Bedeutung?
    Wir lesen das Buch.

24. Das Fahrrad steht beim Eingang.   Bei welchem Eingang steht das Fahrrad?
    Herr Gruber fährt mit dem Auto.
    Wir gehen zur Party.
    Sie kommen aus der Bank.
    Der Lehrer kommt von dem Vorort.
    Seit der Reise hat er kein Geld.

25. Ich glaube dem Jungen.   Ich glaube diesem Jungen.
    Antworte dem Lehrer!
    Komm zu der Haltestelle!
    Was machen wir nach dem Film?
    Sie geben der Verkäuferin fünfzig Mark.
    Wir bringen dem Mädchen ein Geschenk.

26. Welchen Angestellten fragt ihr?   Welche Angestellten fragt ihr?
    Welche Gitarre kaufen Sie?
    Welches Auto gefällt dir?

Welchen Anzug hast du an?

Welches Wort weiß er nicht?

Welchen Tanz hat sie gern?

27. Was zeigt er dieser Dame? Was zeigt er diesen Damen?

Ich gebe es diesem Mädchen.

Er wohnt bei diesem Studenten.

Sie fahren zu diesem Berg.

Wir antworten diesem Lehrer.

Glaubst du diesem Jugendlichen?

28. **Provide the proper endings.**

1. Dies _____ Film gefällt mir gar nicht.
2. Welch _____ Beamten mußt du fragen? Herrn Müller.
3. Wir fahren jed _____ Jahr zu dies _____ Stadt.
4. Welch _____ Koffer brauchen wir denn? Dies _____ zwei.
5. Warum fragen Sie jed _____ Verkäuferin?
6. Wartet bitte bei dies _____ Eingang hier!
7. Welch _____ Studenten studieren dort?
8. Ich weiß jed _____ Aufgabe.
9. Möchten Sie dies _____ Anzug anprobieren?
10. Welch _____ Freunde wirst du besuchen?

29. **Beanwortet die folgenden Fragen!**

Beispiel: *Möchtest du eine Krawatte kaufen?*
Ja, ich möchte diese hier.

1. Möchtest du ein Hemd haben?
2. Möchtest du ein Akkordeon?
3. Möchtest du einen Fernsehapparat kaufen?
4. Möchtest du eine Bluse?
5. Möchtest du einen Pullover haben?

30. **Supply the proper form of *dieser* or *welcher.***

1. _____ Musikinstrument wirst du spielen?
2. Wann sehen Sie _____ Film?
3. _____ Kassetten möchtest du hören?
4. _____ Heft sucht er denn?
5. Ich verstehe _____ Amerikanerin gar nicht.
6. _____ Mannschaft wird gewinnen?
7. Kennst du _____ Sportler? Sie sind sehr bekannt.
8. Zu _____ Städten sollen wir fahren?
9. Habt ihr mit _____ Besuchern viel zu tun?
10. Aus _____ Gebäude kommen _____ Leute?

Lesestück 1

Monika geht gern tanzen

Jede Woche, Donnerstag nachmittags, geht Monika zum Tanzunterricht°. Manchmal geht sie auch am Sonntag in die Tanzschule. *dancing lessons*
Dann können die Jugendlichen dort üben. Heute, am Sonntag, möchte Monika auch etwas üben. Der S-Bahnhof° ist nicht weit von *suburban line station*
ihrem Haus.

Am Bahnhof kauft sie eine Fahrkarte an einem Automaten. Dann entwertet sie ihre Fahrkarte und geht auf den Bahnsteig°. Sie *platform*
muß nicht lange warten bis die S-Bahn kommt. Sie steigt ein. Sonntags° ist die S-Bahn meistens nicht sehr voll° und Monika bekommt *on Sundays/full*
einen Sitzplatz. Monika fährt nur zwei Haltestellen. Die Tanzschule ist gleich in der Nähe vom S-Bahnhof.

Frau Richter, die Besitzerin°, steht hinter einer Theke°. Bei *owner/counter*
ihr muß Monika Eintritt bezahlen. Monikas Freundin Tina ist auch schon da. Beide haben immer viel Spaß zusammen. Peter, Monikas Tanzpartner, kommt heute nicht. Deshalb tanzt sie mit anderen Jungen. Die Musik ist immer sehr gut. Da gibt es Tänze für jeden Geschmack.

Monika geht zum Tanzunterricht.

Mit wem spricht Monika?

Es gibt Tänze für jeden Geschmack.

In der Tanzschule ist es heute sehr heiß. Bei der Hitze kann Monika nicht immer tanzen. Sie muß oftmals° aussetzen°. Jetzt spielt Frau Richter einen Walzer°. Nur wenige tanzen, die meisten tanzen lieber zu schneller Musik. Frau Richter gibt gerade bekannt, daß sie eine Schallplatte mit südamerikanischer° Musik auflegen wird. Diese Musik gefällt Monika am besten. Das weiß auch Bernd. Er fragt Monika, ob° sie mit ihm tanzen möchte. Bei einem Cha-Cha-Cha tanzen die beiden wie° Experten. Nach jedem Tanz muß Monika erst einmal eine Pause machen. Tanzen macht Spaß, aber es strengt sehr an.

often/sit out

waltz

Latin American

if

like

Fragen über das Lesestück

1. Wohin geht Monika einmal die Woche?
2. Was können die Jugendlichen am Sonntag tun?
3. Was macht Monika mit der Fahrkarte?
4. Warum muß Monika in der S-Bahn nicht stehen?
5. Wo ist die Tanzschule?
6. Wer ist Frau Richter?
7. Warum tanzt Monika nicht mit ihrem Tanzpartner?
8. Warum setzt Monika oftmals aus?
9. Warum tanzen nicht viele zu einem Walzer?
10. Welche Musik gefällt Monika am besten?

Erweiterung

31. Beantwortet die folgenden Fragen!

Beispiel: *Spielst du gern Tischtennis? (Fußball)*
Ich spiele lieber Fußball.

1. Spielst du gern Flöte? (Blockflöte)
2. Ißt du gern Käse? (Wurst)
3. Schreibst du gern mit einem Bleistift? (Kuli)
4. Liest du gern eine Zeitung? (Buch)
5. Sprichst du gern Englisch? (Deutsch)
6. Hörst du gern Schallplatten? (Kassetten)

32. Provide an appropriate response in German. Be sure that the whole conversation ties together and becomes meaningful.

1. Von wem hast du dieses Geschenk?
2. Ja, aber er hat doch gar kein Geld.
3. Das glaube ich nicht.

4. Er hat seinen Führerschein?

5. Seit Montag.

33. Define each of the words listed below. Write at least one complete sentence describing each word.

1. Geburtstag
2. Führerschein
3. Klavier
4. Schultasche
5. Schallplatte

34. Beantwortet die Fragen!

Wann hast du Geburtstag?

Was möchtest du zum Geburtstag bekommen?

Hast du einen Führerschein?

Was für ein Musikinstrument spielst du?

Was brauchst du für die Schule?

Gehst du gern tanzen?

Welche Tänze hast du am liebsten?

Spielst du lieber Kassetten oder Schallplatten?

Rückblick

I. **Supply the appropriate German equivalents for the nouns or pronouns as listed in parentheses.**

1. Frau Rübel wohnt bei (the university, a railroad station, a river, the building).
2. Glaubt (him, them, her, me) nicht!
3. Kannst du (the teacher, the girl, the ladies, the saleslady) nicht antworten?
4. Ich werde (her, them, me, him) ein Geschenk kaufen.
5. Warum gehen wir nicht mit (the boyfriend, the girl, them, her) ins Kino?
6. Sie kommen aus (the school, the house, the apartment, the movie theater).
7. Wir geben (you-sg./fam., you-form., them, her, the brother, the girlfriend) das Geld.

II. **Provide the proper form of the verb provided in parentheses.**

1. (sprechen) Mein Freund _____ gut Deutsch.
2. (essen) Was _____ du zum Abendbrot, Michael?
3. (fahren) Der Zug _____ direkt nach Köln.
4. (zugeben) Das stimmt. _____ es doch _____, Kerstin!
5. (gefallen) Wie _____ dir dieses Kleid?
6. (sehen) Wir _____ die Berge schon aus der Entfernung.

7. (tragen) Wer _____ meinen Koffer?

8. (lesen) Die Studenten _____ viele Bücher.

III. Complete the following sentences.

1. Ich kann bei _____ parken.

2. Um wieviel Uhr kommt ihr aus _____?

3. Außer _____ kenne ich auch noch _____.

4. Nach _____ gehen wir zu _____.

5. Wir wohnen schon seit _____ in Hamburg.

6. Hörst du manchmal von _____?

7. Er fährt mit _____.

IV. Write the opposite of each word indicated.

1. wenig: _____

2. gut: _____

3. schnell: _____

4. schwarz: _____

5. langweilig: _____

6. warm: _____

7. klein: _____

8. flach: _____

V. Complete each sentence by using the verb prefixes listed below. You may be able to use the same prefix more than once.

1. Die Jugendlichen räumen das Geschirr _____.

2. Ruf mich doch um fünf Uhr _____!

3. Steigen Sie schnell _____!

4. Meine Mutter bereitet das Essen _____.

5. Angelika probiert den Rock _____.

6. Füllen Sie bitte dieses Formular _____!

7. Wie viele Reiseschecks löst ihr _____?

8. Wir kommen zum Bahnhof _____.

9. Ich kaufe noch schnell in der Stadt _____.

10. Wann kommt dein Bruder _____? Ich muß mit ihm sprechen.

ab   an   aus   ein   mit   zu   zurück

VI. Create a meaningful dialog by giving an appropriate response in German.

1. Grüß dich! Um wieviel Uhr fahren wir zu Sabine?

2. Schon so bald?

3. Ich kaufe noch schnell ein Geschenk.

4. Aber es ist doch ihr Geburtstag!

5. Wer kommt denn noch zur Party?

6. So viele? Die meisten kenne ich gar nicht.

7. Mir ist es recht.

8. Ja, gut. Bis bald!

Lesestück 2

Die BRD — Landschaft

Im Norden grenzt die Bundesrepublik Deutschland an die Nordsee. Direkt auf der anderen Seite vom Festland°, in der Nähe von Kiel, beginnt die Ostsee°.

    Die BRD hat fünf verschiedene Landschaften. Im Norddeutschen *Tiefland*° liegen die Länder Schleswig-Holstein, Hamburg, Bremen, der größte Teil von Niedersachsen und ein Teil von Nordrhein-Westfalen. Die beiden letzten° Länder gehen in das *Mittelgebirgsland*° über°. Die Länder Rheinland-Pfalz, Saarland und Hessen gehören zu° dieser Landschaft. Zum Teil reichen diese Länder aber auch in das West- und Süddeutsche *Stufen- und Bergland*° hinein°. Dort und im Süddeutschen *Alpenvorland*° liegen die Länder Baden-Württemberg und Bayern. Die *Alpen* findet man nur in dem Land Bayern.

    Der höchste Berg ist die Zugspitze (fast 3000 m). Die Zugspitze liegt an der Grenze zu Österreich. Der zweithöchste Berg ist der Watzmann (ungefähr 2700 m). Dieser Berg liegt im Südosten.

    Der Rhein ist der längste Fluß (867 km in der BRD). Er ist eine wichtige° Wasserstraße für den europäischen Verkehr. Der Rhein entspringt° in der Schweiz, fließt durch den Bodensee°, dann durch die BRD und die Niederlande bis in die Nordsee. Der zweitgrößte Fluß in der BRD ist die Donau (647 km). Die Donau entspringt in der Bundesrepublik und fließt von Westen nach Osten bis ins Schwarze Meer°. Der drittgrößte Fluß ist die Elbe (227 km in der BRD, 566 km in der DDR). Die Elbe kommt aus der Tschechoslowakei. Sie fließt durch die DDR, eine kurze Strecke° durch die BRD und dann in die Nordsee.

    Außer den Flüssen ist auch das Kanalsystem° wichtig für den europäischen Wasserverkehr. Der Mittellandkanal zum Beispiel verbindet° die Ems mit der Elbe.

    Der Bodensee ist der größte See. Nur ein Teil vom Bodensee liegt in der BRD. Andere Teile liegen in Österreich und in der Schweiz. Es gibt aber viele kleine Seen. Die meisten Seen liegen in Süddeutschland, wie zum Beispiel der Chiemsee in Bayern oder der Schluchsee im Schwarzwald.

    Die größte Insel° ist Fehmarn. Diese Insel liegt in der Ostsee. Eine Brücke° verbindet Fehmarn mit dem Festland. Fehmarn ist auch eine wichtige Verbindung° für den Verkehr zwischen° der BRD und Dänemark. Die meisten Inseln liegen in der Nordsee. Helgoland zum Beispiel liegt am weitesten vom Festland entfernt und ist ein beliebter Ausflugsort° im Sommer. Viele kleine Inseln liegen ganz in der Nähe vom Festland. Manche° von diesen Inseln kann man bei Ebbe° sogar zu Fuß oder mit Pferden° erreichen.

Glossen:

mainland
Baltic Sea

lowlands

last
central highlands
go into
belong to/reichen…
hinein *reach into*/
terrace and highland country
Alpine foothills

important
originates/*Lake Constance*

Black Sea

stretch

canal system

connects

island
bridge
connection/*between*

excursion area
a few
low tide/*horses*

Der Bodensee ist der größte See.

Die Berge sind im Süden.

Hessen liegt im Mittelgebirgsland.

Fragen über das Lesestück

1. Welche zwei große Seen liegen im Norden der BRD?
2. Wie heißen die fünf Landschaften?
3. Wo liegt die Zugspitze? Wie hoch ist dieser Berg?
4. Fließt der Rhein nur durch die BRD?
5. Fließt die Donau von Norden nach Süden?
6. Welche Flüsse verbindet der Mittellandkanal?
7. Liegt der Bodensee nur in der BRD?
8. Wo sind die meisten Seen?
9. Wie kommt man vom Festland zur Insel Fehmarn?
10. Welche Insel liegt am weitesten vom Festland entfernt?

Sprachspiegel

I. Create a short dialog or narrative describing a party you are attending. Be as creative as possible.

II. Answer each question with at least two or three sentences. Be as descriptive as possible.

1. Was für ein Musikinstrument spielst du? (Wann? Wie oft? Wie lange? etc.)
2. Was bringst du alles in die Schule mit?
3. Was machst du bei einer Party?
4. Gehst du gern tanzen? (Wo? Wie oft? Welche Tänze tanzt du? etc.)
5. Wie sieht die Landschaft aus, wo du wohnst?

Wie sagt man's?

Kommt Tanja nicht?
Nein, sie hat Partys nicht gern.
Das glaub' ich nicht.
Frag sie doch!

Wann ist die Party?
Am Sonnabend um acht. Kommst du?
Wer kommt denn alles?
Bernd und seine Freunde.
Na, dann komme ich auch.

Tanzt du gern?
Ja, besonders zu moderner Musik.
Dann aber 'ran! Britta möchte bestimmt tanzen.
Hoffentlich hast du recht.

Wann beginnt der Tanz?
Um fünf. Hast du Lust mitzukommen?
Heute nicht. Vielleicht das nächste Mal.

Wer ist denn Erikas Tanzpartner?
Rolf. Er tanzt wirklich toll.
Besonders zu amerikanischer Musik.

Frag doch Jutta. Vielleicht tanzt sie mit dir.
Mir gefällt Sabine aber besser.
Warum wartest du dann?
Sie tanzt lieber mit Dieter.

Fährst du schon Auto?
Ja, ich habe jetzt meinen Führerschein.
Prima. Kannst du mich nach Hause fahren?
Na klar!

Tanzt du gern?

Was essen wir denn?
Bist du schon wieder hungrig?
Oh, das Essen sieht so lecker aus.
Ich esse auch etwas.

Zungenbrecher

Hinter Hermann Hannes Haus hängen hundert Hemden 'raus.
(Behind Hermann Hannes' house a hundred shirts are hanging out.)

Kulturecke

Occupations

Since World War II, Germany's economy has relied primarily on heavy industry, such as coal mining and the steel industries. Most of the heavy industry is located in the Northrhine Westphalia region. The Federal Republic of Germany is the third largest automobile producer in the world, following the U.S. and Japan.

Only seven percent of those Germans who are employed are now farmers. In order to be more competitive, most farms now have been consolidated and are part of co-operatives. Many farms are specialized and grow only certain crops such as vegetables or grapes for wine, which grow along the Rhine and Mosel rivers. About a quarter of the Federal Republic's land is forest. The law demands that forest areas must be properly managed. Land laws require forest owners to replant harvested areas or replace dead trees with new ones. Areas like Lower Saxony, Schleswig-Holstein and Bavaria are extensively involved in raising cattle and producing dairy products.

Specially trained personnel are employed in the computer industry and in related areas. Computers have had a tremendous impact on the growth of the economy. Specialists in the computer field are sought after not only by larger firms but even by smaller companies. The importance of computer technology is highly noticeable in the medical profession. There the computer is used in various specialized areas. In the Federal Republic there are about 130,000 doctors; that is one doctor to every 465 inhabitants. This makes the Federal Republic one of the best equipped countries in the world medically. Another health care occupation is the dentist or the dental technician. There are 32,000 dentists, one for every 1,916 Germans. Many pharmaceutical products tested by specialists are sold in pharmacies.

Major emphasis is placed on the importance of education. For many years, an acute shortage of teachers meant that every applicant who passed the proper examinations was accepted with open arms. Now there are many teachers without a job, which poses difficult problems for the country.

Every sixth person is employed by the federal, state or local government, providing services for the communities. For example, there are occupations concerned with public security and order, such as the police. The German Federal Post Office (*Deutsche Bundespost*) constitutes Europe's largest enterprise. Early in the morning, letter carriers can be seen leaving the main post offices to distribute the mail. Postal and telecommunications, in which thousands of people are employed, are part of the German Federal Post Office.

The German monetary system, based on the mark, has become an important factor in international trade. Financial institutions such as banks employ specialists in the different

Service-station attendant *(Tankwart)*.

A tree nursery *(Baumschule)*

Only 7% of employed Germans are farmers.

Handicrafts are traditional, particularly in small towns.

Women now have jobs once considered to be male occupations.

Lektion 8

areas of the complex financial business world. Managers in small and large companies provide the guidance and administration necessary to run their companies more effectively.

Tourism has become an important economic opportunity for Germans. Therefore, it is not surprising to find an abundance of travel agents who plan tours and vacations for groups or individuals. There are about 1.5 million jobs dependent on tourism either directly or indirectly. Some of these jobs, such as a captain on a Rhine ship, require extensive and specialized training. Lufthansa, the German Airline, requires its cabin attendants to speak at least one or two foreign languages. It is no longer rare to see women in jobs which were once considered to be typically male occupations. Almost every second woman is employed outside of the home. Tourists traveling by car have no difficulty finding service stations that can take care of the traveler's needs. Should the automobile need particular attention, authorized dealerships with specially trained auto mechanics can be found everywhere.

Americans going to a German department store with the intention of buying clothes should be aware that all clothing items are sized according to the metric system. However, experienced sales personnel can help foreigners to determine the correct size. Although many Germans go shopping in the local supermarkets today, individual shops are still extremely popular. The store owner and clerks know the individual customers, therefore providing a more personalized atmosphere. Many of these smaller stores, like the local butcher shop, are family-owned. The butcher takes special pride in offering home-made sausages and preparing the meats to the customers' special requests. Two thirds of Germans go shopping once or twice a week at the local markets. Here the clerks offer fresh fruits and vegetables, much preferred over packaged products.

The success of the restaurant business depends to a large extent on the skill of the cook. In Germany there is an abundance of various types of eating establishments, ranging from the very elegant and expensive to the simple and reasonably priced. Restaurant waiters and waitresses can be seen serving in indoor and outdoor restaurants. Many waiters or waitresses are also employed in cafés. Germans love to sit in these cafés, relax and have coffee and delicious German cake.

Germans take pride in keeping everything neat and clean. Some are employed by the sanitation department. Others, such as park attendants and gardeners, have the task of keeping the landscaped park areas beautiful and keeping everyone off the lawn.

Upon entering a town in Germany, the visitor will see a tall pole that is colorfully decorated with figures designating the trades of the town. This traditional pole dates back to the Middle Ages, a time when many apprentices and journeymen would go from town to town searching for jobs. However, times have changed and so have the methods for securing jobs.

Both the folk arts and the formal arts flourish throughout Germany. Handicrafts are traditional, particularly in smaller towns and villages. For example, the visitor will find a number of potters who create unique pottery for sale. Other artists, particularly in the town of Mittenwald, create hand-made violins that are well-respected and recognized throughout the world. In Southern Germany, the art of woodcarving is practiced by artisans who demonstrate great skill.

A woodcarver (Holzschnitzer).

Vokabeln

das **Akkordeon,-s** accordion
als than
an on
anstrengen to exert
    Es strengt an. It is exhausting.
auflegen to put on
aussetzen to sit out
der **Bahnsteig,-e** platform
bei with
bekanntmachen to announce
die **Besitzerin,-nen** owner (female)
der **Cha-Cha-Cha** cha-cha
der **Eintritt** admission
entwerten to cancel (tickets)
das **Essen** meal, food
europäisch European
der **Experte,-n** expert
die **Fahrprüfung,-en** driver's test
die **Flöte,-n** flute
der **Führerschein,-e** driver's license
die **Geige,-n** violin
das **Geschenk,-e** present
der **Glückwunsch,-̈e** congratulations (pl.)
    Herzlichen Glückwunsch zum
    Geburtstag! Happy Birthday!
das **Heft,-e** notebook
herzlich sincere, cordial
hinter behind
die **Hitze** heat
    bei der Hitze in this heat
der **Kartoffelsalat** potato salad
die **Klarinette,-n** clarinet
das **Klavier,-e** piano
der **Kuli,-s** (ballpoint) pen
die **Landschaft,-en** landscape
lecker delicious
das **Lineal,-e** ruler
das **Musikinstrument,-e** musical
    instrument
nämlich namely
ob if, whether
oftmals often
das **Papier** paper
die **Party,-s** party
die **Pause,-n** break
    eine Pause machen to take a break
der **Radiergummi,-s** eraser
'ran: 'Ran an die Arbeit!
    Let's go to work!
der **S-Bahnhof,-̈e** suburban line station
die **Schallplatte,-n** record
die **Schultasche,-n** school bag
sicher safe, secure
der **Sitzplatz,-̈e** seat

sonntags on Sundays
südamerikanisch South American
der **Tanz,-̈e** dance
der **Tanzpartner,-** dancing partner
der **Tanzschule,-n** dancing school
die **Theke,-n** counter
die **Trompete,-n** trumpet
der **Walzer,-** waltz
warnen to warn
die **Wasserstraße,-n** waterway
der **Wasserverkehr** water traffic
wie like

Dialog

Beim Sportwettbewerb

UWE:	Heute ist der große Tag. Ich hoffe, ich erreiche meine Bestleistung.
ACHIM:	Beim Weitsprung bist du immer klasse.
UWE:	Das letzte Mal hast du mich aber geschlagen.
ACHIM:	Da hab' ich mehr Glück als Verstand gehabt.
UWE:	Du hast recht. Ich bin etwas zu früh gesprungen. Dabei habe ich mindestens 15 Zentimeter verloren.
ACHIM:	Ich glaube, Daniel ist in bester Form. Er hat viel trainiert.
UWE:	Wie weit bist du denn vorhin gesprungen, Daniel?
DANIEL:	Ich bin auf 5,80 gekommen.
ACHIM:	Jetzt bin ich dran.
UWE:	Zeig, was du kannst!
ACHIM:	Ich versuche mein Bestes.
DANIEL:	Viel Glück! . . . *(Achim springt.)* . . . Phantastisch! . . . Nicht schlecht . . . 5,66.
UWE:	Das werde ich kaum übertreffen.
DANIEL:	Du kannst es sicherlich schaffen.
UWE:	Hoffentlich. Hier kommt meine letzte Chance.
UWE:	Du bist doch besser als ich gewesen.
ACHIM:	Aber nicht der Beste. Daniel hat uns beide geschlagen.
ANSAGER:	Das Endergebnis im Weitsprung . . . Erster — Daniel Kästner, Zweiter — Achim Lehmann und Dritter — Uwe Schmidt.
UWE:	Herzlichen Glückwunsch!

Fragen über den Dialog

1. Wer ist beim Weitsprung meistens sehr gut?
2. Warum hat Uwe das letzte Mal verloren?
3. Warum ist Daniel in bester Form?
4. Wie weit ist Daniel gesprungen?
5. Wie weit springt Achim?
6. Wer ist dieses Mal der Beste?

At the Sports Competition

UWE: Today is the big day. I hope I can match my best performance.

ACHIM: In the broad jump you're always great.

UWE: But you beat me the last time.

ACHIM: I had more luck than brains.

UWE: You're right. I jumped a bit too early. That made me lose at least 15 centimeters.

ACHIM: I think Daniel is in great form. He has practiced a lot.

UWE: How far did you jump before, Daniel?

DANIEL: I got to 5.80 (5 meters and 80 centimeters).

ACHIM: It's my turn now.

UWE: Show what you can do.

ACHIM: I'll try my best.

DANIEL: Lots of luck! . . . (Achim jumps.) . . . Fantastic! . . . Not bad . . . 5.66.

UWE: I'll hardly beat that.

DANIEL: You can certainly make it, too.

UWE: I hope so. Here is my last chance.

UWE: You were better than I was.

ACHIM: But not the best. Daniel beat both of us.

ANNOUNCER: The final result in broad jump . . . First — Daniel Kästner, second — Achim Lehmann and third — Uwe Schmidt.

UWE: Congratulations!

Nützliche Ausdrücke

Er hat mich geschlagen.	He beat me.
Du hast mehr Glück als Verstand.	You have more luck than brains.
Sie sind in bester Form.	They are in great form.
Ich bin dran.	It's my turn.
Kannst du das übertreffen?	Can you beat that?
Herzlichen Glückwunsch!	Congratulations!
Wann findet das Spiel statt?	When does the game take place?
Machst du mit?	Are you participating?
Sie sieht auf ihre Uhr.	She looks at her watch.
Er ist an der Spitze.	He is in front.
Sieht sie müde aus?	Does she look tired?
Wer wird es wohl sein?	Who could it be?

Ergänzung

1. Welche Sportart treibst du?

   Ich spiele Fußball. (Korbball oder Basketball, Federball, Hockey, Tennis, Tischtennis, Golf).

   Was machst du sonst noch gern?

   Ich schwimme gern.

   Ich laufe gern Ski.

   Ich fahre gern Rad.

   Ich laufe gern Schlittschuh.

   Ich wandere gern.

   Was hast du gestern gemacht?

   Ich habe Tennis gespielt.

   Ich bin gewandert.

Golf

Tennis

Hockey

Tischtennis

Korbball
Basketball

Fußball

Federball

2. Was möchtest du trinken?

   Ich möchte eine Cola trinken.
   (eine Tasse Kaffee, eine Tasse Tee, eine Tasse Kakao, ein Glas Wasser, Bier, Wein, Milch, Limonade)

197

Ausspracheübung

initial /r/	middle /r/	final /r/
Rad	andere	Sportler
rüber	unsere	Sommer
recht	Jahre	Nummer
Regal	Klarinette	später
rufen	interessant	hier
Reise	während	Uhr
Röcke	Europa	mir
Ruhe	fahren	vor
rot	Österreich	Tür
Frau	Marathon	aber
Bruder	warten	für
braun	fahren	Läufer
Freund	morgen	dort
fragen	Karte	Ort
groß	dürfen	Wort
drüben	Norden	Dorf
Straße	Arbeit	darf
Krawatte	vorbei	fährt

Übungen

Present Perfect Tense

The present perfect is used more frequently in German conversation than in English. It is often called the "conversational past."

Regular verbs

haben + (*ge* + 3rd person singular)
er hat gefragt. (He has asked.)
NOTE: In English two forms (*He has asked* or *He asked*) may be used. To simplify the presentation, only the present perfect form is used throughout.

The form *gefragt* (asked) is called the past participle, which in German is placed at the end of the sentence.

Example: *Ich habe meinen Vater gefragt.*
(I have asked my father.)

Irregular verbs
The irregular verbs, as the term suggests, do not follow the pattern above in forming their past participle. Some of them use *sein* instead of *haben*. Therefore, you must learn each present perfect form individually.

Examples: *Sie hat den Kaffee getrunken.*
(She has drunk the coffee.)
Sie ist nach Hause gefahren.
(She has driven home.)

NOTE: Verbs which use a form of *sein* must both
— indicate motion or change of condition *and*
— be intransitive, i.e. a verb that cannot have a direct object.

Here are the irregular forms for most of the verbs you have learned so far:

Infinitive	Past Participle
beginnen (to begin)	begonnen
bieten (to offer)	geboten
bleiben (to stay)	ist geblieben
bringen (to bring)	gebracht
denken (to think)	gedacht
essen (to eat)	gegessen
fahren (to drive)	ist gefahren
finden (to find)	gefunden
geben (to give)	gegeben
gefallen (to like)	gefallen
gehen (to go)	ist gegangen
gewinnen (to win)	gewonnen
haben (to have)	gehabt
helfen (to help)	geholfen
kennen (to know)	gekannt
kommen (to come)	ist gekommen
laufen (to run)	ist gelaufen
lesen (to read)	gelesen
liegen (to lie, be located)	gelegen
schlagen (to beat)	geschlagen
schreiben (to write)	geschrieben
schwimmen (to swim)	ist geschwommen
sehen (to see)	gesehen
sein (to be)	ist gewesen
sitzen (to sit)	gesessen
sprechen (to speak)	gesprochen
springen (to jump)	ist gesprungen
stehen (to stand)	gestanden
tragen (to carry)	getragen
trinken (to drink)	getrunken
tun (to do)	getan
verlassen (to leave)	verlassen
verlieren (to lose)	verloren
verstehen (to understand)	verstanden
wissen (to know)	gewußt

Verbs ending in *-ieren*

Verbs ending in *-ieren* do not have the *ge-* in the past participle.

Examples: *Maria hat Englisch studiert.*
(Maria has studied English.)
Die Studenten haben oft darüber diskutiert.
(The students have often discussed it.)

Folgt den Beispielen!

1. Hast du ihn gefragt?   Ja, ich habe ihn gefragt.
   Hast du sie gesucht?
   Hast du die Wurst gekauft?
   Hast du ihr geglaubt?
   Hast du Fußball gespielt?
   Hast du vor dem Kino gewartet?

2. Die Reise dauert vier Studen.   Die Reise hat vier Stunden gedauert.
   Die Zuschauer hören die Musik.
   Wir lernen Deutsch.
   Michael parkt das Auto.
   Es regnet nicht.
   Die Fahrräder kosten viel.
   Die Sportler üben oft.

3. Wohnen Sie in Hamburg?   Haben Sie in Hamburg gewohnt?
   Wann tanzt ihr denn?
   Kochst du das Essen?
   Paßt der Anzug gut?
   Stempelt er den Ausweis?
   Was machen die Jungen?

4. Was hast du am Montag gemacht?   Am Montag habe ich Fußball gespielt.
      (Fußball spielen)
   Was hast du am Samstag gemacht?
      (zu Hause arbeiten)
   Was hast du am Donnerstag gemacht?
      (eine Kassette kaufen)
   Was hast du am Sonntag gemacht?
      (spät frühstücken)
   Was hast du am Dienstag gemacht?
      (die Aufgaben machen)

5. Ich höre diese Musik. Und du?   Ich habe diese Musik schon gehört.
   Ich lese die Zeitung. Und du?

Ich esse Abendbrot. Und du?

Ich trage den Koffer. Und du?

Ich trinke Milch. Und du?

Ich verstehe ihn. Und du?

6. Achim bringt mir ein Geschenk.   Achim hat mir ein Geschenk gebracht.

   Hast du viel Zeit?

   Was denkt ihr?

   Wir schreiben eine Arbeit.

   Ich gebe dir meine Karte.

   Die Sportler verlieren nicht.

7. Das Mädchen — schwimmen   Das Mädchen ist geschwommen.

    Die Studenten — fahren

    Der Besucher — bleiben

    Meine Tante — gehen

    Daniel und Uwe — laufen

    ich — kommen

8. Gehen Sie zu Fuß?   Sind Sie zu Fuß gegangen?

   Die Touristen fahren nach Deutschland.

   Das Spiel ist sehr interessant.

   Wie weit springst du?

   Daniel kommt später.

   Wir schwimmen gern.

9. Provide the correct form of *haben* or *sein*.

1. Wann _____ ihr nach Hause gekommen?

2. Die Jugendlichen _____ Tennis gespielt.

3. Es _____ gestern viel geschneit.

4. Angelika _____ mir die Schultasche gebracht.

5. Die Studenten _____ zwei Stunden im Sprachlabor gewesen.

6. Der Lehrer _____ lange vor dem Bahnhof gewartet.

7. Um wieviel Uhr _____ ihr Abendbrot gegessen?

8. _____ Sie mit dem Zug gefahren?

9. Was _____ du am Abend getrunken?

10. _____ ihr zur Uni gelaufen?

10. *Was hast du gestern gemacht?* Beantwortet diese Frage! Folgt dem Beispiel!

   Beispiel: *ein Buch lesen*

          Ich habe ein Buch gelesen.

1. eine Trompete kaufen

2. Fußball spielen

3. in der Stadt sein

4. eine Reise machen

5. mit meinem Auto fahren

6. zum Sportwettbewerb gehen

7. deiner Freundin schreiben

11. Change the following sentences from the present to the present perfect.

1. Daniel springt weiter als Achim.

2. Was ist deine Bestleistung?

3. Ich habe viel Glück.

4. Verstehen Sie Deutsch?

5. Wir gehen um acht Uhr ins Kino.

6. Die Sportler laufen zehn Kilometer.

7. Am Sonntag regnet es nicht.

8. Warum glaubst du ihm denn?

9. Die Zuschauer hören die Musik.

10. Tragen die Touristen ihr Gepäck?

11. Der Ansager gibt das Startsignal.

12. Weißt du, wann die Vorstellung beginnt?

12. Complete each sentence by using the proper form of *haben* or *sein* as well as one of the verbs from the columns below. Be sure to use the proper form of the past participle.

1. Die Reise _____ acht Stunden _____.

2. Manche Läufer _____ älter als 50 Jahre _____.

3. Wie _____ euch der Film _____?

4. _____ die Studenten Englisch _____?

5. Ich _____ eine Tasse Kaffee _____.

6. Am Sonnabend _____ wir ins Kino _____.

7. _____ du diese Zeitung _____?

8. _____ ihr mit dem Auto _____?

9. Die Zuschauer _____ beim Sportwettbewerb _____.

10. _____ Sie die Kalte Platte schon _____?

11. _____ du deine Freundin um zwei Uhr _____?

12. Er _____ kein Wort _____.

dauern	essen
sein	sehen
trinken	fahren
lesen	gehen
gefallen	sprechen
klatschen	sagen

13. Complete the following sentences using a different verb (in the present perfect tense) each time.

1. Am Dienstag haben wir _____.

2. Warum sind die Zuschauer _____?

3. Mein Freund hat _____.

4. Hast du _____?
5. Ich bin gestern _____.
6. Die Sportler sind _____.
7. Haben die Studenten _____?
8. Uwe hat _____.

Possessive Adjectives (Dative)

	Dative Singular			Plural
	masculine	*feminine*	*neuter*	
ich	meinem	meiner	meinem	meinen
du	deinem	deiner	deinem	deinen
er	seinem	seiner	seinem	seinen
sie	ihrem	ihrer	ihrem	ihren
es	seinem	seiner	seinem	seinen
wir	unserem	unserer	unserem	unseren
ihr	euerem	euerer	euerem	eueren
sie	ihrem	ihrer	ihrem	ihren
Sie	Ihrem	Ihrer	Ihrem	Ihren

The endings for the dative possessive adjectives are the same as for the indefinite article (*ein*-words).

Folgt den Beispielen!

14. Was gibst du deiner Schwester?
    (eine Schallplatte)

    Ich gebe meiner Schwester eine Schallplatte.

    Was kaufst du deiner Freudin?
    (eine Bluse)

    Was bringst du deinem Lehrer?
    (das Wörterbuch)

    Was sagst du deinem Freund?
    (kein Wort)

    Was kochst du deiner Mutter?
    (das Essen)

15. Mit wem sprichst du denn?
    (meine Tante)

    Mit meiner Tante.

    Wem antwortest du denn?
    (sein Bruder)

    Von wem hast du denn gehört?
    (ihre Freundin)

    Wem hast du denn geglaubt?
    (deine Mutter)

    Aus welchem Gebäude werdet ihr denn
       kommen?
    (unser Haus)

16. Ich wohne nicht weit von meiner Schule.
    euer — Straße
    ihr — Schwester
    dein — Freund
    unser — Wohnung
    sein — Onkel

Ich wohne nicht weit von meiner Schule.

17. Wie geht es deinem Vater?
    euer — Großmutter
    Ihr — Sohn
    sein — Angestellter
    unser — Freundin
    mein — Lehrer

Wie geht es deinem Vater?

18. Sie spricht viel von ihrem Bruder.
    Hast du deiner Tante geschrieben?
    Ich glaube seiner Tochter.
    Er sagt es unserem Lehrer.
    Kommt doch mit euerem Freund!
    Ich habe von Ihrem Sohn gehört.

Sie spricht viel von ihren Brüdern.

19. Er spricht viel von seiner Reise.
    Buch
    Freundin
    Lehrer
    Schallplatte
    Auto

Er spricht viel von seinen Reisen.

20. **Supply the German equivalents for the words in parentheses.**

    1. Ich bringe (my aunt, his mother, their uncle, her girlfriends) _____ ein Geschenk.
    2. Gehst du zu (my teacher, our grandmother, his house) _____?
    3. Wie weit ist es von (our university, her apartment, their school) _____?
    4. Wir haben das (his sons, their father, her aunt) _____ nicht geglaubt.
    5. Antworte (your teacher, your brothers, your mother) _____, Michael!

21. **Form complete sentences using the information provided.**

    1. Peter / kaufen / seine Freundin / Kassette
    2. Wann / werden / Angelika / mit / ihr Lehrer / sprechen
    3. Die Angestellten / kommen / vier Uhr / aus / ihre Geschäfte
    4. Geben / du / dein Freund / ein Kugelschreiber
    5. Außer / meine Tante / besuchen / wir / unser Onkel
    6. Ansager / sprechen / viel / von / seine Sportler
    7. Student / gehen / zu / sein Zimmer

Lesestück 1

Marathonlauf in Leipzig

Jedes Jahr findet der KMU°-Marathonlauf in Leipzig statt. Mehr als 600 Sportler° machen bei diesem Sportwettbewerb mit. Schon eine Stunde vor dem Start kommen die Läufer° zur Karl-Marx-Universität. Dort wird der Marathonlauf beginnen. Manche Teilnehmer° studieren noch einmal die Strecke. Sie ist mehr als 40 Kilometer lang.

Karl-Marx-Universität
athletes
runners

participants

Ein paar Minuten vor zwei Uhr stehen alle Läufer am Start. Die Polizei sperrt den Verkehr ab°. Niemand° darf jetzt an der Universität vorbeifahren°. Das Rote Kreuz steht auch schon bereit°. Die Zuschauer° warten ungeduldig. Es ist zwei Uhr.

sperrt…ab blocks off/no one drive by/steht… bereit is ready spectators

Ein Ansager gibt das Zeichen° zum Start. Zuerst starten acht Rollstuhlfahrer°. Fünf Minuten später hört man den Ansager wieder. Jetzt gibt er das Startsignal für die Läufer. Alle Teilnehmer laufen sofort los°. Sie sind in bester Form. Aber wie viele werden es schaffen, mehr als 40 Kilometer zu laufen? Vom Start laufen sie erst zweimal um die Universität herum°. Der Leiter° für den Marathonlauf sieht manchmal auf seine Uhr. Er weiß genau, wann

signal
wheel chair drivers

laufen…los start running

around/person in charge

Die Teilnehmer sind in bester Form.

Wo findet der Marathonlauf statt?

Seine Kameraden gratulieren dem Sieger.

die Läufer wieder vorbeikommen°. Es dauert auch nicht lange, da kommen schon die ersten Läufer. Andreas Sprenger, Nummer 203, ist an der Spitze. Er hat schon die letzten zwei Jahre hier gewonnen. Wird er es auch dieses Mal schaffen? *come by*

Nach ein paar Kilometern laufen die Sportler nicht mehr so dicht° zusammen. Außer den Männern° starten auch mehr als 40 Frauen diesen Marathonlauf. Manche Läufer sind sogar älter als 60 Jahre. *close/men*

Die Richter° notieren° die Namen von den Läufern, sobald° sie vorbeikommen. Es gibt auch Aufseher°. Sie stehen auf der Straße und passen auf°, daß die Strecke für die Läufer frei bleibt. Einige Radfahrer° stehen bereit und wollen ihrer Mannschaft° helfen°. *judges/jot down/ as soon as attendants watch bicycle rider/team help*

Auf der Strecke gibt es einige Stellen°, wo die Sportler etwas trinken° können. Dort stehen auch Wasserbehälter°. Bei der Hitze können sich die Läufer dort etwas abkühlen°. *places drink/water containers cool off*

Nummer 203 ist noch immer an erster Stelle. Er ist jetzt schon mehr als 35 Kilometer gelaufen. Andreas Sprenger läuft sehr schnell. Er sieht gar nicht müde aus. Am Ziel° sagt der Ansager den Zuschauern, daß der erste Läufer bald ankommen wird. Wer wird es wohl sein? Plötzlich° hört man die Zuschauer klatschen°. Der erste Sportler läuft dem Ziel entgegen°. Der Sieger° heißt auch dieses Jahr wieder Andreas Sprenger. Er hat zum dritten Mal gewonnen. Seine Kameraden° gratulieren° ihm. Er hat den Marathonlauf in der Zeit von 2 Stunden und 17 Minuten gewonnen. *finish line suddenly/applaud towards/winner buddies/congratulate*

Fragen über das Lesestück

1. Wie viele Sportler kommen zum Marathonlauf in Leipzig?
2. Wo beginnt der Marathonlauf?
3. Was macht die Polizei ein paar Minuten vor dem Start?
4. Wer startet zuerst?
5. Wo laufen die Sportler zuerst?
6. Wer hat den Marathonlauf schon zweimal gewonnen?
7. Wie viele Frauen starten im KMU-Marathonlauf?
8. Wie alt sind die ältesten Sportler?
9. Was machen die Richter? Und die Aufseher?
10. Was müssen die Läufer bei der Hitze manchmal tun?
11. Warum sieht Andreas Sprenger nicht sehr müde aus?
12. Warum klatschen die Zuschauer?
13. Wer gewinnt den Marathonlauf?
14. Wie lange ist der Sieger gelaufen?

Erweiterung

22. Wie heißt das auf deutsch?

1. Will he participate?
2. Did you beat him? No, he is much better than I am.
3. I like to play tennis.
4. Did you hike yesterday?
5. She would like to drink a glass of water.
6. It's his turn.
7. He doesn't look tired.
8. The spectators are applauding.
9. They congratulate her.
10. Who won?
11. The police are blocking off the street.
12. The athletes are waiting at the finish line.

23. Beantwortet die Fragen!

Welche Sportart treibst du?

Warum hast du diesen Sport gern?

Welcher Sport ist in deiner Schule sehr beliebt?

Kommen viele Zuschauer zu den Sportwettbewerben in deiner Schule? Warum?

Was trinkst du gern zum Mittagessen?

Rückblick

I. Complete the comparison by providing the comparative and the superlative.

1. Heute morgen ist es kalt. Später ist es _____. Am Abend ist es_____.
2. Das Museum ist alt. Das Rathaus ist _____. Das Schloß ist _____.
3. Die BRD ist klein. Die DDR ist _____. Österreich ist _____.
4. Frankfurt ist weit von München. Berlin ist _____ von München. Hamburg ist _____.
5. Das Fahrrad fährt schnell. Der Bus fährt _____. Der Zug fährt _____.
6. Die Elbe ist lang. Der Rhein ist _____. Die Donau ist _____.

II. Provide the proper form of the possessive adjective in each sentence.

1. Er geht mit (his girlfriend) _____ ins Kino.
2. Sie sind zu (their parents) _____ gefahren.
3. (Her blouse) _____ ist sehr teuer.
4. Ich antworte (my teachers) _____.

5. Wir spielen (our music) _____ sehr gern.

6. Kauf (your brothers) _____ ein paar Karten, Daniel!

7. Wir essen gern bei (your mother) _____, Kerstin und Jörg.

III. Choose the most appropriate verb from the list below to complete each phrase.

1. den Sportwettbewerb _____

2. Auto _____

3. Schach _____

4. ein Glas Limonade _____

5. Glück _____

6. einen Walzer _____

7. die Lektion _____

8. meine Hausaufgaben _____

9. Abendbrot _____

10. eine Frage _____

fahren	spielen
trinken	tanzen
haben	gewinnen
beantworten	verstehen
essen	machen

IV. Supply the appropriate forms of *dieser, jeder, welcher.*

1. _____ Buch hast du gelesen?

2. Ich habe fast _____ Film gesehen.

3. _____ Mäntel sind sehr teuer.

4. _____ Hemd kostet 40 DM.

5. _____ Karten hast du gekauft?

6. Was machst du mit _____ Kassette?

7. Er ist aus _____ Museum gekommen.

8. _____ Fahrrad habt ihr gekauft?

Lesestück 2

Die DDR — Land und Städte

Die Deutsche Demokratische Republik grenzt im Osten an Polen, im Südosten an die Tschechoslowakei und im Westen an die Bundesrepublik Deutschland. Im Norden bildet° die Ostsee eine natürliche Grenze. Zwei Drittel der DDR bestehen aus dem *Tiefland* (im Norden) und ein Drittel besteht aus dem *Mittelgebirgsland* (im Süden). Das Erzgebirge liegt im Süden und reicht° bis in die Tschechoslowakei. Der Fichtelberg (1 214 m) ist der höchste Berg. Im Südwesten liegt der Thüringer Wald. Der Harz liegt im Westen der DDR und reicht bis in die BRD. Der höchste Berg im Harz ist der Brocken (1 142 m).

forms

reaches

75% der Bevölkerung wohnt in Städten. (Stralsund)

Die Elbe ist der längste Fluß.

Im Norden ist das Tiefland.

Die Elbe ist der längste Fluß. Die Elbe erreicht in der DDR eine Länge von 566 Kilometern. Nach der Elbe kommt die Saale mit 427 Kilometern. Der drittlängste Fluß ist die Oder (162 km). Die Oder bildet die natürliche Grenze zwischen der DDR und Polen. Der Oder-Spree-Kanal (84 km) ist der längste Kanal°. *canal*

In der DDR leben° fast 17 Millionen Menschen. 75 Prozent° der Bevölkerung° wohnt in Städten. Die größte Stadt ist Berlin (Ost), die Hauptstadt der DDR. Berlin (Ost) liegt im Osten der DDR und hat ungefähr 1,2 Millionen Einwohner. Die zweitgrößte Stadt, Leipzig (560 000 Einwohner), liegt im Süden. Jedes Jahr kommen eine halbe Million Besucher zur Messe° (Frühling und Herbst). Die nächstgrößte Stadt, Dresden (515 000 Einwohner), liegt im Südosten. Dresden hat viele Museen° und historische Gebäude. Nach Dresden kommt Karl-Marx-Stadt (315 000 Einwohner). Karl-Marx-Stadt liegt im Süden und ist eine wichtige Industriestadt°. Wie Dresden liegt auch Magdeburg an der Elbe. Magdeburg (290 000 Einwohner) liegt im Westen der DDR. *live/percent* *population* *Trade Fair* *museums* *industrial city*

Die Insel Rügen ist die größte Insel der DDR. Jedes Jahr verbringen° über 700 000 Menschen ihre Ferien° auf dieser beliebten Insel. *spend/vacation*

Fragen über das Lesestück

1. Welche Länder grenzen an die DDR?
2. Wie heißen die zwei Landschaften?
3. Wie heißt der höchste Berg und wie hoch ist er?
4. Wie heißen die drei größten Flüsse?
5. Wie viele Menschen wohnen in Städten?
6. Wie heißen die drei größten Städte und wo liegen sie?
7. Was für Sehenswürdigkeiten gibt es in Dresden?
8. Welche zwei Städte liegen an der Elbe.
9. Wie heißt die größte Insel und was machen viele Besucher dort jedes Jahr?

Sprachspiegel

I. Describe your favorite sport in one or two paragraphs. Your description might include such items as: When do you participate (time of season)? Where do you do your sport? With whom do you play? How long have you participated in this sport?

II. Write at least one sentence in German defining the following:

1. Sportwettbewerb
2. Weitsprung
3. Ansager
4. Zuschauer
5. Sportler

III. Schreib einen kurzen Aufsatz über das Thema *Ein Marathonlauf!*

der Ansager (Leipzig)

Wie sagt man's?

Wie schnell bist du denn gelaufen?
13 Sekunden.
Im Hundert-Meter Lauf bist du immer klasse.

Kannst du 10 Kilometer schaffen?
Mit dem Auto ja, aber nicht zu Fuß.
Das kann jeder.
Aber nicht jeder hat ein Auto.

Ich habe schon viel trainiert?
Für das Tennisspiel?
Nein, wir spielen morgen Fußball.
Na, dann viel Glück!

Diesmal bist du besser gewesen.
Ich habe eben Glück gehabt.
Nein, du bist in guter Form.

Wann findet das Fußballspiel statt?
Am Freitag, um vier.
Gehst du hin?
Vielleicht.

Hast du Paul geholfen?
Er braucht meine Hilfe nicht.
Warum nicht?
Er trainiert viel mehr als früher.

Gehst du zum Sportwettbewerb?
Ich glaube nicht.
Angelika soll die Beste sein.
Im Weitsprung?
Nein, im Tausend-Meter-Lauf.

Zungenbrecher

Hundert hurtige Hunde hetzen hinter hundert hurtigen Hasen her.
(A hundred speedy dogs are racing after a hundred speedy rabbits.)

Kulturecke

Sports

Germans have become more and more concerned about physical fitness. Running, jogging, hiking and walking are just some of the sports supported by the German Sports Federation *(DSB-Deutscher Sportbund)* for people of all ages. Throughout Germany, usually in a forest or park area, you can find designated exercise areas marked *"TRIMM-DICH-PFAD"* (literally meaning "Slim Down Path"). To keep physically fit or to participate in organized sports, Germans join local sports clubs. Every fourth person in the Federal Republic is a member of a sports club.

Soccer *(Fußball)* is by far the most popular sport. During the soccer season, from August to May, millions of people watch the games in the various stadiums around the country or on television at home. The national team of the Federal Republic is considered one of the best in the world.

Germany has produced world-class athletes in track and field competition *(Leicht-athletik)* as well. Meets between various countries are scheduled continuously to compare athletic achievements with the rest of the world. The sport with the longest tradition in Germany is gymnastics *(Turnen)*, which became popular in the early 19th century and is today the second most popular sport with almost three million Germans participating. The sport of handball *(Handball)* is not the same as we know it. The German handball is an indoor or outdoor sport played with a ball slightly smaller than a soccer ball. Similar to soccer, the object is to get the ball down between the goal posts.

For many decades in Germany, tennis *(Tennis)* was reserved only for the upper class. This is no longer true today. Tennis courts, which typically have a clay surface, are now found in all cities and most smaller towns as well. It is difficult to find golf courses in Germany. The sport of golf *(Golf)* is played by few Germans who belong to private clubs. However, the recreational sport of miniature golf *(Minigolf* or *Kleingolf)* is played by Germans everywhere. There are even championships in which the best players participate.

Various types of horse races *(Pferderennen)* take place in major cities from early spring through late fall. Horseback riding *(Reiten)* has been popular for centuries. However, this sport is expensive and practiced by only a few. In horsemanship competition, German riders have done extremely well in international competition, winning many medals in the Olympics over the last two to three decades.

The water sports, such as sailing *(Segeln)*, enjoy a tremendous popularity among Germans. The famous annual *Kieler Woche,* an international sailing regatta, has the best sailors compete for the grand prize. Others enjoy sailing more as a leisure-time sport. Sailing is particularly popular on the North Sea and Baltic Sea as well as in the few sailing lakes that Germany has to offer. Recently, surfing *(Surfen)* has been enthusiastically received by Germans. There are over one million people who participate in this sport. Those who enjoy more treacherous waters are involved in white water canoeing *(Wildwasser fahren)*, which was officially introduced as a sport in the 1972 Olympic Games held in Germany.

Over a million Germans belong to rifle and pistol clubs *(Schützenvereine)*. Many of the members enjoy the marksmanship training as well as hunting *(Jagen)* in areas that are leased to trained and licensed hunters. A less expensive sport is fishing *(Angeln)*. Germans fish not only in the lakes but also in the various rivers.

Most cities have indoor or outdoor skating facilities. Here Germans can practice and improve their skill. Germany has produced several world-class figure skaters *(Eiskunstläufer)* during the past three decades. Ice hockey *(Eishockey)* was relatively unknown twenty years ago. During the last few years, however, Germany has done quite well in international com-

Marathonlauf (Leipzig)

Segeln ist sehr beliebt.

ein Trimm-Dich-Pfad

Was machen diese Leute? (Bayern)

Leichtathletik (Jena)

Hochsprung

Handball

Lektion 9

petition. Most sports organizations also have a youth program. During the winter months, many Germans head for the mountains in Southern Germany and go skiing *(Ski laufen)*. Those who master the skill after years of hard training can compete in local, national or even international competition. Endurance is tested not only in downhill skiing but also in cross-country skiing *(Skilanglauf)*. Some of these competitive races cover distances of up to 30 miles. Another winter sport is curling, seen mostly in the southern part of Germany.

Gliding *(Segelfliegen)* is also a popular sport in Southern Germany. There the hills and mountains provide the favorable air currents needed to stay in the air for a long time. Those who are most daring participate in a new sport called hang-gliding *(Drachen fliegen)* in which these sporting people push themselves off cliffs or hills and sit on a rod strapped to a kite-like sail. Finally, the sport of mountaineering *(Bergsteigen)* is practiced in the mountainous regions of Germany. Those who become experts eventually climb the many challenging peaks found in the Alps.

Drachen fliegen

Ski laufen

Skilanglauf

Vokabeln

sich **abkühlen** to cool off
absperren to block off
der **Ansager,-** announcer
aufpassen to watch, keep an eye on
something
der **Aufseher,-** attendant
der **Basketball,-̈e** basketball
bereitstehen to be ready, stand ready
die **Bestleistung,-en** best performance
das **Bier,-e** beer
der **Bleistift,-e** pencil
die **Blockflöte,-n** recorder
die **Chance,-n** chance
dabei in the process, while doing that
dicht close
dran sein to be one's turn
Ich bin dran. It's my turn.
das **Endergebnis,-se** final result
entgegenlaufen to run towards
der **Federball,-̈e** badminton
die **Form-en** form, shape
früh early
gestern yesterday
das **Glas,-̈er** glass
das **Golf** golf
gratulieren to congratulate
helfen to help
herumlaufen to run around
das **Hockey** hockey
hoffentlich hopefully
der **Kakao** hot chocolate, cocoa
der **Kamerad,-en** buddy
kaum hardly
klatschen to applaud
der **Korbball,-̈e** basketball
lang long
der **Läufer,-** runner
der **Leiter,-** head, person in charge
loslaufen to start running
die **Limonade,-n** soft drink
das **Mal,-e** time(s)
der **Mann,-̈er** man
die **Mannschaft,-en** team
der **Marathonlauf,-̈er** marathon run
mindestens at least
mitmachen to participate
niemand nobody, noone
notieren to jot down, make a note of
die **Nummer,-n** number
phantastisch fantastic, great
plötzlich suddenly
die **Polizei** police
das **Prozent,-e** percent

der **Radfahrer,-** bicycle rider
der **Richter,-** judge
der **Rollstuhlfahrer,-** wheel chair driver
das **Rote Kreuz** Red Cross
schaffen to manage (it), make (it)
schlagen to beat
Schlittschuh laufen to skate
schwimmen to swim
der **Sieger,-** winner
Ski laufen to ski
sobald as soon as
sonst besides, otherwise
die **Spitze,-n** top
an der Spitze sein to be in front
die **Sportart,-en** kind of sport
der **Sportwettbewerb,-e** sports competition
springen to jump
der **Start,-e** start
starten to start
das **Startsignal,-e** starting signal
stattfinden to take place
die **Stelle,-n** place, spot
die **Tasse,-n** cup
der **Teilnehmer,-** participant
das **Tennis** tennis
trainieren to train, practice
treiben to drive, do
Sport treiben to participate in
sports
trinken to drink
übertreffen to surpass, beat
der **Verstand** reason, mind
mehr Glück als Verstand haben
to have more luck than brains
versuchen to try
vorbeifahren to drive by
vorbeikommen to come by
vorhin before, earlier
der **Wasserbehälter,-** water container
der **Wein,-e** wine
der **Weitsprung,-̈e** broad jump
das **Zeichen,-** signal, sign
der **Zentimeter,-** centimeter
das **Ziel,-e** finish (line)
der **Zuschauer,-** spectator

Dialog

Beim Reisebüro

ANGESTELLTE: Bitteschön?

KUNDE: Meine Frau und ich möchten eine Reise machen.

ANGESTELLTE: Wissen Sie schon, wohin?

KUNDE: In den sonnigen Süden. Es kommt aber ganz auf den Preis an.

ANGESTELLTE: Wir haben gerade ein Sonderangebot...zwei Wochen in Mallorca.

KUNDE: Das klingt ja ganz interessant.

ANGESTELLTE: Sehen Sie! Unser Prospekt beschreibt alles...zwei Wochen, einschließlich Flug, Hotel und zwei Mahlzeiten pro Tag.

KUNDE: Sie machen mir schon richtig den Mund wässerig. Hm, der Preis ist sehr günstig. Haben Sie im Juli noch etwas frei?

ANGESTELLTE: Das kann ich gleich mal nachsehen...Ja, wir haben noch ein Doppelzimmer, Abfahrt am 9. Juli. Soll ich zwei Plätze für Sie buchen?

KUNDE: Ja, bitte, auf den Namen Krüger.

ANGESTELLTE: Schön, Herr Krüger. Es geht in Ordnung.

ANGESTELLTE: Sie müssen die Reise einen Monat vor der Abfahrt bezahlen.

KUNDE: Ich nehme an, Sie schicken mir die Rechnung zu.

ANGESTELLTE: Die bekommen Sie in ein paar Tagen. Nehmen Sie doch noch diesen Prospekt mit! Ich wünsche Ihnen eine gute Reise.

KUNDE: Vielen Dank.

Fragen über den Dialog

1. Wohin möchten Herr und Frau Krüger fahren?
2. Von welchem Sonderangebot spricht die Angestellte?
3. Wo können sie alles über Mallorca lesen?
4. Wie findet Herr Krüger den Preis für die Reise?
5. Wann möchten Krügers die Reise machen?
6. Wann muß Herr Krüger die Reise bezahlen?
7. Was wird das Reisebüro in ein paar Tagen tun?

At the Travel Agency

CLERK: Can I help you?

CUSTOMER: My wife and I would like to take a trip.

CLERK: Do you know where to?

CUSTOMER: To the sunny south. It depends entirely on the price.

CLERK: We're just having a special offer…two weeks in Mallorca.

CUSTOMER: That sounds quite interesting.

CLERK: Look! Our brochure describes everything…two weeks, including flight, hotel and two meals a day.

CUSTOMER: You're already making my mouth water. Hm, the price is very reasonable. Do you still have something available in July?

CLERK: I can check that right away…Yes, we still have a double room, departure July 9th. Should I book two seats for you?

CUSTOMER: Yes, please, in the name of Krüger.

CLERK: Fine, Mr. Krüger. It will be taken care of.

CLERK: You'll have to pay the trip a month before departure.

CUSTOMER: I assume you'll send me the bill.

CLERK: You'll get it in a few days. Why don't you take this brochure along? I hope you have a good trip.

CUSTOMER: Thank you.

Nützliche Ausdrücke

Bitteschön?	Can I help you?
Es kommt auf den Preis an.	It depends on the price.
Das klingt gut.	That sounds good.
Ich sehe mal nach.	I'll check it.
Es geht in Ordnung.	It will be taken care of. That's O.K.
Ich nehme an…	I assume…
Gute Reise!	Have a good trip!
Er hält an.	He is stopping.
Wir müssen umsteigen.	We have to transfer.
Sie machen eine Rast.	They take a rest.
Wir sitzen im Freien.	We are sitting outside.

Ergänzung

Metric—U.S. Conversion

German Metric		U.S.
1	Gramm (g)	0.035 ounce
1	Pfund (Pfd)	1.1 pounds
1	Kilogramm - *or* Kilo (kg)	2.2 pounds
1	Zentimeter (cm)	0.3937 inch
2,54	Zentimeter	1 inch
1	Meter (m)	3.281 feet
1609,3	Meter	1 mile
1	Kilometer (km)	1.094 yards
1	Liter (l)	2.113 pints

Thermometer Readings

German thermometers use the centigrade scale. To convert Fahrenheit to centigrade, subtract 32, then multiply by 5 and divide by 9. To convert centigrade to Fahrenheit, multiply by 9, divide by 5 and add 32. The chart below gives some sample readings with the conversion.

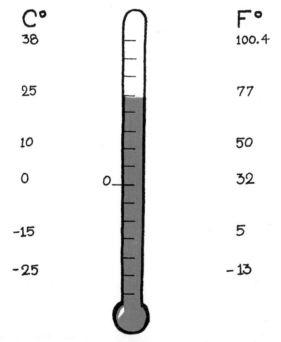

C°	F°
38	100.4
25	77
10	50
0	32
−15	5
−25	−13

Metric Units	
1 Pfund	500 Gramm
2 Pfund	1 Kilogramm (or: 1 000 Gramm)
1 Meter	100 Zentimeter
1 000 Meter	1 Kilometer

Ausspracheübung

/ ai /	/ oi /	/ au /
bei	neun	aus
drei	Leute	blau
Mai	teuer	kauft
weiß	euch	Auto
heißt	deutsch	laufen
Teil	heute	genau
weit	Freund	auf
ein	Läufer	brauchen
klein	Häuser	August
Zeit	Bedeutung	Haus

Übungen

Verbs with Separable Prefixes

With modal auxiliaries
When you use modal auxiliaries in a sentence, combine the separable prefix with the verb.

Examples: *Er muß um sechs Uhr **aufstehen**.*
*Sie **will** ihre Freundin **mitbringen**.*

Present perfect tense
In the present perfect, add the separable prefix to the past participle for regular and irregular verbs.

Examples: *Ich habe meinen Freund **angerufen**.*
*Er hat heute nichts **vorgehabt**.*

As you have seen in the previous lesson, you must learn the present perfect form of all irregular verbs individually. You need only learn the past participle of a particular verb, regardless of the addition of various prefixes, since the prefix changes the meaning but not the structure.

Examples: *Wir sind nicht **mitgekommen**.* (We didn't come along.)
*Ich bin heute morgen **vorbeigekommen**.* (I came by this morning.)
*Bist du früh **angekommen**?* (Did you arrive early?)

NOTE: The accent or emphasis is always on the separable prefix.

Here is a list of the most important irregular separable prefix verbs that you have learned so far:

Infinitive	Past Participle
anhaben (to have on)	angehabt
anhalten (to stop)	angehalten
ankommen (to arrive)	ist angekommen
annehmen (to assume)	angenommen
anrufen (to call, phone)	angerufen
aufstehen (to get up)	ist aufgestanden
aussehen (to look)	ausgesehen
aussteigen (to get off)	ist ausgestiegen
einsteigen (to get in)	ist eingestiegen
herumfahren (to drive around)	ist herumgefahren
hineingehen (to go inside)	ist hineingegangen
hierherkommen (to come here)	ist hierhergekommen
loslaufen (to start running)	ist losgelaufen
mitbringen (to bring along)	mitgebracht
mitkommen (to come along)	ist mitgekommen
mitnehmen (to take along)	mitgenommen
nachsehen (to check)	nachgesehen
stattfinden (to take place)	stattgefunden
umsteigen (to transfer)	ist umgestiegen
vorbeifahren (to drive by)	ist vorbeigefahren
vorbeikommen (to come by)	ist vorbeigekommen
vorhaben (to plan)	vorgehabt
weiterfahren (to continue driving)	ist weitergefahren
zugeben (to admit)	zugegeben
zurückgehen (to go back)	ist zurückgegangen
zurückfahren (to drive back)	ist zurückgefahren

Folgt den Beispielen!

1. Was hast du an?   Ich habe einen Anzug an.
    (einen Anzug)
    Wann kommst du vorbei?
    (um sieben Uhr)
    Wer steigt ein?
    (die Touristen)
    Wen ruft er an? (Sabine)
    Was räumen die Jungen ab?
    (das Geschirr)
    Was löst der Ausländer ein?
    (einen Reisescheck)
    Wann machst du sauber?
    (später)

2. Stehst du um halb sieben auf?   Ja, ich stehe um halb sieben auf.
    Kommst du heute nachmittag rüber?

Legst du die Schallplatte auf?

Hast du am Samstag etwas vor?

Hält der Zug dort an?

Steigen die Besucher beim Museum
aus?

Bringt er seine Freundin mit?

3. Uwe kommt mit.   Uwe möchte mitkommen.

   Der Kunde probiert es an.

   Die Leute fahren zurück.

   Wir steigen aus.

   Ich schicke dir das Geschenk zu.

   Frau Müller bereitet das Essen zu.

   Sie kaufen heute ein.

4. Wann kommt das Flugzeug an?   Wann soll das Flugzeug ankommen?

   Was zieht der Kunde an?

   Machst du dein Zimmer sauber?

   Um wieviel Uhr findet die Vorstellung
   statt?

   Warum geht ihr da hinein?

   Wie sieht die Dame aus?

   Paßt du nicht auf?

5. Ich habe den Tisch abgeräumt.   Ich habe den Tisch nicht abgeräumt.
   Und du?

   Ich habe meinen Eltern zugewinkt.
   Und du?

   Ich habe beim Spiel mitgemacht.
   Und du?

   Ich habe es ausgefüllt. Und du?

   Ich habe das Abendbrot zubereitet.
   Und du?

   Ich habe den Reisescheck eingelöst.
   Und du?

6. Wir haben es mitgebracht.   Wir haben es mitgebracht.
   anziehen   Wir haben es angezogen.
   vorhaben
   zugeben
   mitnehmen
   annehmen

7. Sie steigen dort aus.   Sie sind dort ausgestiegen.
   Ich fahre dort weiter.
   Steigt er dort ein?
   Wann kommst du dort an?
   Die Familie fährt dort vorbei.
   Wir gehen dort hinein.

8. Paßt ihr nicht auf?   Habt ihr nicht aufgepaßt?
   Kaufst du heute ein?
   Was hast du denn vor?
   Bereitet er es gut zu?
   Ziehst du diese Hose an?
   Gibt sie es zu?
   Machen sie alles sauber?

9. **Change the following sentences from the present to the present perfect tense.**

   > **Beispiel:** *Die Leute kommen mit dem Flugzeug an.*
   > *Die Leute sind mit dem Flugzeug angekommen.*

   1. Ich sehe gleich einmal nach.
   2. Das Spiel findet um drei Uhr statt.
   3. Sie steigen schnell in die S-Bahn ein.
   4. Um wieviel Uhr ruft Angelika an?
   5. Am Nachmittag fahre ich in die Stadt mit.
   6. Warum löst du alle Reiseschecks ein?
   7. Die Schüler bringen ihre Musikinstrumente mit.
   8. Was haben Sie am Sonntag vor?
   9. Die Polizei sperrt die Straßen ab.
   10. Die Besucher winken ihnen zu.

10. **Supply the proper verb form in its appropriate tense (present or present perfect) from the list below. Be sure to separate the prefix, where appropriate.**

   1. Wann _____ du heute morgen _____?
   2. Willst du in der Stadt _____? Die Auswahl ist dort viel besser.
   3. Zuerst muß ich die Mahlzeit _____.
   4. Ich _____ das Kleid _____. Es paßt sehr gut.
   5. Peter _____ nicht _____. Jetzt kann er die Frage nicht beantworten.
   6. _____ du ihn _____? Ja, er kommt mit.
   7. Die Touristen _____ am Fernsehturm _____.
   8. Wir sollen dieses Anmeldeformular _____.
   9. Wie _____ er denn _____? Er ist sehr groß.
   10. Könnt ihr euer Zimmer _____? Wir haben keine Lust.

aufpassen	ausfüllen
aussehen	aufstehen
einkaufen	anrufen
aussteigen	zubereiten
saubermachen	anprobieren

11. **Complete each of the following sentences by using an appropriate prefix.**

   1. Die Straßenbahn steht schon da. Er steigt gleich _____.
   2. Warum ziehst du die Hose nicht _____? Vielleicht paßt sie.

3. Leg doch eine Schallplatte _____! Ich möchte etwas Musik hören.
4. Sie sind zu weit gegangen. Gehen Sie wieder _____!
5. Die Vorstellung findet um acht Uhr _____.
6. Wir werden Fußball spielen. Machst du _____?
7. Die Jugendlichen räumen das Geschirr _____.
8. Steh bitte jetzt _____! Es ist schon neun Uhr.
9. Die Schüler bringen ihre Bücher _____.
10. Meine Mutter bereitet noch schnell das Essen _____.

Verbs with Inseparable Prefixes

Present tense
There are a number of inseparable prefixes in German that remain with the verb.

Examples: *Er entwertet die Farhrkarte.*
            Bezahlst du das?

As you can see from these examples, the verbs containing inseparable prefixes are treated the same way as those without prefixes.

Present perfect tense
The past participle of regular verbs with inseparable prefixes has the same form as the third person singular of the present tense.

Examples: *Er hat die Fahrkarte entwertet.*
            Hast du das bezahlt?

Again you must learn the past participle of irregular verbs with inseparable prefixes. The list below includes the most important verbs with inseparable prefixes learned up to now. You will notice that some past participles are identical to those learned in the previous lesson, except that the prefix replaces *ge*.

Infinitive	Past Participle
beginnen (to begin)	begonnen
bekommen (to get)	bekommen
beschreiben (to describe)	beschrieben
besprechen (to discuss)	besprochen
bestehen (to consist)	bestanden
verbringen (to spend—time)	verbracht
verlassen (to leave)	verlassen
verlieren (to lose)	verloren
verstehen (to understand)	verstanden

NOTE: The accent is never on the inseparable prefix, but always on the stem of the verb.

Folgt den Beispielen!

12. Ich bekomme kein Geld.   Ich habe kein Geld bekommen.
    Er bespricht die Lektion.
    Wann verläßt du dein Haus?
    Erreicht sie das?

Die Jungen verlieren das Spiel.
Wir bezahlen an der Kasse.

13. Hast du es beantwortet?
    begrüßen
    beschreiben
    verlieren
    entwerten
    verstehen

Hast du es beantwortet?
Hast du es begrüßt?

14. Form complete sentences using the present perfect tense.

    Beispiel: *Wann / zurückfahren / ihr*
                     Wann seid ihr zurückgefahren?

  1. Studenten / beantworten / Fragen
  2. Leute / entwerten / Fahrkarten
  3. Herr / umsteigen / bei / Bahnhof
  4. Warum / du / Spiel / verlieren
  5. Bus / anhalten / dort drüben
  6. Was / vorhaben / Sie / gestern
  7. Besichtigen / ihr / Stadt
  8. Verstehen / er / Dialog
  9. Ich / mitnehmen / Schultasche
10. Bekommen / du / Geld

Accusative Prepositions

The accusative case always follows these prepositions:

durch	through
für	for
gegen	against
ohne	without
um	around

Contractions

These accusative prepositions and articles are contracted as long as there is no special emphasis on the article.

durch	+	das	=	durchs
für	+	das	=	fürs
um	+	das	=	ums

Folgt den Beispielen!

15. Wir sind durch die Stadt gegangen.

    Museum
    Universität
    Tanzschule
    Rathaus
    Bahnhof

    Wir sind durch die Stadt gegangen.
    Wir sind durchs Museum gegangen.

16. Fährst du um das Haus? (Schule)
    Gehst du um das Gebäude? (Ecke)
    Läufst du um den Parkplatz? (Rathaus)
    Gehst du um die Jugendherberge?
      (Museum)
    Fährst du um die Bank? (Reisebüro)

    Nein, ich fahre um die Schule.

17. Für wen ist das Geld? (Freund)
    Für wen ist diese Kassette? (Bruder)
    Für wen ist dieser Platz?
      (Großmutter)
    Für wen ist die Karte? (Freundin)
    Für wen ist das Geschenk? (Onkel)
    Für wen ist dieses Zimmer?
      (Schwester)

    Für meinen Freund.

18. Warum kommst du ohne dein Buch?

    Fahrrad
    Geld
    Gitarre
    Freund
    Karte

    Warum kommst du ohne dein Buch?
    Warum kommst du ohne dein Fahrrad?

19. Sie spielt gegen ihre Schwester.

    Freundin
    Lehrer
    Mannschaft
    Mutter
    Bruder

    Sie spielt gegen ihre Schwester.
    Sie spielt gegen ihre Freundin.

20. Replace the italicized words with those listed in parentheses.

    1. Wir spielen lieber ohne *ihn*. (ihr Bruder, mein Freund, du, ihr)
    2. Viele Besucher kommen durch *die Stadt*. (Rathaus, Ort, Museum, Straße, Gebäude)

3. Er fährt mit seinem Auto gegen *das Haus.* (Fahrrad, Stadtmauer, Turm, Tor)

4. Kaufst du ein Geschenk für *deinen Freund?* (er, ich, sein Onkel, ihre Tante)

5. Gehen wir lieber um *die Ecke.* (Stadttor, Kino, Universität, Bahnhof, Geschäft)

21. Complete the following sentences.

1. Ich will nicht ohne _____.

2. Das Reisebüro ist gleich um _____.

3. Für meine Schwester _____.

4. Ich möchte nicht gern gegen _____.

5. Auf unserer Reise sind wir durch _____.

6. Sie kaufen die Geschenke für _____.

7. Kannst du ohne _____?

8. Haben Sie etwas gegen _____?

Lesestück 1

Auf zur Zugspitze!

Die Alpen sind zu jeder Jahreszeit beliebt. Besonders gern besuchen viele Deutsche und Ausländer° jedes Jahr die Gegend um die Zugspitze. Die Zugspitze ist fast 3 000 m hoch und der höchste Berg in Deutschland. Sollen wir einmal eine Reise zur Zugspitze machen? Warum nicht. Also°, auf zur Zugspitze!

foreigners

O.K. then…

Grainau liegt in der Nähe von Garmisch-Partenkirchen.

Wir fahren direkt in die Alpen zu dem Ort° Grainau, in der *town*
Nähe von Garmisch-Partenkirchen. Schon bei der Ankunft in
Grainau begrüßt uns die Zugspitze aus der Entfernung. Der
Bahnhof ist sehr klein. Von hier können wir mit der Zahnradbahn° *cog-wheel train*
fast bis auf die Spitze fahren. Die Bahn fährt jede Stunde und kommt
immer pünktlich. Viele Touristen warten schon. Wir fahren ungefähr zehn Minuten bis zur nächsten Station—Eibsee. Auch hier
steigen noch einige Leute ein. Vom Eibsee fahren wir noch eine
halbe Stunde. Wir halten jetzt nicht mehr an. Unterwegs° haben wir *on the way*
einen schönen Blick auf den Eibsee. Er sieht wirklich märchenhaft° *fairy tale-like*
aus. Endlich kommen wir am Schneefernerhaus an°. Die Zahnrad- kommen…an *arrive*
bahn fährt nicht mehr weiter. Wir müssen in eine Seilbahn° um- *cable car*
steigen.

Endlich sind wir da. Heute haben wir Glück. Das Wetter ist
ausgezeichnet°. Der Himmel° ist blau und es gibt nur ein paar *excellent/sky*
Wolken°. Viele Touristen sind schon da. Hier oben° gibt es viel *clouds/on top*
zu sehen. Manche Leute sind sogar ganz auf die Spitze ge-
stiegen° und machen dort oben eine Rast. Andere gehen ein paar *climbed*
Meter weiter und kommen so nach Österreich. Die Grenze ist
direkt auf der Zugspitze. Natürlich sind wir nach einer Weile
etwas hungrig. Auf der Zugspitze gibt es ein Restaurant. Kein

Was kann man alles auf der Zugspitze sehen?

anderes deutsches Restaurant liegt so hoch wie dieses. Wir können hier an einem Tisch im Freien sitzen und eine Mahlzeit essen.

Am Nachmittag fahren wir wieder mit einer Seilbahn Richtung° Eibsee. Der Eibsee ist bei den Touristen sehr beliebt. Manche kommen nur einen Tag hierher°, wandern in der Gegend oder fahren mit Booten auf dem See. Andere bleiben eine Woche oder länger am Eibsee und übernachten in den Hotels am See.

to

kommen...hierher *come here*

Die Abfahrtszeiten° vom Eibsee nach Grainau stehen deutlich° auf dem Fahrplan am Bahnhof. Eine Zahnradbahn fährt uns nach Grainau zurück°. Viele Touristen steigen in Grainau aus°, aber manche fahren direkt bis nach Garmisch-Partenkirchen weiter.

departure times

clearly

fährt...zurück *drives back*/steigen...aus *get off*

Fragen über das Lesestück

1. Wo liegt die Zugspitze? Wie hoch ist dieser Berg?
2. Wie kommt man von Grainau zur Zugspitze?
3. Wie oft fährt die Bahn?
4. Was kann man unterwegs sehen?
5. Wo müssen wir umsteigen? Warum?
6. Wie ist das Wetter heute?
7. Was machen die Touristen dort oben?
8. Welche Grenze ist direkt auf der Zugspitze?
9. Was machen die Touristen am Eibsee?
10. Warum steigen nicht alle Touristen in Grainau aus?

Erweiterung

22. Beantwortet diese Fragen!

1. Hast du in den letzten zwei oder drei Jahren eine Reise gemacht? Wohin?
2. Was hast du auf der Reise gemacht?
3. Wann hast du eine Reise gemacht?
4. Wo habt ihr übernachtet?
5. Wie weit bist du gefahren?

23. Use a complete sentence to define each word in German.

1. Sonderangebot
2. Prospekt
3. Rechnung

4. Reisebüro

5. Restaurant

6. Tourist

24. Provide a logical response to each statement or question.

1. Bitteschön?

2. Wohin wollen Sie denn fahren?

3. Ja, dort ist es immer schön warm.

4. So teuer ist diese Reise nicht.

5. Ja, das kann ich tun. Einen Moment, bitte.

25. Wie heißt das auf deutsch?

1. It depends on the time.

2. This book describes everything.

3. Do you have a room available?

4. Send me a brochure.

5. Why is he stopping?

6. We'll have to transfer.

7. We are very hungry.

8. I would like to eat a meal.

9. Should we sit outside?

10. The tourists are getting off in Munich.

26. Complete the following information.

1. 7 kg = _____ g

2. 18 Pfund = _____ kg

3. 2,5 m = _____ cm

4. 12 000 cm = _____ km

5. 15° C = _____ ° F

6. 4 lbs. = _____ g

7. 1 ft. = _____ cm

27. Beantwortet die Fragen!

Wohin möchtest du eine Reise machen?

Warum brauchst du einen Prospekt?

Warum sitzt du im Freien?

Wie sieht das Land in deiner Gegend aus?

Wie kommst du jeden Tag zur Schule?

Rückblick

I. Change these sentences from the present to the present perfect tense.

Beispiel: *Am Abend essen wir meistens Wurst.*
Am Abend haben wir meistens Wurst gegessen.

1. Der Tourist fragt den Beamten.
2. Wann bist du beim Stadttor?
3. Trinkst du den Tee?
4. Mein Vater kommt um fünf Uhr nach Hause.
5. Wie gefällt dir dieses Spiel?
6. Bekommt ihr noch Karten?
7. Haben wir heute Hausaufgaben?
8. Sprechen die Ausländer deutsch?
9. Bringen Sie mir ein Geschenk?
10. Ich sage es nicht.
11. Sie fahren nach Deutschland.
12. Bezahlst du für diese Reise?

II. Supply the proper forms for the present, future or present perfect tense. Use the verbs provided in parentheses. Make sure that the whole sentence is meaningful.

1. (gehen) Die Mädchen _____ letzten Samstag zum Sportwettbewerb _____.
2. (sehen) Wir _____ diesen Film nächste Woche _____.
3. (kommen) Wann _____ du zu uns?
4. (kaufen) Was _____ wir ihm morgen zum Geburtstag _____?
5. (fahren) Heute ist der 15. Mai. Schmidts _____ am 19. Mai nach Europa _____.
6. (gefallen) Dieser Mantel _____ mir nicht.
7. (warten) Erika kommt immer spät. Ich _____ das letzte Mal eine halbe Stunde auf sie _____.
8. (sein) Es ist sechs Uhr. In zwei Stunden _____ das Flugzeug hier _____.
9. (helfen) Warum _____ du ihm nicht?
10. (wissen) Köln liegt am Rhein. Das _____ ich nicht _____.

III. Supply the proper plural forms and their corresponding definite articles.

1. Die Verkäuferin zeigt ihr (Hemd, Bluse, Prospekt, Buch, Mantel).
2. Wir fahren zu (Stadt, Berg, Haus, Gebäude, Turm).
3. Die Leute kommen schon aus (Kino, Bahnhof, Theater, Museum, Reisebüro).
4. Kaufst du (Heft, Kugelschreiber, Bleistift, Buch)?
5. (Straßenbahn, Zug, Auto, Fahrrad) stehen da drüben.
6. Ich brauche die Karten für (Lehrer, Kunde, Mädchen, Dame).

IV. Supply the proper forms after the dative and accusative prepositions. The singular or plural forms in parentheses are given in the nominative case.

Beispiel: *Sprichst du mit (er) _____?*
Sprichst du mit ihm?

1. Er kommt von (die Bank) _____.
2. Wir spielen gegen (euere Klasse) _____.
3. Warum geht ihr nicht ohne (ich) _____?
4. Um fünf Uhr kommen sie aus (die Tanzschule) _____.
5. Nach (das Spiel) _____ können wir in die Stadt gehen.
6. Wir müssen um (der Marktplatz) _____ fahren.

7. Sie wohnt bei (ihre Eltern) _____.
8. Hat er etwas Geld für (wir) _____?
9. Die Touristen gehen durch (das Stadttor) _____.
10. Spielst du gern mit (dein Bruder) _____?
11. Sie fahren zu (ihre Freunde) _____.
12. Außer (ich) _____ spielt auch Ursula Klavier.

Lesestück 2

Die Romantische Straße

Zwischen Würzburg und Füssen liegt die ,,Romantische Straße''. Diese Straße ist ungefähr 360 Kilometer lang. Millionen von Deutschen und Ausländern besuchen jedes Jahr die historischen Städte wie Würzburg, Rothenburg, Dinkelsbühl und Nördlingen. Stellen wir uns einmal eine Reise auf der Romantischen Straße vor°. Unsere Reise beginnt in Würzburg.

stellen…vor *imagine*

Würzburg ist eine Bischofs- und Universitätsstadt. Schon aus der Entfernung sehen wir die Festung° Marienburg. Diese Festung ist fast 800 Jahre alt. Sie steht hoch auf einem Hügel° und überblickt° den Main. Eine Brücke (Die Alte Mainbrücke) — man hat sie von 1453 bis 1543 erbaut° — führt° direkt in die Stadt. Verkehrsschilder° zeigen deutlich die Richtung zur Romantischen Straße.

fortress
hill
overlooks
built/leads
traffic signs

Nach ungefähr einer Stunde Fahrt° kommen wir nach Weikersheim. Wie die anderen Städte in dieser Gegend erinnert uns auch Weikersheim an° das Mittelalter°. Diese Stadt ist früher bei den Fürsten° sehr beliebt gewesen. Sie haben Weikersheim oft besucht und manchmal auch dort gewohnt. Nur ungefähr 15 Kilometer weit von Weikersheim entfernt liegt das Städtchen Creglingen. Viele Touristen besuchen dort jedes Jahr den Marienaltar° in der Herrgottskirche. Er ist sehr berühmt°.

trip
erinnert…an *reminds of/Middle Ages*
princes

Altar of the Virgin Mary
famous

Rothenburg ob der Tauber ist für viele Deutsche und Ausländer der Lieblingsort° an der Romantischen Straße. Eine Stadtmauer° umgibt° diese Stadt aus dem Mittelalter. Man kann nur durch vier oder fünf Tore° in die Stadt fahren. Alle Busse müssen vor der Stadtmauer parken. In der Stadt gibt es fast keine Parkplätze.

favorite place
city wall/surrounds
gates

Der Mittelpunkt von Rothenburg ist der Marktplatz. Das Rathaus ist schon mehr als 500 Jahre alt. Der Turm hinter dem Rathaus ist sogar noch älter. Rechts° vom Rathaus steht die Ratstrinkstube. Dreimal am Tag führen zwei Figuren neben° einer Uhr den ,,Meistertrunk'' vor°. Dieser hat eine besondere geschichtliche Bedeutung für Rothenburg. Links vom Rathaus steht der St. Georgs-Brunnen. Der Brunnen° hat die Einwohner schon 1446 mit Wasser versorgt°.

to the right
next to
führen…vor *stage*

fountain
supplied

Dinkelsbühl

Die Häuser in Rothenburg
sehen märchenhaft aus.

Nördlingen

Man kann durch vier oder fünf Tore in
die Stadt Rothenburg fahren.

Schloß
Weikersheim

Die Straßen und Häuser in Rothenburg sehen märchenhaft aus. Viele Blumen° verzieren° die Fenster° von den Häusern. Auf dem Weg zum Stadttor° kommen wir zum Plönlein. Dieser Stadtteil mit dem Fachwerkhaus° am Brunnen und dem Stadttor ist weltberühmt°.

Von Rothenburg führt eine Landstraße an Feldern°, Bauernhöfen° und Dörfern vorbei°. Kurz vor Dinkelsbühl stehen einige Hotelschilder°. Diese geben uns Informationen über die verschiedenen Möglichkeiten, dort zu übernachten. Wie Rothenburg winkt uns auch Dinkelsbühl märchenhaft aus der Entfernung zu°. Dinkelsbühl ist mehr als eintausend Jahre alt. Heute ist diese Stadt für Besucher ein besonderer Anziehungspunkt°. Viele Häuser aus dem Mittelalter stehen noch immer dort.

Weiter geht es auf der Romantischen Straße in Richtung Nördlingen, ungefähr 30 Kilometer von Dinkelsbühl entfernt. Die Stadtmauer hat drei Tore, zwei für Autos und eins für Fußgänger°. Ein Stadtplan° am Rathaus bezeichnet° diese Stadt mit den Worten „NÖRDLINGEN—DIE LEBENDE° STADT DES MITTELALTERS". Der Stadtplan zeigt deutlich, wo die Sehenswürdigkeiten sind. Wie die meisten Städte an der Romantischen Straße hat auch Nördlingen seinen mittelalterlichen° Charakter bewahrt°. Die Verkehrsschilder in der Innenstadt zeigen uns, auf welcher Straße wir weiterfahren müssen.

Wir verlassen Nördlingen und kommen ein paar Minuten später am Schloß Harburg vorbei. Das Schloß ist heute ein Museum. Dort kann man Kunstschätze° aus früheren Zeiten besichtigen°. Donauwörth ist eine Kleinstadt an der Donau. Viele Touristen beenden° ihre Reise hier in Donauwörth. Andere setzen ihre Reise auf der Romantischen Straße fort° und fahren über Augsburg, Landsberg, Schongau nach Füssen. Auch auf dieser Strecke können wir noch viele andere Sehenswürdigkeiten finden.

flowers/decorate/ windows
city gate
half-timbered house
world-famous

fields
farms/führt...vorbei goes by
hotel signs

winkt...zu waves at

attraction

pedestrians/city map/labels living

medieval
preserved

art treasures
view
end
setzen...fort continue

Fragen über das Lesestück

1. Wo liegt die Romantische Straße und wie lang ist sie?
2. Was kann man alles in Würzburg sehen?
3. Wer hat früher Weikersheim oft besucht?
4. Was gibt es in Creglingen zu sehen?
5. Warum können die Busse nicht in der Stadt Rothenburg parken?
6. Was ist der Mittelpunkt von Rothenburg? Was gibt es da alles zu sehen?
7. Wie sehen die Straßen und Häuser in Rothenburg aus?
8. Was findet man kurz vor Dinkelsbühl? Warum?
9. Wie weit ist Nördlingen von Dinkelsbühl entfernt?
10. Was steht auf dem Stadtplan von Nördlingen?

11. Wohnt heute noch ein Fürst im Schloß Harburg?
12. Wo liegt Donauwörth?
13. Welche anderen Städte gibt es noch an der Romantischen Straße?

Sprachspiegel

I. Develop a dialog situation or a narrative based on the topic *"Ich möchte eine Reise machen."*

In order for you to decide on a specific trip, you may have to inquire at a travel agency, talk to your friends and/or parents and other sources. Be as creative as possible.

II. Express the answers to the following questions using only the metric system. You may have to do some figuring to come up with the right answer.

1. Wie warm ist es heute?
2. Wie groß bist du?
3. Wie weit wohnt deine Freundin

Wie sagt man's?

Wir möchten einen Ausflug auf dem Rhein machen.
Wie viele Personen?
Zwei. Was kostet die Reise?
Achtzehn Mark pro Person.

Wohin geht denn die Reise?
In den Schwarzwald.
Wie schön. Wir sind letztes Jahr dort gewesen.
Ja, es soll märchenhaft sein.

Hast du heute abend etwas vor?
Nein, ich glaube nicht.
Wollen wir ins Kino gehen?
Was läuft im Filmpalast?
Ein Spielfilm aus England.

Ich möchte nach Garmisch-Partenkirchen fahren.
Da müssen Sie in München umsteigen.
Haben Sie einen Fahrplan?
Ja, bitte schön, für Sie!

Ich nehme diesen Prospekt mit.
Darin finden Sie alles, was Sie wissen wollen.
Haben Sie Sonderangebote?
Nur während der Wintermonate.

Wir fahren nächste Woche nach Deutschland.
Ich nehme an, ihr habt alles schon geplant.
Na klar.
Wohin fahrt ihr denn?
Nach München und dann weiter in die Alpen.

Wie lange dauert die Reise?
Drei Stunden mit dem Flugzeug und zwei Stunden mit dem Bus.
Wer kommt denn alles mit?
Meine Eltern und meine Schwester.

Zungenbrecher

Der Potsdamer Postkutscher putzt den Potsdamer Postkutschkasten.
(The Potsdam stagecoach driver is cleaning the Potsdam stagecoach.)

Kulturecke

Vacationing

Almost half the Germans go on vacation in their own country and approximately 22 million foreign tourists visit Germany every year as well. It is not surprising, therefore, to see innumerable travel agencies *(Reisebüros)* throughout the country. What are the favorite spots that tourists like to visit?

A number of islands dot the coast line of the German North Sea shore *(Nordseeküste)*. During the summer months, many Germans head north to such islands as *Sylt* or *Norderney* or take short weekend trips to the island of *Helgoland.* Along the shore of the North and the Baltic Seas *(Nord- und Ostsee)* are beautiful sandy beaches where Germans go to vacation for one or two weeks at a time. The area of *Glücksburg* near the Danish border is a particularly popular spot because of its famous castle *(Schloß Glücksburg)*, which attracts visitors from all over the world.

Located south of Hamburg is a restful area, the *Lüneburger Heide.* This heather-covered region has only a few small towns. It is one of the very few secluded sections of Germany where you can hike for a long time without meeting another person. Much of it is a wildlife refuge.

Most Germans do not stay in hotels during their vacation. Instead they look for quiet, peaceful places. Vacationing on farms has become particularly popular. There the adults as well as the youngsters often have the opportunity to explore the countryside on horseback. Many of the young adults, vacationing with their classmates or friends, travel throughout Germany or stay at summer camps for two or three weeks. Wherever there are resort areas, there are modern facilities awaiting visitors. Outdoor swimming pools can be found everywhere. Of course, these resort areas also offer indoor swimming pools, including many that can make artificial waves for the enjoyment of their guests.

Along the *Rhein,* legends and fairy tales come alive for visitors passing the many castles between the cities of *Mainz* and *Koblenz.* Excursion boats provide music and other entertainment and add to the colorful surroundings. The *Mosel,* sometimes referred to as the sister of the Rhein, is another peaceful place to spend your vacation. The Mosel is located in the western part of Germany. Most tourists visit here during the months of September and October — the peak of the wine season and the festivals associated with it. One of the most popular places is the area of *Bernkastel*, where the surroundings take you back centuries.

During the summer, Germans go to lakes and rivers to explore with their own motor boats or in their kayaks. Some enjoy sitting along the river's edge and trying their fishing skill. The *Neckar River* is particularly popular on warm summer days. And, of course, the 14th century castle in *Heidelberg*, overlooking the Neckar River, is the landmark of the city.

Those who don't stay in hotels or guest-houses *(Pensionen)* travel in their own campers. Camping is the least expensive way of vacationing in Germany. There are about 1,700 camping sites to choose from. Hiking always ranks high among Germans vacationing anywhere in the country. Detailed maps of the hiking paths are usually found right at the entrance of the park or forest area. Most hikers familiarize themselves with the maps before tackling the sometimes long and strenuous hiking paths.

One of the most frequently visited towns is *Rothenburg*, located along the *Romantische Straße*. Rothenburg is a well-preserved medieval town with an encircling wall and over 30 gates and towers. Not far away from Rothenburg is *Dinkelsbühl*, a town that is more than one thousand years old.

Camping in den Alpen

an der Ostsee

Youngsters explore
the countryside
on horseback.
(Schwarzwald)

ein Picknick
im Schwarzwald

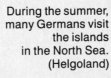

During the summer,
many Germans visit
the islands
in the North Sea.
(Helgoland)

Was machen diese
Leute? (Friedrichsau)

The Black Forest *(Schwarzwald)*, located in southwestern Germany, is just what its name implies. It really is a forest, and the trees are exceptionally dark because of their density. This vast mountain forest has a number of popular resort areas, like the town and lake of *Titisee*. The lake offers numerous opportunities for excursion rides and boating. Within 20 miles of Titisee you'll find another lake, the *Schluchsee,* which is a paradise for surfing and sailing. The sport of surfing has enjoyed a tremendous popularity during the past few years. Many vacationers visit not only the smaller peaceful lakes but also such large lakes as the *Bodensee,* located in the southwestern corner of Germany. The Bodensee is a favorite vacation spot due to its convenient location, close to Switzerland and Austria. The island of *Mainau* has one of the most beautifully landscaped parks found anywhere in Germany. The park facilities, an important prerequisite for most vacationers, are plentiful. People can be seen sitting on the benches reading a paper or book, or just watching the world go by.

For many vacationers, Bavaria *(Bayern)* is still the favorite place to spend their vacation. In recent years, a trip on the *Isar* River has been the thing to do. More than 50 people can float down this river on a raft, while being entertained by a small band. Besides the numerous attractions offered in the Bavarian capital of *München,* many people visit the various castles further south, such as *Neuschwanstein.* This castle has been immortalized in several books and movies. The Alps have numerous vacation spots. An example is the quaint little town of *Berchtesgaden,* located in the vicinity of the *Watzmann,* Germany's second largest mountain. More and more people come to the South during the winter for the skiing opportunities for all skill levels in this Alpine region. The area of the *Zugspitze,* near *Garmisch-Partenkirchen,* attracts many vacationers during the winter season. And, of course, the traditional sleigh rides in these mountain resorts, like *Mittenwald,* are still considered among the most popular activities for the visitors.

Vokabeln

die **Abfahrt,-en** departure
die **Abfahrtszeit,-en** departure time
also O.K. then…
anhalten to stop
ankommen to arrive
annehmen to assume
ausgezeichnet excellent
der **Ausländer,-** foreigner
aussteigen to get off
die **Bahn,-en** train
beschreiben to describe
dienen to serve
das **Doppelzimmer,-** double room
die **Fahrt,-en** trip
die **Figur,-en** figure
der **Flug,-̈e** flight
die **Frau,-en** wife
der **Fürst,-en** prince
gerade just
geschichtlich historical
das **Gramm,-e** gram
günstig favorable, reasonable
hierherkommen to come here
der **Himmel** sky
die **Information,-en** information
klein small
die **Kleinstadt,-̈e** small town
klingen to sound
der **Kunde,-n** customer
die **Landstraße,-n** two-lane highway
die **Mahlzeit,-en** meal
märchenhaft legendary, fairy tale-like
der **Meter,-** meter
mitnehmen to take along
der **Mund,-̈er** mouth
nachsehen to check
oben on top
die **Ordnung,-en** order
Es geht in Ordnung. It will be taken care of.
der **Ort,-e** town, place
das **Pfund,-e** pound
pro per
der **Prospekt,-e** brochure
die **Rast,-en** rest, break
eine Rast machen to take a rest
die **Rechnung,-en** bill, invoice
das **Reisebüro,-s** travel agency
richtig really, correct
die **Richtung,-en** direction
die **Seilbahn,-en** cable car
das **Sonderangebot,-e** special offer
sonnig sunny
der **Sportler,-** athlete

die **Station,-en** station
steigen to climb
tausend thousand
umsteigen to transfer
unterwegs on the way
vorher before, in advance
wässerig watery
weiterfahren to continue (driving)
die **Wolke,-n** cloud
womit with what
wünschen to wish
die **Zahnradbahn,-en** cog-wheel train
zurückfahren to drive back
zuschicken to send, mail (to)

Lesestück 1

In der Stadt

Jeden Samstag, außer dem ersten Samstag im Monat, sind die Geschäfte nur bis 14 Uhr geöffnet. Deshalb ist am Samstag in der Stadt immer besonders viel Verkehr. Die Leute wollen noch schnell vor 14 Uhr einkaufen.

Stephanie, Tina und Ursel gehen samstags auch gern in die Stadt. Oft treffen sie sich° vor dem Kino. Das Kino ist direkt in der Stadtmitte. Viele Geschäfte sind in der Nähe vom Kino. Die Mädchen haben noch etwas Zeit, sich die Schaufenster anzusehen°. Manchmal kaufen sie auch ein paar Kleinigkeiten°. Heute haben die drei Mädchen vor, in der Stadt zu essen. Sie kommen bei Hillers vorbei. Hillers ist eine Imbißstube°. Dort ist es immer preiswert, und das Essen schmeckt° auch gut. Auf einer Tafel° können sie auswählen°, was sie essen möchten. Alle drei essen dieses Mal Bratwurst mit Brot. Außer der Bratwurst bestellen° sie noch Cola.

Während der Mittagszeit° ist es in der Imbißstube sehr voll. Die Mädchen haben aber Glück, einen Tisch in der Ecke zu finden. Sie sprechen oft über ihre Freunde und Freundinnen. Stephanie möchte wissen, was sie ihrem Freund Georg kaufen soll. In zwei Wochen gibt Georg eine Party. Er wird dann mit seinem Abitur° fertig sein. Tina glaubt, daß Georg einen Kugelschreiber gebrauchen kann. Ursel hat einen anderen Vorschlag. „Georg kann ein Fotoalbum besser gebrauchen," sagt sie. Dieser Vorschlag gefällt auch Stephanie und Tina. Georg fotografiert° gern. Sie hoffen, daß ein Fotoalbum nicht zu teuer sein wird.

Nach dem Essen wollen sie noch schnell zu einem Kaufhaus° gehen. Das Kaufhaus ist gleich in der Nähe von der Imbißstube. Sie müssen sich beeilen. Es ist schon Viertel vor zwei und die Geschäfte machen bald zu°.

treffen…sich meet

sich…anzusehen to look at
small items

snack bar

tastes/board
select
order

noon time

final examination

takes pictures

department store

machen…zu close

Fragen über das Lesestück

1. Warum ist am Samstag meistens viel Verkehr in der Stadt?
2. Wo sind viele Geschäfte?
3. Wo wollen sie heute essen?
4. Was bestellen sie dort?
5. Warum wird Georg eine Party haben?
6. Was will Stephanie Georg kaufen?

Lesestück 2

Wolfgang und Günter fahren zur Jugendherberge

Wolfgang und Günter haben schon seit Wochen geplant°, eine Reise durch Süddeutschland zu machen. Sie wollen mit Wolfgangs Motorrad fahren. Sie haben genug Geld gespart° und haben vor, zwei Wochen lang durch die Gegend zu fahren. Sobald sie in einem Ort ankommen, suchen sie zuerst die Jugendherberge. Dort kann man immer preiswert übernachten. Meistens sehen sie ein Schild. Es zeigt ihnen, wo die Jugendherberge ist. Manchmal müssen sie aber fragen.

planned

saved

Heute kommen sie in Nürnberg an. Wie in den meisten Städten ist auch in dieser Stadt die Jugendherberge groß. Hier können mehr als 200 Jugendliche übernachten. Ein paar Motorräder, ein paar Autos und drei Busse stehen schon da. Wolfgang stellt sein Motorrad neben den Eingang. Dann gehen sie beide in die Jugendherberge hinein.

Sie müssen dem Herbergsvater ihren Jugendherbergsausweis zeigen. Der Herbergsvater zeigt den beiden Jungen die Jugendherberge. Die Jugendherberge ist sehr modern. Sie hat viele Schlafzimmer und auch zwei große Speisesäle. Sie können hier für zwölf Mark pro Person übernachten. Gleich in der Nähe von der Jugendherberge ist ein Sportplatz°. Dort spielen immer viele Fußball. Andere bleiben in der Jugendherberge und spielen Tischtennis, Karten, Schach oder andere Spiele. Ein Mädchen spielt sogar Gitarre und einige Jugendliche singen.

athletic field

Viele Jugendliche kommen in kleinen oder großen Gruppen°. Für Wolfgang und Günter ist es nicht schwer, andere Jungen und Mädchen kennenzulernen°. Es ist besonders interessant, denn die Jugendlichen kommen aus allen Teilen Deutschlands und sogar aus anderen Ländern. Außer Deutsch hören sie noch Englisch und Französisch. Wolfgang und Günter bleiben hier nur einen Tag und fahren dann in Richtung München weiter.

groups

to get to know

Fragen über das Lesestück

1. Wohin fahren Wolfgang und Günter?
2. Was suchen sie zuerst in einem Ort?
3. Wie finden sie eine Jugendherberge?
4. Was steht alles vor der Jugendherberge?
5. Was müssen sie dem Herbergsvater zeigen?
6. Was machen die Jugendlichen in der Jugendherberge?
7. Woher kommen die Jugendlichen?

Wo ist die
Jugendherberge?

ein Jugendherbergsausweis

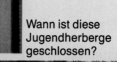

eine Jugendherberge

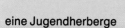

Wann ist diese
Jugendherberge
geschlossen?

In diesem
Buch stehen
alle deutschen
Jugendherbergen.

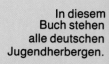

Dialog

Auf dem Weg in die Stadt

FRAU SENDER: Guten Tag, Frau Böll. Wohin gehen Sie denn so früh am Morgen?

FRAU BÖLL: Guten Tag, Frau Sender. Ich will in die Stadt gehen und ein Geschenk für meinen Mann kaufen. Er hat morgen Geburtstag.

FRAU SENDER: Fahren Sie mit der Straßenbahn?

FRAU BÖLL: Nein, ich gehe zu Fuß. Es dauert nur eine halbe Stunde, bis ich in der Stadt bin.

FRAU SENDER: Was kaufen Sie Ihrem Mann denn?

FRAU BÖLL: Das weiß ich noch nicht genau. Vielleicht ein Hemd und eine Krawatte oder ein Buch.

FRAU SENDER: Das ist eine gute Idee. Mein Bruder hat nächste Woche Geburtstag. Er liest auch sehr gern Bücher.

FRAU BÖLL: Wollen Sie mitkommen?

FRAU SENDER: Nein, heute habe ich leider keine Zeit.

Fragen über den Dialog

1. Was will Frau Böll für ihren Mann kaufen?
2. Warum will sie etwas kaufen?
3. Wie kommt Frau Böll in die Stadt?
4. Was möchte Frau Sender kaufen?
5. Warum kann Frau Sender heute nicht mit Frau Böll in die Stadt gehen?

Übungen

I. **Provide an appropriate response in German. Be sure that the whole conversation ties together and becomes meaningful.**

A. Heute habe ich wirklich Lust, an den See zu gehen.

B: Ich habe heute leider keine Zeit mitzukommen.

A: _____

B: Ich muß mit meinen Eltern zum Bahnhof fahren.

A: _____

B: Mein Onkel und meine Tante.

A: _____

B: Aus Stuttgart.

A: _____

B: Sie bleiben ungefähr drei Wochen bei uns.

A: _____

II. Form complete sentences using first the future and then the present perfect tense.

1. Jungen / spielen / Montag / Tennis
2. Familie Lesemann / fahren / Sommer / Österreich
3. Ich / kaufen / Hose / und / Hemd
4. Sprechen / du / Deutsch / oder / Englisch
5. Wir / Spiel / gewinnen
6. Welcher / Film / ihr / sehen
7. Zug / acht Uhr / München / ankommen

III. Define each of the following words in German. Form at least one complete sentence describing each word.

1. die Stadt
2. der Tag
3. die Imbißstube
4. das Reisebüro
5. der Zug
6. das Geld
7. die Universität
8. die Mutter
9. das Wort
10. das Kino

IV. Complete each sentence by supplying the correct form of the possessive adjective indicated.

1. Hast du (my) _____ Bruder gesehen?
2. Wo habt ihr (our) _____ Karten gekauft?
3. Ich kann (his) _____ Schwester nicht verstehen.
4. Der Lehrer wird den Schülern (their) _____ Bücher geben.
5. Wohin haben Sie (your) _____ Frau gefahren, Herr Wiemann?

das Reisebüro

6. Sie kommt mit (her) _____ Eltern nach Europa.

7. Maria bekommt das Buch von (her) _____ Freunden.

8. Seit zwei Jahren habe ich (your) _____ Onkel nicht gesehen, Walter.

9. Ich habe von (your) _____ Brüdern lange nicht gehört, Elisabeth und Barbara.

10. Was machen Sie denn nach (your) _____ Reise?

11. Haben Sie mit (my) _____ Mutter gesprochen?

12. Peter hat (his) _____ Freundin nichts von dem Geschenk gesagt.

V. Find the matching word pairs using the words listed below.

1. Tischtennis: _____

2. Walzer: _____

3. Mittwoch: _____

4. Mahlzeit: _____

5. Reisescheck: _____

6. Wasser: _____

7. Herbst: _____

8. Blockflöte: _____

9. Straßenbahn: _____

10. Zimmer: _____

11. Rock: _____

12. Film: _____

Tag	Musikinstrument	Jahreszeit
Bank	Verkehrsmittel	Kleidungsstück
Kino	Fluß	Restaurant
Sport	Tanz	Hotel

VI. Change the following sentences to the present perfect tense.

1. Herr Schmidt spricht gut Deutsch.

2. Ich werde ein paar Prospekte mitbringen.

3. Seine Eltern sind nicht zu Hause.

4. Werden sie heute in Köln ankommen?

5. Wir besuchen die Stadtmauer.

6. Habt ihr die Karten?

7. Um wieviel Uhr wirst du aufstehen?

8. Wo bleibt er denn nur?

9. Ich finde das Buch sehr schwer.

10. Warum fragst du ihn nicht?

VII. Supply the proper present tense forms of the verbs provided in parentheses.

Beispiel: *(sprechen) _____ du Deutsch?*
Sprichst du Deutsch?

1. (geben): _____ er dir sein Fahrrad?

2. (lesen): Paul _____ das Buch. Es ist toll.

3. (anhalten): Der Bus _____ hier _____.

4. (fahren): Familie Meier _____ in die Schweiz.

5. (sehen): _____ du das Flugzeug?

6. (mitnehmen): Petra _____ ihre Schwester in die Stadt _____.

7. (essen): Was _____ ihr denn?

8. (gefallen) Diese Stadt _____ mir besonders gut.

VIII. Substitute the proper form of one of the three words which best completes the sentence.

1. Sie _____ zu Fuß in die Stadt. (fahren, gehen, sehen)

2. Ich möchte gern diesen Film _____. (laufen, sehen, spielen)

3. Die Dame will einen Platz _____. (lesen, machen, buchen)

4. Wir können die Vokabeln nicht _____. (verstehen, kaufen, kommen)

5. _____ wir am besten unsere Reise! (warten, gehen, besprechen)

6. Die Prospekte _____ die mittelalterliche Stadt sehr gut. (sagen, einkaufen, beschreiben)

7. In Mainz müssen wir in einen anderen Zug _____. (umsteigen, gehen, anrufen)

8. Meine Mutter wird das Essen _____. (anprobieren, einsteigen, zubereiten)

9. Wir wollen meinen Onkel _____. (glauben, besuchen, interessieren)

10. Mußt du das Gepäck _____? (liegen, versuchen, tragen)

Welche Filme zeigt man in diesen Kinos?

Sie haben
viel Spaß.

Nützliche Ausdrücke

Here are some phrases that are particularly helpful when buying clothing items:

Bitte sehr?	May I help you?
Ich möchte ein paar Schuhe, Größe 41, bitte.	I would like a pair of shoes, size 9, please.
Welche Größe haben Sie?	What size do you wear?
Welche Farbe?	Which color?
Wollen Sie das Kleid anprobieren?	Do you wish to try the dress on?
Gehen Sie bitte in die Kabine.	Please go to the fitting room.
Es ist zu eng.	It is too tight.
Was kostet das?	What does that cost?

Cultural Notes

Popular English Words in the German Language

German borrowed many words from English. Here are some of the English words with their corresponding German articles. The pronunciation of these words in German is usually as close to English as possible, depending on the speaker's familiarity with English.

die Band	das Happening	der Manager	das Sit-in
die City	das Hobby	die Party	die Snackbar
der Computer	die Jeans	die Pipeline	der Teenager
das Feature	der Job	das Popcorn	der Trend
der Gag (joke)	das Makeup	die Publicity	das Understatement

Hier kann man Jeans kaufen.

Was kauft man in diesem Geschäft?

Welcher Film läuft hier?

Origin of Town Names

Many town and city names in Germany have suffixes that can easily identify their origin. Once you know a little about their origin, you may look at these places with different eyes. Many town names go back to the Roman and Germanic times.

The ending syllable *-furt* (as in Frankfurt) means that the town originated at a ford, where a river could be crossed by wading or with a wagon.

Some German town names end or begin with *-reuth, -reut, -reute, -rode, -rod,* or *-rath* (as *Bayreuth, Wernigerode* or *Benrath*). These towns originated in a wooded area that had to be cleared of trees and stumps (*"roden"* in German) before houses could be built and fields could be made arable.

Many towns in southern and western Germany originated as Roman settlements in the earliest centuries A.D. The end syllable *-kastel* (as in *Bernkastel*) goes back to the Latin "castellum" (castle, fortified camp).

If a name ends with *-burg* (as *Hamburg*), this shows that the town grew near or around a *Burg,* a castle.

Towns originating around abbeys, convents, etc. often still carry the word *Kloster* (cloister) or *Mönch* (monk) in their names (*Klosterreichenbach, München*).

Town names ending with *-ingen* (Sigmaringen) usually lie in Swabia, those with *-ing* (Dingolfing) in Bavaria. The name *Sigmaringen* tells that the settlement was founded by a Teuton called Sigmar and his kin.

Wie heißen die Städte auf dem Schild?

Kloster Ettal (Bayern)

Ravensburg grew near a *Burg*.

At a German Hotel

Finding a Room

The safest way to get a room is to reserve one in advance. However, if you arrive without a room reservation, in most German cities you can make use of the services of a room referral agency, called *"Zimmernachweis"* which often is in or near the railroad station. It charges a small fee for locating a room for you.

Bath Must be Ordered

Moderately priced German hotels do not furnish soap and wash cloths. All hotels supply towels, but only the more expensive ones supply soap. Rooms with a private bath and toilet must be specifically ordered; they cost usually about 50% more than a room without these facilities. Usually, there is at least one bathroom with shower at the disposal of all hotel guests. However, hotel guests have to let the hotel know when they want to use it, as a fee will be charged. A toilet is generally found on each floor and can be used by those who do not have one included in their room.

Registration

Every hotel guest must fill out a hotel registration form, which is not as detailed and complex as it used to be. Some hotels have even abolished lengthy registration forms.

Paying the Bill

In all German hotels you pay when you check out. A service charge will be included in the bill.

Continental Breakfast

The "continental breakfast" is the traditional German breakfast served in German hotels. It consists of *Kaffee* or *Tee* (your choice), *Brötchen, Schwarzbrot* (brown bread), *Marmelade* (jam) and, on requests, a soft boiled egg *(weich gekochtes Ei),* served in a little egg cup. In some hotels you may also find a small assortment of *Aufschnitt* (assorted cold cuts and cheese) for breakfast. Most hotels expect you to have breakfast at their hotel. Consequently, breakfast is usually included in the hotel bill.

Zimmernachweis oder Tourist Information

Hotels usually furnish towels
but not always soap.

Personal Pronouns

SINGULAR	Nominative	Accusative	Dative
1st person	ich	mich	mir
2nd person	du	dich	dir
3rd person	er sie es	ihn sie es	ihm ihr ihm
PLURAL			
1st person	wir	uns	uns
2nd person	ihr	euch	euch
3rd person	sie	sie	ihnen
formal form (plural or singular)	Sie	Sie	Ihnen

Definite Article

	Singular			Plural
	Masculine	*Feminine*	*Neuter*	
Nominative	der	die	das	die
Accusative	den	die	das	die
Dative	dem	der	dem	den

Der-Words

	Singular			Plural
	Masculine	*Feminine*	*Neuter*	
Nominative	dieser	diese	dieses	diese
Accusative	diesen	diese	dieses	diese
Dative	diesem	dieser	diesem	diesen

Other *der*-words introduced here are *welcher* and *jeder*.

Question Words: *Wer? Was?*

Nominative	wer	was
Accusative	wen	was
Dative	wem	

Indefinite Article

	Singular			Plural
	Masculine	*Feminine*	*Neuter*	
Nominative	ein	eine	ein	keine
Accusative	einen	eine	ein	keine
Dative	einem	einer	einem	keinen

Regular Verb Forms — Present Tense

	gehen	finden	heißen
ich	gehe	finde	heiße
du	gehst	findest	heißt
er, sie, es	geht	findet	heißt
wir	gehen	finden	heißen
ihr	geht	findet	heißt
sie, Sie	gehen	finden	heißen

Irregular Verb Forms — Present Tense

	haben	sein	wissen
ich	habe	bin	weiß
du	hast	bist	weißt
er, sie, es	hat	ist	weiß
wir	haben	sind	wissen
ihr	habt	seid	wißt
sie, Sie	haben	sind	wissen

Command Forms

Familiar (singular)	Geh!	Warte!	Sei!	Hab!
Familiar (plural)	Geht!	Wartet!	Seid!	Habt!
Formal (singular/plural)	Gehen Sie!	Warten Sie!	Seien Sie!	Haben Sie!
Wir-**form** **(Let's…)**	Gehen wir!	Warten wir!	Seien wir!	Haben wir!

Plural of Nouns

	Singular	Plural
no change or add umlaut	das Zimmer die Mutter	die Zimmer die Mütter
add -*n*, -*en*, or -*nen*	die Ecke der Automat die Freundin	die Ecken die Automaten die Freundinnen
add -*e* or ¨*e*	der Tag die Stadt	die Tage die Städte
add ¨*er*	das Buch	die Bücher
add -*s* (adopted foreign words)	das Café das Büro	die Cafés die Büros

Inverted Word Order

1. Formation of questions beginning with the verb
   Spielst du heute Fußball?
2. Formation of questions beginning with a question word
   Wohin gehen Sie heute nachmittag?
3. Command forms
   Hab keine Angst!
   Lauft schnell!
   Passen Sie auf!
   Gehen wir!
4. Sentence beginning with a word other than the subject
   Am Sonntag fahren wir zu meiner Tante.

Negation

Verbs *(nicht)*   Kommen Sie nicht zu uns?
Nouns *(kein)*   Ich habe keine Karte.

Modal Auxiliaries

	dürfen	können	mögen	müssen	sollen	wollen
ich	darf	kann	mag	muß	soll	will
du	darfst	kannst	magst	mußt	sollst	willst
er, sie, es	darf	kann	mag	muß	soll	will
wir	dürfen	können	mögen	müssen	sollen	wollen
ihr	dürft	könnt	mögt	müßt	sollt	wollt
sie, Sie	dürfen	können	mögen	müssen	sollen	wollen

Future tense *(werden* + infinitive)

ich	werde
du	wirst
er, sie, es	wird
wir	werden
ihr	werdet
sie, Sie	werden

Sie werden nächstes Jahr nach Deutschland fahren.
Wirst du morgen ins Kino gehen?

Verbs with Stem Vowel Change (2nd & 3rd person singular only)

	a to *ä*	*e* to *i*	*e* to *ie*
ich	fahre	spreche	sehe
du	fährst	sprichst	siehst
er, sie, es	fährt	spricht	sieht
wir	fahren	sprechen	sehen
ihr	fahrt	sprecht	seht
sie, Sie	fahren	sprechen	sehen

Prepositions

Dative	Accusative	Contraction
aus	durch	durch das = durchs
außer	für	für das = fürs
bei	gegen	bei dem = beim
mit	ohne	—
nach	um	um das = ums
seit		—
von		von dem = vom
zu		zu dem = zum / zu der = zur

Verbs Followed by Dative Case

helfen antworten gefallen passen glauben
Gabi hilft ihrer Mutter.
Der Anzug gefällt mir.

The verb *glauben* may take either the dative or accusative. If used with a person, the dative follows *(Ich glaube ihm)*. If used with an object, the accusative is used *(Ich glaube das nicht)*.

Possessive Adjectives

	Singular			Plural
	Masculine	*Feminine*	*Neuter*	
Nominative	mein	meine	mein	meine
Accusative	meinen	meine	mein	meine
Dative	meinem	meiner	meinem	meinen

The endings of possessive adjectives are the same as those of the indefinite article *(ein-*words). Possessive adjectives are *mein, dein, sein, ihr, sein, unser, euer, ihr, Ihr.*

Comparison of Adjectives and Adverbs

Adjective/Adverb	schnell	warm	gut	hoch
Comparative	schneller	wärmer	besser	höher
Superlative	schnellst-	wärmst-	best-	höchst-

Numbers

0 = null	11 = elf	22 = zweiundzwanzig
1 = eins	12 = zwölf	30 = dreißig
2 = zwei	13 = dreizehn	40 = vierzig
3 = drei	14 = vierzehn	50 = fünfzig
4 = vier	15 = fünfzehn	60 = sechzig
5 = fünf	16 = sechzehn	70 = siebzig
6 = sechs	17 = siebzehn	80 = achtzig
7 = sieben	18 = achtzehn	90 = neunzig
8 = acht	19 = neunzehn	100 = einhundert
9 = neun	20 = zwanzig	101 = hunderteins
10 = zehn	21 = einundzwanzig	

Time

 1:00 Es ist ein Uhr.
 2:00 Es ist zwei Uhr.
 3:30 Es ist halb vier Uhr.
10:15 Es ist Viertel nach zehn.
11:45 Es ist Viertel vor zwölf.
 5:10 Es ist zehn Minuten nach fünf.
 7:58 Es ist zwei Minuten vor acht.

Irregular Verbs — Present Perfect Tense (Past Participle)

The following list contains all the irregular verbs used in *DEUTSCH: AKTUELL 1*. Verbs with separable or inseparable prefixes are not included when the basic verb form has been introduced (Example: *kommen, ankommen*). If the basic verb has not been introduced, then the verb is included with its prefix. Verbs with stem vowel changes have also been indicated.

Infinitive	Stem Vowel Change	Past Participle	Meaning
anhalten	hält an	angehalten	to stop
anrufen		angerufen	to call (phone)
anziehen		angezogen	to put on (clothes)
beginnen		begonnen	to begin
bekommen		bekommen	to get
beschreiben		beschrieben	to describe
bieten		geboten	to offer
bleiben		ist geblieben	to stay, remain
bringen		gebracht	to bring
denken		gedacht	to think
essen	ißt	gegessen	to eat
fahren	fährt	ist gefahren	to drive, go
finden		gefunden	to find
fließen		ist geflossen	to flow, run
geben	gibt	gegeben	to give
gefallen	gefällt	gefallen	to like
gehen		ist gegangen	to go, walk
gewinnen		gewonnen	to win
haben	hat	gehabt	to have
heißen		geheißen	to be called
helfen	hilft	geholfen	to help
kennen		gekannt	to know (a person)
klingen		geklungen	to sound
kommen		ist gekommen	to come
laufen	läuft	ist gelaufen	to run, walk
lesen	liest	gelesen	to read
liegen		gelegen	to lie
nehmen	nimmt	genommen	to take
scheinen		geschienen	to shine
schlagen	schlägt	geschlagen	to beat, hit
schreiben		geschrieben	to write
schwimmen		ist geschwommen	to swim
sehen	sieht	gesehen	to see
sein	ist	ist gewesen	to be
singen		gesungen	to sing
sitzen		gesessen	to sit
sprechen	spricht	gesprochen	to speak, talk
springen		ist gesprungen	to jump
stehen		gestanden	to stand
steigen		ist gestiegen	to climb
tragen	trägt	getragen	to carry

Infinitive	Stem Vowel Change	Past Participle	Meaning
treffen	trifft	getroffen	to meet
treiben		getrieben	to do (sports)
trinken		getrunken	to drink
tun		getan	to do
verlassen	verläßt	verlassen	to leave
verlieren		verloren	to lose
verbinden		verbunden	to connect
wissen	weiß	gewußt	to know

All the words introduced in DEUTSCH: AKTUELL 1 have been summarized in this section. The numbers following the meaning of individual words or phrases indicate the particular lesson in which they appear for the first time. In cases in which there is more than one meaning for a word or phrase and it has appeared in different lessons, both lesson numbers are listed. (Example: die *Frau,-en* Mrs., woman 1; wife 5)

Nouns have been listed with their respective articles and plural forms.

A

der **Abend,-e** evening 2
das **Abendbrot** supper 5
  aber but 2
die **Abfahrt,-en** departure 10
die **Abfahrtszeit,-en** departure time 10
der **Abgeordnete,-n** representative 7
das **Abitur,-e** final examination (secondary school) B
sich **abkühlen** to cool off 9
  abräumen to clear 7
der **Abschnitt,-e** slip (of paper) 6
  absperren to block off 9
  acht eight 1
  achtzehn eighteen 2
das **Akkordeon,-s** accordion 8
  alle all 2; everyone 8
  alles everything 3
die **Alpen** Alps 5
das **Alpenvorland** Alpine foothills 8
  als than 8
  also O.K. then... 10
  alt old 4
  ältest- oldest 7
  am (or: **an dem**) at the, on the 2
  Amerika America 5
der **Amerikaner,-** American (male) A
die **Amerikanerin,-nen** American (female) A
  an at 3; on 8
  ander- other, different 4
der **Angestellte,-n** employee (male) 6
die **Angst,¨e** fear 2; *Hab keine Angst!* Don't worry! Don't be afraid! 2
  anhaben to have on 6
  anhalten to stop 10
  ankommen to arrive 10
die **Ankunft,¨e** arrival 7
das **Anmeldeformular,-e** registration form 7
  anprobieren to try on 6
  anrufen to call up 5

der **Ansager,-** announcer 9
sich **ansehen** to look at B
  anstrengen to exert 8; *Es strengt an.* It is exhausting. 8
  antworten to answer 3
  anziehen to put on (clothes); dress 6
der **Anziehungspunkt,-e** attraction 10
der **Anzug,¨e** suit 6
das **Apfelmus** apple sauce A
der **April** April 4
die **Arbeit,-en** work 2; *eine Arbeit schreiben* to take a test 2
  arbeiten to work 5
  auch also, too 1
  auf to, on 2
die **Aufgabe,-n** problem, exercise 4
  auflegen to put on 8
  aufpassen to watch, keep an eye on something 9
der **Aufsatz,¨e** essay, composition A
der **Aufseher,-** attendant 9
  aufstehen to get up A
der **August** August 4
  aus from, out of 2
der **Ausdruck,¨e** expression 4
der **Ausflugsort,-e** excursion area 8
  ausfüllen to fill out 7
  ausgezeichnet excellent 10
der **Ausländer,-** foreigner 10
  ausreichend sufficient 4
  aussehen to look, appear 7
  außer besides, except 6
  außerhalb outside 5
  aussetzen to sit out 8
  aussteigen to get off 10
die **Auswahl** selection, choice 6
  auswählen to choose, select B
der **Ausweis,-e** identification (card) 7
  auswendig lernen to memorize, learn by heart 4
das **Auto,-s** car 5

der **Automat,-en** automat 3

B

die **Bahn,-en** train 10
der **Bahnhof,¨e** (train) station 3
der **Bahnsteig,-e** platform 8
  bald soon 2
die **Bank,¨e** bench 4
die **Bank,-en** bank 6
der **Basketball,¨e** basketball 9
der **Bauernhof,¨e** farm 10
  beantworten to answer A; *eine Frage beantworten* to answer a question A
die **Bedeutung,-en** meaning, significance 4
sich **beeilen** to hurry 3; *Beeilen wir uns!* Let's hurry. 3
  beenden to end, finish 10
  befriedigend satisfactory 4
  beginnen to begin 3
  begrüßen to greet 3
  begutachten to look over, evaluate 6
  bei at 5; with 8
  beide both 2
das **Beispiel,-e** example 7; *zum Beispiel* for example 7
  bekannt well-known 5
  bekanntgeben to announce 8
  Belgien Belgium 3
  beliebt popular 5
  bekommen to get, receive 2
  bequem comfortable 3
  bereitstehen to be ready, stand ready 9
der **Berg,-e** mountain 5
  berühmt famous 10
  beschreiben to describe 10
die **Beschreibung,-en** description 4
  besichtigen to view, look over 10

die **Besitzerin,-nen** owner (female) 8

besonder- special, unusual 4

besonders especially 4

besprechen to discuss 4

best- best 7; *am besten* the best is 7

bestehen aus to consist of 4

bestellen order B

bestimmt undoubtedly, certainly 6

die **Bestleistung,-en** best performance 9

besuchen to visit 5

der **Besucher,-** visitor 6

der **Betrag,-̈e** amount 6

das **Bett,-en** bed 5; *Er muß ins Bett.* He has to go to bed. 5

die **Bevölkerung,-en** population 9

bewahren to preserve 10

bezahlen to pay 6

bezeichnen to label, designate 10

das **Bier,-e** beer 9

bieten to offer 7

bilden to form 9

die **Biologie** biology 4

bis until 2

bitte please 6

blau blue 6

bleiben to stay, remain 2

der **Bleistift,-e** pencil 8

der **Blick** view 4

die **Blockflöte,-n** recorder 9

die **Blume,-n** flower 10

die **Bluse,-n** blouse 6

der **Bodensee** Lake Constance 8

das **Boot,-e** boat 7

die **Bratwurst,-̈e** bratwurst, fried sausage B

brauchen to need 2

braun brown 6

der **Briefkasten,-̈** mailbox 7

der **Briefmarkenautomat,-en** stamp automat 7

bringen to bring A

das **Brot,-e** bread A

die **Brücke,-n** bridge 8

der **Bruder,-̈** brother 5

der **Brunnen,-** fountain, well 10

das **Buch,-̈er** book 4

buchen to book 10

die **Bücherabteilung,-en** book department 6

die **Bundeshauptstadt** federal capital 7

das **Bundeshaus** Federal Building (in Bonn) 7

das **Bundeshochhaus** Federal Office Building for Representatives 7

das **Bundesland,-̈er** Federal State 5

der **Bundespräsident** Federal President 7

der **Bundesrat** similar to Senate 7

die **Bundesrepublik Deutschland** Federal Republic of Germany 3

der **Bundestag** similar to the House of Representatives 7

bunt colorful 6

das **Büro,-s** office 4

der **Bus,-se** bus 4

die **Butter** butter A

C

das **Café,-s** café, coffee shop 5

der **Cha-Cha-Cha** cha-cha 8

die **Chance,-n** chance 9

der **Charakter,-e** character 10

die **Chemie** chemistry 4

die **Cola,-s** cola 2

der **Computer,-** computer 3

D

da there 1; *da drüben* over there 1

dabei in the process, while doing that 9

dafür for that, for it 4

die **Dame,-n** lady 6

die **Damenabteilung,-en** ladies' department 6

Dänemark Denmark 3

der **Dank** thanks 10; *Vielen Dank.* Many thanks. 10

danke thanks 1; *Danke schön.* Thank you 5

dann then 2

das the, that 1

daß that 6

dasselbe the same 7

das **Datum, Daten** date (calendar) 5

dauern to last, take (time) 3

dazu with it A

decken to cover A; *den Tisch decken* to set the table A

dein your 4

denken to think 7

denn used for emphasis 2; *Wieviel Geld brauchst du denn?* Well, how much money do you need? 2

deshalb therefore 6

deutlich clearly 10

deutsch German 1

das **Deutsch** German (the language, subject in school) 4

die **Deutsche Demokratische Republik** German Democratic Republic 3

Deutschland Germany 3

der **Dezember** December 4

dicht close 9

der **Dienstag** Tuesday 2

diese (form of **dieser**) this 3

dieser this 3

direkt direct, immediate, straight 6

doch used for emphasis 3

der **Dollar,-s** dollar 6

die **Donau** Danube 5

der **Donnerstag** Thursday 2

das **Doppelzimmer,-** double room 10

dort there 3

dorthin (to) there 5

dran sein to be one's turn 9; *Ich bin dran.* It's my turn. 9

drei three 1

dreizehn thirteen 2

du you (familiar singular) 1

durch through 5

dürfen to be permitted to, may 5

E

die **Ebbe,-n** low tide 8

eben just 4

die **Ecke,-n** corner 1

eigentlich actual(ly), real(ly) 3

ein(e) a, an 2

einfach simple, one-way (ticket) 3

der **Eingang,-̈e** entrance 6

einige a few, several 7

einkaufen to shop 5; *einkaufen gehen* to go shopping 5

einlösen to cash (in) 6

einmal once 3; *wieder einmal* once again 3; *noch einmal* one more time 5

eins one 1

einschließlich including 10

einsteigen to get in(to), board 2

der **Eintritt** admission 8

der **Einwohner,-** inhabitant 3

die **Eisdiele,-n** ice cream parlor 2

elegant elegant 7

elf eleven 2

die **Eltern** (pl.) parents 5

das **Ende** end 3

das **Endergebnis,-se** final result 9

endlich finally 2
England England 4
das **Englisch** English (language, subject in school) 4
englisch English 4
der **Enkel,-** grandson 5
die **Enkelin,-nen** granddaughter 5
entfernt away, distant 4
die **Entfernung,-en** distance 3
entgegenlaufen to run towards 9
entspringen to originate (river) 8
entwerten to cancel (tickets) 8
er he 1
erbauen to build, construct 10
die **Erbse,-n** pea A
die **Erdkunde** geography 4
das **Ereignis,-se** event 7
erinnern an to remind of 10
erreichen to reach 6
erst only, first 5
es it 1
das **Essen** meal A; food 8
essen to eat 5
die **Essenausgabe,-n** serving counter 7
etwas some, a little 2
Europa Europe 5
europäisch European 8
der **Experte,-n** expert 8

F

das **Fach,-̈er** (school) subject 4
das **Fachwerkhaus,-̈er** half-timbered house 10
fahren to drive, go 3
die **Fahrkarte,-n** ticket 3
der **Fahrplan,-̈e** schedule 3
die **Fahrprüfung,-en** driver's test 8
das **Fahrrad,-̈er** bicycle 7
der **Fahrstuhl,-̈e** elevator 7
die **Fahrt,-en** trip 10
die **Familie,-n** family 5
die **Farbe,-n** color 6
der **Faschismus** fascism 7
fast almost 5
der **Februar** February 4
der **Federball,-̈e** badminton 9
das **Feld,-er** field 10
der **Feldweg,-e** field path 4
das **Fenster,-** window 10
die **Ferien** (pl.) vacation 9
das **Ferienland,-̈er** vacation country 5
der **Fernsehapparat,-e** television set 7

Fernsehen: im Fernsehen on TV A
fernsehen to watch TV 5
der **Fernsehturm,-̈e** television tower 7
fertig ready, done, finished 5
das **Festland,-̈er** mainland 8
die **Festung,-en** fortress 10
die **Figur,-en** figure 10
der **Film,-e** movie, film 5
finden to find 4
flach flat 5
die **Fläche,-n** area, surface 3
fleißig hard-working, industrious 4
fließen to flow, run 5
die **Flöte,-n** flute 8
der **Flug,-̈e** flight 10
das **Flugzeug,-e** airplane 7
der **Fluß,-̈sse** river 5
folgen to follow 7
die **Form,-en** form, shape 9
die **Formel,-n** formula 4
fortsetzen to continue 10; *eine Reise fortsetzen* to continue a trip 10
das **Fotoalbum,-ben** photo album B
fotografieren to photograph B
die **Frage,-n** question A
fragen to ask 2
Frankreich France 3
Französisch French (language) 6
die **Frau,-en** Mrs., woman 1; wife 10
das **Fräulein,-** Miss 1
frei free, available 7
Freie: ins Freie outside 7; *im Freien* outdoors 10
der **Freitag** Friday 2
die **Fremdsprache,-n** foreign language 4
der **Freund,-e** boyfriend, friend 1
die **Freundin,-nen** girlfriend 3
froh happy, glad 2
früh early 9
der **Frühling,-e** spring 4
frühstücken to have breakfast 5
führen to lead 10
der **Führerschein,-e** driver's license 8
fünf five 1
fünfzehn fifteen 2
für for 3
der **Fürst,-en** prince 10
der **Fuß,-̈e** foot 3; *zu Fuß* on foot, walk 3; *zu Fuß gehen* to walk 3
der **Fußball,-̈e** soccer 7
der **Fußgänger,-** pedestrian 10

G

ganz quite 3; whole 7
gar nicht not at all 4
das **Gebäude,-** building 7
geben to give 4; *es gibt* there is (are) 4
gebrauchen to use, apply 4
die **Gebühr,-en** fee 4
die **Geburtsstadt,-̈e** native town, city of birth 7
der **Geburtstag,-e** birthday 5
gefallen to like 6; *Es gefällt ihr.* She likes it. 6
die **Gegend,-en** area 5
gegenüber across 7
gehen to go 1; *Wie geht's?* How are you? (familiar) 1; *zu Fuß gehen* to walk 3; *Das geht.* That's possible. 7
gehen über to go into, merge with 8
gehören zu to belong to 8
die **Geige,-n** violin 8
gelb yellow 6
das **Geld** money 2
das **Gemälde,-** painting 7
gemütlich pleasant 7
genau exact 7
genauso wie just like/as 4
geöffnet open B; *Das Geschäft ist geöffnet.* The store is open. B
das **Gepäck** luggage, baggage 3
gerade just 10
gern gladly, with pleasure 4; *gern gehen* like (enjoy) to walk 4
das **Geschäft,-e** store 6
das **Geschenk,-e** present 8
die **Geschichte** history 4
geschichtlich historical 10
das **Geschirr** dishes 7
der **Geschmack,-̈e** taste 8
die **Geschwister** (pl.) siblings 5
gespannt sein to wonder, be curious 5
gestern yesterday 9
das **Getränk,-̈e** beverage 7
gewinnen to win 5
die **Gitarre,-n** guitar A
das **Glas,-̈er** glass 9
glauben to believe, think 3
gleich immediately, right away 1; *gleich um die Ecke* right around the corner 1
das **Gleis,-e** track 3
das **Glück** luck 2; *Glück haben* to be lucky 2

der **Glückwunsch,-̈e** congratulations (pl.) 8; *Herzlichen Glückwunsch zum Geburtstag!* Happy Birthday! 8; *Herzlichen Glückwunsch!* Congratulations! 9

gold gold 4

das **Golf** golf 9

das **Gramm,-e** gram 10

gratulieren to congratulate 9

grau gray 6

die **Grenze,-n** border 6

grenzen an to border on 4

groß big, large 3

größt- biggest, largest 4

die **Großeltern** (pl.) grandparents 5

die **Großmutter,-̈** grandmother 5

der **Großvater,-̈** grandfather 5

grün green 6

gründlich thorough, careful 4

die **Gruppe,-n** group B

Grüß dich! Hi! 1; *Grüß Gott!* Hello! 5

günstig favorable, reasonable 10

gut good, well, O.K. 1

die **Güte** goodness 7; *Du meine Güte!* My goodness! 7

das **Gymnasium,-sien** secondary school 2; *Sie geht auf ein Gymnasium.* She goes to a secondary school. 2

H

haben to have 2

häkeln to crochet 5

halb half 3

die **Haltestelle,-n** stop (for bus or streetcar) 2

der **Handschuh,-e** glove 6

die **Handtasche,-n** purse 6

die **Hauptstadt,-̈e** capital (city) 3

das **Haus,-̈er** house 2; *nach Hause gehen* to go home 2; *zu Hause* at home 2

die **Hausaufgabe,-n** homework 5; *die Hausaufgaben machen* to do homework 5

das **Heft,-e** notebook 8

heiß hot 7

heißen to be called, named 1; *Wie heißt du?* What's your name? 1

helfen to help 9

das **Hemd,-en** shirt 6

der **Herbergsvater,-̈** youth hostel director 7

der **Herbst,-e** fall, autumn 4

der **Herr,-en** Mr., gentleman 1

herumfahren to drive (ride) around 7

herumlaufen to run around 9

herzlich sincere, cordial 8

heute today 2; *heute abend* this evening, tonight 2

hier here 1

hierherkommen to come here 10

die **Hilfe** help, assistance 4

der **Himmel** sky 10

hin und zurück round trip 3

hineingehen to go inside 7

hineinreichen to reach into 8

hinter behind 8

historisch historical, historic 7

die **Hitze** heat 8; *bei der Hitze* in this heat 8

hoch high 5

höchst- highest 5

das **Hockey** hockey 9

hoffen to hope 6

hoffentlich hopefully 9

die **Höhe,-n** height 6

die **HO-Kaufhalle,-n** (government-owned) supermarket 5

hören to listen, hear 4

die **Hose,-n** pants, slacks 6

das **Hotel,-s** hotel 7

das **Hotelschild,-er** hotel sign 10

der **Hügel,-** hill 10

der **Hunger** hunger 7; *Hunger haben* to be hungry 7

hungrig hungry 4

I

ich I 1

die **Idee,-n** idea 2

ihn it, him 5

ihr you (familiar plural) 1, their 4, her A

Ihr your (formal) 6

im (or: **in dem**) in the 4

die **Imbißstube,-n** snack bar B

immer always 2; *immer wieder* again and again 7

in in 1

die **Industriestadt,-̈e** industrial city 9

die **Information,-en** information 10

die **Innenstadt,-̈e** downtown, center of city 6

ins (or: **in das**) in(to) the 4

die **Insel,-n** island 8

interessant interesting 7

das **Interesse,-n** interest A

interessieren to interest A

ist is 1

Italien Italy 5

Italienisch Italian (language) 6

J

ja yes 1

das **Jahr,-e** year 2

die **Jahreszeit,-en** season 4

der **Januar** January 4

die **Jeans** (pl.) jeans 6

jeden form of **jeder** each, every 2

jeder each, every 7

jetzt now 1

die **Jugendherberge,-n** youth hostel 7

der **Jugendherbergsausweis,-e** youth hostel identification (card) 7

der **Jugendliche,-n** youngster, teenager, youth 7

Jugoslawien Yugoslavia 5

der **Juli** July 4

der **Junge,-n** boy 1

der **Juni** June 4

K

der **Kaffee** coffee A

der **Kakao** hot chocolate, cocoa 9

kalt cold 7

die **Kalte Platte** cold-cut platter 5

der **Kamerad,-en** buddy 9

der **Kanal,-̈e** canal 9

das **Kanalsystem,-e** canal system 8

die **Karte,-n** ticket 5, map 6; card B

die **Kartoffel,-n** potato A

der **Kartoffelsalat** potato salad 8

der **Käse** cheese A

die **Kasse,-n** cashier's counter 6

die **Kassette,-n** cassette 4

kaufen to buy 3

das **Kaufhaus,-̈er** department store B

der **Kaufhof** name of department store 6

kaum hardly 9

kein no 2; *keine Zeit* no time 2

kennen to know (someone) 1

kennenlernen to get to know B

der **Kilometer,-** kilometer 3

das **Kino,-s** movie theater 5

der **Kiosk,-e** kiosk 2

die **Kirche,-n** church 7

klar clear, O.K. 3

die **Klarinette,-n** clarinet 8

die **Klasse,-n** class 3; *zweiter Klasse* second class 3

klasse sein to be great 5

der **Klassenausflug,-̈e** class trip 7

klatschen to applaud 9
das **Klavier,-e** piano 8
das **Kleid,-er** dress 6
das **Kleidungsstück,-e** article of clothing 6
klein small, little 10
die **Kleinigkeit,-en** small item, thing B
kleinst- smallest 4
die **Kleinstadt,̈e** small town 10
klingeln to ring 4; *an der Tür klingeln* to ring the doorbell 4
klingen to sound 10
klug smart 3
kochen to cook A
der **Koffer,-** suitcase 3
der **Koffer-Kuli,-s** luggage cart 3
kommen to come 1; *Komm doch mit.* Why don't you come along? 1; *Es kommt auf... an.* It depends on... 10
können to be able to, can 5
der **Korbball,̈e** basketball 9
kosten to cost 4
die **Krawatte,-n** tie 6
das **Kreuz,-e** cross 6
die **Küche,-n** kitchen 5
kühl cool 7
der **Kuli,-s** (ballpoint) pen 8
kulturell cultural 7
der **Kunde,-n** customer 10
die **Kunst** art 4
der **Kunstschatz,̈e** art treasure 10
der **Kurs,-e** exchange 6
kurz short(ly) A

L

das **Land,̈er** country, land 3; "state" in the *BRD* 4
die **Landschaft,-en** landscape 8
die **Landstraße,-n** two-lane highway 10
lang long 9
lange long 3
die **Länge,-n** length 5
langsam slow(ly) A
längst- longest 5
langweilig boring 2
laufen to run 5
die **Läufer,-** runner 9
leben to live 9
lebend living 10
lecker delicious 8
leer empty 5
der **Lehrer,-** teacher 7
leicht easy 3
leider unfortunately B

der **Leiter,-** head, person in charge 9
lernen to learn 4; *auswendig lernen* to memorize, learn by heart 4
lesen to read 4
letzt- last 8
die **Leute** (pl.) people 7
lieber rather 5
der **Lieblingsort,-e** favorite place 10
Liechtenstein Liechtenstein 5
liegen to lie, be located 3
die **Limonade,-n** soft drink 9
das **Lineal,-e** ruler 8
links left, on(to) the left 7
los: was ist los? What's the matter? 2; *Los!* Come on! 5; *Los, kommt!* Come on, let's go! 5
lösen to solve 4
loslaufen to start running 9
die **Lust** pleasure, joy 2; *Sie hat Lust...* She would like to... 2
Luxemburg Luxembourg 3

M

machen to do, make 1; *Das macht fünf Mark.* That's five marks. 3
das **Mädchen,-** girl 1
die **Mahlzeit,-en** meal 10
das **Mahnmal** memorial 7
der **Mai** May 4
mal times 3
das **Mal,-e** time(s) 9
man one, they, you, people 3
manche a few 8
manchmal sometimes 4
mangelhaft inadequate 4
der **Mann,̈er** man 9
die **Mannschaft,-en** team 9
der **Mantel,̈** coat 6
der **Marathonlauf,̈e** marathon run 9
märchenhaft legendary, fairy tale-like 10
die **Mark** mark (German monetary unit) 2
der **Markt,̈e** market 7
der **Marktplatz,̈e** market square 7
der **Markttag,-e** market day 7
die **Marmelade,-n** jam A
der **März** March 4
die **Matheaufgabe** math problem 3
die **Mathematik** (or: **Mathe**) mathematics 4
mehr als more than 5
mein my 1
die **meisten** most 7
meistens mostly, most of the time 5

der **Mensch,-en** person, human being 6
die **Messe,-n** trade fair 9
der **Meter,-** meter 10
das **Mietshaus,̈er** apartment building 5
die **Milch** milk A
die **Million,-en** million 3
mindestens at least 9
minus minus, less 2
die **Minute,-n** minute 2
mit with 3
mitbringen to bring along 7
mitkommen to come along 5
mitmachen to participate 9
mitnehmen to take along 10
der **Mittag,-e** noon 2
das **Mittagessen** lunch A
die **Mittagszeit,-en** noon time, lunch time B
die **Mitte,-n** middle, center 4
das **Mittelalter** Middle Ages 10
mittelalterlich medieval 10
das **Mittelgebirgsland** central highlands 8
der **Mittelpunkt,-e** focal point 7
der **Mittwoch** Wednesday 2
möchten would like to 5
modern modern B
mögen to like 5
möglich possible 2
die **Möglichkeit,-en** possibility 7
der **Moment,-e** moment 3
der **Monat,-e** month 2
der **Montag** Monday 2
morgen tomorrow 2
der **Morgen** morning 2; *heute morgen* this morning 2
das **Motorrad,̈er** motorcycle 7
müde tired A
der **Mund,̈er** mouth 10
das **Münster,-** cathedral 7
munter awake A
das **Museum,-seen** museum 9
die **Musik** music 4
das **Musikfest,-e** music festival 5
das **Musikinstrument,-e** musical instrument 8
müssen must, to have to 5
die **Mutter,̈** mother 5
die **Muttersprache,-n** mother tongue 5

N

na well 2
nach to, after 3

das **Nachbarland,-̈er** neighboring country 3

der **Nachmittag,-e** afternoon 2

die **Nachrichten** (pl.) news A

nachsehen to check 10

nächst next 4

der **Nachtisch,-e** dessert A

die **Nähe** nearness, proximity 2; *in der Nähe* nearby 2

der **Name,-n** name 1

nämlich namely 8

die **Nationalfahne,-n** national flag 4

natürlich of course, natural(ly) 4

neben next to, besides 10

nein no 1

neu new 4

neun nine 1

neunzehn nineteen 2

nicht not 1

die **Niederlande** Netherlands 3

niemand nobody, noone 9

noch still, yet 2

nochmal once more 5

der **Norden** north 3

die **Nordsee** North Sea 6

die **Note,-n** (school) grade, mark 4

notieren to jot down, make a note of 9

der **November** November 4

null zero 1

die **Nummer,-n** number 9

nur only, just 3

O

ob if, whether 8

oben on top 10

oder or 5

oft often 2

oftmals often 8

ohne without 3

der **Oktober** October 4

der **Onkel,-** uncle 5

das **Opfer,-** victim 7

orange orange 6

die **Ordnung,-en** order 10; *Es geht in Ordnung.* It will be taken care of. 10

der **Ort,-e** town, place 10

der **Osten** east 3

Österreich Austria 3

die **Ostsee** Baltic Sea 8

P

paar: ein paar a few, some 3

das **Paar,-e** pair 6

das **Papier** paper 8

das **Paradies,-e** paradise 6

parken to park 6

der **Parkplatz,-̈e** parking space, parking lot 6

die **Parkuhr,-en** parking meter 6

die **Party,-s** party 8

der **Paß,-̈sse** passport 6

passen to fit 3

die **Pause,-n** break 8; *eine Pause machen* to take a break 8

die **Person,-en** person 7

das **Pferd,-e** horse 8

das **Pfund,-e** pound 10

phantastisch fantastic, great 9

die **Physik** physics 4

die **Physikaufgabe,-n** physics problem 4

planen to plan B

der **Platz,-̈e** seat, place 3

der **Platzanweiser,-** usher 5

plötzlich suddenly 9

plus plus 1

politisch political 7

die **Polizei** police 9

praktisch practical 4

der **Preis,-e** price 6

preiswert reasonable 6

prima great, splendid 3

pro per 10

das **Programm,-e** program A

der **Prospekt,-e** brochure 10

das **Prozent,-e** per cent 9

der **Pullover,-** pullover 5

pünktlich punctual, on time 2

R

der **Radfahrer,-** bicycle rider 9

der **Radiergummi,-s** eraser 8

'ran: 'Ran an die Arbeit! Let's go to work! 9

die **Rast,-en** rest, break 10; *eine Rast machen* to take a rest 10

das **Rathaus,-̈er** city hall 7

die **Realschule,-n** secondary school (grades 5-10) A

die **Rechnung,-en** bill, invoice 10

recht right 1; *Das ist mir recht.* That's all right (O.K.) with me. 1; *Du hast recht.* You're right. 3

rechts right, on(to) the right 10

das **Regal,-e** shelf 4

das **Regierungsgebäude,-** government building 7

regnen to rain 7

reichen to reach, extend 9

die **Reihe,-n** row 6; *Er ist an der Reihe.* It's his turn. 6

die **Reise,-n** trip 4

das **Reisebüro,-s** travel agency 10

der **Reisescheck,-s** traveler's check 6

renovieren to renovate 7

die **Republik,-en** republic 5

das **Restaurant,-s** restaurant 7

der **Richter,-** judge 9

richtig really, correct 10

die **Richtung,-en** direction 10

der **Rock,-̈e** skirt 6

der **Rollstuhlfahrer,-** wheel chair driver 9

rosa pink 6

rot red 4

das **Rote Kreuz** Red Cross 9

rüberkommen (colloquial) to come over 2

die **Ruhe** peace, silence 3; *Immer mit der Ruhe!* Take it easy. 3

ruhig quiet, peaceful 4

S

die **S-Bahn,-en** city train, suburban express train 2

der **S-Bahnhof,-̈e** suburban line station 8

sagen to say, 2

die **Sammlung,-en** collection 7

der **Samstag** Saturday 2

saubermachen to clean 7

sauer angry, annoyed 4

das **Schach** chess 7

schade too bad 2

schaffen to manage (it), make (it) 9

die **Schallplatte,-n** record 8

der **Schalter,-** (ticket) counter 3

das **Schaufenster,-** display window 6

scheinen to shine 7

das **Schiff,-e** ship, boat 7

das **Schild,-er** sign 7

der **Schinken** ham A

das **Schlafzimmer,-** bedroom 5

schlagen to beat 9

der **Schlaukopf,-̈e** genius, smartie 4

schlecht bad 1

Schlittschuh laufen to skate 9

das **Schloß,-̈sser** castle 7

schmecken to taste B

schneien to snow 7

schnell fast, quick(ly) 2

schon already 2; *schon wieder* again 2

schön beautiful 4

schreiben to write *2*
der **Schuh,-e** shoe *6*
die **Schuld** fault *5*
die **Schule,-n** school *2*
der **Schüler,-** pupil, student (at elementary and secondary school) *4*
die **Schultasche,-n** school bag *8*
der **Schulweg,-e** way to school *3*
schwarz black *4*
das **Schwarze Meer** Black Sea *8*
der **Schwarzwald** Black Forest *6*
die **Schweiz** Switzerland *3*
schwer difficult, hard *3*
die **Schwester,-n** sister *5*
schwimmen to swim *9*
sechs six *1*
sechzehn sixteen *2*
der **See,-n** lake *5*
sehen to see, look *3; Mal sehen…* Let's see… *3; Seht mal!* Look! *4; sehen auf* to look at *4*
die **Sehenswürdigkeit,-en** sight(s) *7*
sehr very *3*
die **Seilbahn,-en** cable car *10*
sein to be *3*
sein his *5*
seit since, for *A*
die **Seite,-n** page *4;* side *7*
die **Sekunde,-n** second *2*
der **September** September *4*
sicher safe, secure *8*
sie she, they *1*
Sie you (formal) *1*
sieben seven *1*
siebzehn seventeen *2*
der **Sieger,-** winner *9*
singen to sing *B*
sitzen to sit *4*
der **Sitzplatz,-̈e** seat *8*
Ski laufen to ski *9*
so so *3*
so… wie as… as *3*
sobald as soon as *9*
die **Socke,-n** sock *6*
sofort right away, immediately *6*
sogar even *7*
der **Sohn,-̈e** son *5*
sollen to be supposed to, should *5*
der **Sommer,-** summer *4*
der **Sommermonat,-e** summer month *6*
das **Sonderangebot,-e** special offer *10*
sondern but *7; nicht nur… sondern auch* not only… but also *7*
der **Sonnabend** Saturday *2*

die **Sonne** sun *7*
sonnig sunny *10*
der **Sonntag** Sunday *2*
sonntags on Sundays *8*
sonst besides, otherwise *9*
die **Soße,-n** gravy *A*
sowie as well as *10*
sowieso anyhow, anyway *6*
sparen to save *B*
der **Spaß** fun *6; Viel Spaß!* Have fun! *6; Es macht Spaß.* It is fun. *8*
spät late *2; Wie spät ist es?* What time is it? How late is it? *2*
später later *2*
der **Speisesaal,-säle** dining hall *7*
das **Spiel,-e** game *5*
spielen to play *5*
der **Spielfilm,-e** feature film *A*
die **Spitze,-n** top *9; an der Spitze sein* to be in front *9*
der **Sport** sport *4*
die **Sportart,-en** kind of sport *9*
der **Sportler,-** athlete *9*
der **Sportplatz,-̈e** athletic field *B*
der **Sportwettbewerb,-e** sports competition *9*
die **Sprache,-n** language *6*
das **Sprachlabor,-s** language lab *4*
sprechen to speak, talk *2; sprechen über* to talk about *2*
springen to jump *9*
der **Staat,-en** state *3*
die **Staatsoper** State Opera *7*
das **Staatsratsgebäude** Council of State Building (DDR) *7*
die **Stadt,-̈e** city *1; in die Stadt gehen* to go downtown *1*
das **Städtische Kunstmuseum** City Art Museum *7*
die **Stadtmauer,-n** city wall *10*
der **Stadtplan,-̈e** city map *10*
das **Stadttor,-e** city gate *10*
der **Start,-s** start *9*
starten to start *9*
das **Startsignal,-e** starting signal *9*
die **Station,-en** station *10*
stattfinden to take place *9*
der **Status** status *4*
stehen to stand, be located *4; Es steht ihr gut.* She looks good in it. *6*
steigen to climb *10*
steigen: Sie steigt ein. She gets in(to). *2*
die **Stelle,-n** place, spot *9*
stellen to put, place *A*
stempeln to stamp *7*

stimmen to be correct *7; Das stimmt.* That's right. That's true. *7*
die **Straße,-n** street *4*
die **Straßenbahn,-en** streetcar *3*
die **Strecke,-n** stretch, distance *8; auf der Strecke* on the track (road) *9*
stricken to knit *A*
der **Strumpf,-̈e** stocking *6*
der **Student,-en** student (at university) *4*
studieren to study (at university) *4*
das **Studium, -dien** studies *4*
das **Stufen- und Bergland** terrace and highland country *8*
die **Stunde,-n** hour *2*
suchen to look for, search *4*
südamerikanisch South American, Latin American *8*
der **Süden** south *3*
die **Süßigkeiten** (pl.) sweets *7*
das **Symbol,-e** symbol *7*

T

die **Tafel,-n** board *B*
der **Tag,-e** day *1; Tag!* Hello! (conversational), Hi! *1; Guten Tag!* Hello! *1*
die **Tante,-n** aunt *5*
der **Tanz,-̈e** dance *8*
tanzen to dance *8*
der **Tanzpartner,-** dancing partner *8*
die **Tanzschule,-n** dancing school *8*
der **Tanzunterricht** dancing lessons (pl.) *8*
die **Tasche,-n** bag *3*
die **Tasse,-n** cup *9*
tausend thousand *10*
der **Tee** tea *A*
der **Teil,-e** part, section *5; zum größten Teil* for the most part, mostly *5; zum Teil* partly, in part *8*
der **Teilnehmer,-** participant *9*
das **Telefon,-e** telephone *2*
die **Telefonzelle,-n** telephone booth *7*
das **Tennis** tennis *9*
teuer expensive *6*
das **Theater,-** theater *7*
die **Theke,-n** counter *8*
das **Tiefland** lowlands *8*
der **Tisch,-e** table *5*
das **Tischtennis** table tennis *7*
die **Tochter,-̈** daughter *5*
toll fantastic, wild, terrific *5*

die **Tomate,-n** tomato *A*

das **Tor,-e** gate *10*

der **Tourist,-en** tourist *5*

tragen to carry *3*

trainieren to train, practice *9*

sich **treffen** to meet *B*

treiben to drive, do *9; Sport treiben* to participate in sports *9*

trinken to drink *9*

die **Trompete,-n** trumpet *8*

die **Tschechoslowakei** Czechoslovakia *3*

Tschüs! See you! (sometimes spelled Tschüss! or Tschüß!) *2*

tun to do *2*

die **Tür,-en** door *4*

der **Turm,-̈e** tower *7*

typisch typical *A*

U

üben to practice *4*

über over, above *3;* about *10*

überblicken to overlook *10*

übernachten to stay overnight *7*

die **Übernachtung,-en** (overnight) accommodation *7*

übertreffen to surpass, beat *9*

die **Übung,-en** exercise, practice *4; Übung macht den Meister!* Practice makes perfect. *4*

die **Uhr,-en** clock, watch *2; Wieviel Uhr ist es?* What time is it? *2; Es ist vier Uhr.* It's four o'clock. *2*

um at *2;* around *1;* in order to, to *7; Um wieviel Uhr?* At what time? *2*

umgeben to surround *10*

die **Umgebung,-en** surrounding, vicinity *5*

die **Umkleidekabine,-n** fitting room *6*

umsteigen to transfer *10*

und and *1*

Ungarn Hungary *5*

ungeduldig impatient *4*

ungefähr approximate(ly) *3*

ungenügend unsatisfactory *4*

die **Uni** "U" (abbreviation for **Universität**) university *4*

die **Universität,-en** university *4*

unpünktlich late, not on time *5*

uns us *5*

unsere (form of **unser**) our *5*

unterdessen meanwhile, in the meantime *5*

unterwegs on the way *10*

V

der **Vater,-̈** father *5*

verärgert angry *2*

verbinden to connect *8*

die **Verbindung,-en** connection *8*

verbringen to spend (a vacation) *9*

die **Vereinigten Staaten** United States *3*

die **Verkäuferin,-nen** sales clerk (female) *5*

der **Verkehr** traffic *4*

das **Verkehrsmittel,-** means of transportation *7*

das **Verkehrsschild,-er** traffic sign *10*

verlassen to leave *A*

verlaufen to run, extend *6*

verlieren to lose *4; Verlier keine Worte!* Don't waste any words! *4*

sich **versammeln** to gather, meet *7*

verschieden different, various *7*

versorgen to supply, provide *10*

der **Verstand** reason, mind *9; mehr Glück als Verstand haben* to have more luck than brains *9*

verstehen to understand *4*

versuchen to try *9*

verzieren to decorate *10*

viel much *2*

viele many *4*

vielleicht perhaps *4*

vier four *1*

das **Viertel,-** quarter *3; Es ist Viertel nach acht.* It's a quarter after eight. *3*

vierzehn fourteen *2*

die **Vokabel,-n** (vocabulary) word *4*

voll full *3*

von from, of *2*

vor in front of, before *5*

vorbeifahren to drive by *9*

vorbeiführen to go past *10*

vorbeikommen to come by *9*

vorführen to perform, stage *10*

vorhaben to plan, intend *6*

vorher before, in advance *10*

vorhin before, earlier *9*

der **Vormittag,-e** forenoon *2*

der **Vorort,-e** suburb *3*

der **Vorschlag,-̈e** suggestion *4*

sich **vorstellen** to imagine *10*

die **Vorstellung,-en** performance, show *5*

W

die **Wachablösung** changing of the guard *7*

der **Wagen,-** car *6*

während during *5*

der **Wald,-̈er** forest *7*

der **Walzer,-** waltz *8*

wandern to hike *6*

wann when *2*

die **Ware,-n** product, goods *6*

warm warm *7*

warnen to warn *8*

warten to wait *2; warten auf* to wait for *A*

warum why *2*

was what *1*

was für what kind of *4*

der **Wasserbehälter,-** water container *9*

wässerig watery *10*

die **Wasserstraße,-n** waterway *8*

der **Wasserverkehr** water traffic *8*

der **Weg,-e** way *2; auf dem Weg* on the way *2*

die **Weile** while *2; eine Weile* a while *2*

der **Wein,-e** wine *9*

weiß white *5*

weiter further *4; Sie gehen weiter.* They keep going. *4*

weiterfahren to continue (driving) *10*

weitest- farthest *3*

der **Weitsprung,-̈e** broad jump *9*

welcher which *2*

die **Welt,-en** world *7*

weltberühmt world-famous *10*

die **Weltzeituhr** World Time Clock *7*

wenig little *4*

wenige few *7*

wenigstens at least *6*

wer who *2*

der **Westen** west *3*

das **Wetter** weather *7*

wichtig important *8*

wie how *1;* like *8; Wie geht's?* How are you? (familiar) *1; wie viele?* how many *3*

wieder again *2*

wiederholen to repeat *A*

wieviel how much? *2; Um wieviel Uhr?* At what time? *2*

der **Winter,-** winter *4*

der **Wintermonat,-e** winter month 6

der **Wintersportler,-** winter sports-man 5

wir we 1

wirklich really 4

wissen to know, be familiar with 3

wo where 1

woher where from 4

wohin where to 4

wohnen to live 1

die **Wohnung,-en** apartment 4

das **Wohnviertel,-** residential area 7

das **Wohnzimmer,-** living room 5

die **Wolke,-n** cloud 10

wollen to want to 5

womit with what 10

das **Wort,-e** word (saying, quotation) 4; *Verlier keine Worte!* Don't waste any words. 4

das **Wort,-er** word 4

das **Wörterbuch,-er** dictionary 4

wünschen to wish 10

die **Wurst,-e** sausage A

Z

die **Zahnradbahn,-en** cog-wheel train 10

zehn ten 1

das **Zeichen,-** signal, sign 9

zeigen to show 3; *zeigen auf* to point to 6

die **Zeit,-en** time 2

die **Zeitung,-en** newspaper 5

der **Zentimeter,-** centimeter 9

das **Zentrum, -tren** center 6

das **Ziel,-e** finish (line) 9

das **Zimmer,-** room 2

der **Zimmerschlüssel,-** room key 7

zu at, too, to 2; *zu Hause* at home 2

zubereiten to prepare (a meal) 7

zuerst first 5

der **Zug,-e** train 3

zugeben to admit 6

zum (or: **zu dem**) to the 5

zumachen to close B

zur (or: **zu der**) to the 2

zurückbekommen to get back 2

zurückfahren to drive back 10

zurückgehen to go back 6

zusammen together 2

der **Zuschauer,-** spectator 9

zuschicken to send, mail (to) 10

zuwinken to wave at 10

zwanzig twenty 2

zwei two 1

zwischen between 8

zwölf twelve 2

All the words introduced in DEUTSCH: AKTUELL 1 have been summarized in this section. The numbers following the meaning of individual words or phrases indicate the particular lesson in which they appear for the first time. In cases in which there is more than one meaning for a word or phrase and it has appeared in different lessons, the corresponding lesson numbers are listed.

A

a eine(e) *2*
able: to be able to können *5*
about über *10*
above über *3*
accommodations (overnight) die Übernachtung,-en *7*
accordion das Akkordeon,-s *8*
across gegenüber *7*
actual(ly) eigentlich *3*
admission der Eintritt *8*
to **admit** zugeben *7*
afraid: to be afraid Angst haben *2*
after nach *3*
afternoon der Nachmittag,-e *2*
again wieder *2; again and again* immer wieder *7*
airplane das Flugzeug,-e *7*
all alle *2*
almost fast *5*
Alps die Alpen *5*
already schon *2*
also auch *1*
always immer *2*
America Amerika *5*
American der Amerikaner,- (male), die Amerikanerin,-nen (female) *A*
amount der Betrag,"e *6*
an ein(e) *2*
and und *1*
angry verärgert *2;* sauer *4*
to **announce** bekanntgeben *8*
announcer der Ansager,- *9*
annoyed sauer *4*
to **answer** antworten *3;* beantworten *A; to answer a question* eine Frage beantworten *A*
anyhow sowieso *6*
anyway sowieso *6*
apartment die Wohnung,-en *4*
apartment building das Mietshaus,"er *5*

to **applaud** klatschen *9*
apple sauce das Apfelmus *A*
approximate(ly) ungefähr *3*
April der April *4*
area die Fläche,-n *3;* die Gegend,-en *5*
around um *1*
arrival die Ankunft,"e *7*
to **arrive** ankommen *10*
art die Kunst *4*
article of clothing das Kleidungsstück,-e *6*
art treasure der Kunstschatz,"e *10*
as... as so... wie *3*
to **ask** fragen *2*
to **assume** annehmen *10*
at um, an *2;* bei *5; At what time?* Um wieviel Uhr? *2; at home* zu Hause *2*
athlete der Sportler,- *9*
athletic field der Sportplatz,"e *B*
attendant der Aufseher,- *9*
attraction der Anziehungspunkt,-e *10*
August der August *4*
aunt die Tante,-n *5*
Austria Österreich *3*
automat der Automat,-en *3*
available frei *7*
awake munter *A*
away entfernt *4*

B

bad schlecht *1; too bad* schade *2*
badminton der Federball,"e *9*
bag die Tasche,-n *3*
baggage das Gepäck *3*
ballpoint pen der Kuli,-s *8*
Baltic Sea die Ostsee *8*

bank die Bank,-en *6*
basketball der Basketball,"e; der Korbball,"e *9*
to **be** sein *3*
to **beat** übertreffen *9;* schlagen *9*
beautiful schön *4*
bed das Bett,-en *5*
bedroom das Schlafzimmer,- *5*
beer das Bier,-e *9*
before vor *5;* vorher *10*
to **begin** beginnen *3*
behind hinter *8*
Belgium Belgien *3*
to **believe** glauben *3*
to **belong to** gehören zu *8*
bench die Bank,"e *4*
beside neben *10*
besides außer *6;* sonst *9*
best best- *7; the best is* am besten *7*
between zwischen *8*
beverage das Getränk,-e *7*
bicycle das Fahrrad,"er *7*
bicycle rider der Radfahrer,- *9*
big groß *3*
bill die Rechnung,-en *10*
biology die Biologie *4*
birthday der Geburtstag,-e *5 Happy Birthday!* Herzlichen Glückwunsch zum Geburtstag! *8*
black schwarz *4*
Black Forest der Schwarzwald *6*
Black Sea das Schwarze Meer *6*
to **block off** absperren *9*
blouse die Bluse,-n *6*
blue blau *6*
board die Tafel,-n *B*
boat das Boot,-e *7;* das Schiff,-e *7*
book das Buch,"er *4; book department* die Bücherabteilung,-en *6*
to **book** buchen *10*

border die Grenze,-n 6
to **border on** grenzen an 4
boring langweilig 2
both beide 2
boy der Junge,-n 1
boyfriend der Freund,-e 1
bratwurst die Bratwurst,-̈e B
bread das Brot,-e A
break die Pause,-n 8; *to take a break* eine Pause machen 8
breakfast: to have breakfast frühstücken 5
bridge die Brücke,-n 8
to **bring** bringen A
to **bring along** mitbringen 7
broad jump der Weitsprung,-̈e 9
brochure der Prospekt,-e 10
brother der Bruder,-̈ 5
brown braun 6
buddy der Kamerad,-en 9
to **build** erbauen 10
building das Gebäude,- 7
bus der Bus,-se 4
but aber 2; sondern 7; *not only... but also* nicht nur... sondern auch 7
butter die Butter A
to **buy** kaufen 3

C

cable car die Seilbahn,-en 10
café das Café,-s 5
to **call (up)** anrufen 5
called: to be called heißen 1
can können 5
canal der Kanal,-̈e 9
canal system das Kanalsystem,-e 8
to **cancel (tickets)** entwerten 8
capital (city) die Hauptstadt,-̈e 3
car das Auto,-s 5; der Wagen,- 6
card die Karte,-n B
to **carry** tragen 3
to **cash (in)** einlösen 6
cashier's counter die Kasse,-n 6
cassette die Kassette,-n 4
castle das Schloß,-̈sser 7
cathedral das Münster,- 7
center die Mitte,-n 4; das Zentrum,-tren 6
centimeter der Zentimeter,- 9
certainly bestimmt 6
chance die Chance,-n 9
character der Charakter,-e 10
to **check** nachsehen 10

cheese der Käse A
chemistry die Chemie 4
chess das Schach 7
chocolate: hot chocolate der Kakao 9
choice die Auswahl 6
to **choose** auswählen B
church die Kirche,-n 7
city die Stadt,-̈e 1
city gate das Stadttor,-e 10
city hall das Rathaus,-̈er 7
city map der Stadtplan,-̈e 10
city wall die Stadtmauer,-n 10
clarinet die Klarinette,-n 8
class die Klasse,-n 3; *second class* zweiter Klasse 3
class trip der Klassenausflug,-̈e 7
to **clean** saubermachen 7
clear klar 3
to **clear** abräumen 7
clearly deutlich 10
to **climb** steigen 10
clock die Uhr,-en 2
close dicht 9
to **close** zumachen B
cloud die Wolke,-n 10
coat der Mantel,-̈ 6
cocoa der Kakao 9
coffee der Kaffee A
cog-wheel train die Zahnradbahn,-en 10
cola die Cola,-s 2
cold kalt 7
cold-cut platter die Kalte Platte 5
collection die Sammlung,-en 7
color die Farbe,-n 6
colorful bunt 6
to **come** kommen 1; *Come on!* Los! 5
to **come along** mitkommen 5
to **come by** vorbeikommen 9
to **come here** hierherkommen 10
to **come over** rüberkommen 2
comfortable bequem 3
competition der Wettbewerb,-e 9; *sports competition* der Sportwettbewerb 9
composition der Aufsatz,-̈e A
computer der Computer,- 3
to **congratulate** gratulieren 9
congratulations (pl.) der Glückwunsch,-̈e 8; *Congratulations!* Herzlichen Glückwunsch! 9
to **connect** verbinden 8
connection die Verbindung,-en 8
to **consist of** bestehen aus 4
to **construct** erbauen 10

to **continue** fortsetzen 10; *to continue a trip* eine Reise fortsetzen 10; *to continue (driving)* weiterfahren 10
to **cook** kochen A
cool kühl 7
to **cool off** sich abkühlen 9
corner die Ecke,-n 1
correct richtig 10; *to be correct* stimmen 7
to **cost** kosten 4
counter die Theke,-n 8; *counter (ticket)* der Schalter,- 3
country das Land,-̈er 3
course: of course natürlich 4
to **cover** decken A
to **crochet** häkeln 5
cross das Kreuz,-e 6
cultural kulturell 7
cup die Tasse,-n 9
customer der Kunde,-n 10
Czechoslovakia die Tschechoslowakei 3

D

dance der Tanz,-̈e 8
to **dance** tanzen 8
dancing lessons (pl.) der Tanzunterricht 8
dancing partner der Tanzpartner,- 8
dancing school die Tanzschule,-n 8
Danube die Donau 5
date (calendar) das Datum, Daten 5
daughter die Tochter,-̈ 5
day der Tag,-e 1
December der Dezember 4
to **decorate** verzieren 10
delicious lecker 8
Denmark Dänemark 3
department store das Kaufhaus,-̈er B
departure die Abfahrt,-en 10
departure time die Abfahrtszeit,-en 10
to **describe** beschreiben 10
description die Beschreibung,-en 4
to **designate** bezeichnen 10
dessert der Nachtisch,-e A
dictionary das Wörterbuch,-̈er 4
different verschieden 7
difficult schwer 3
dining hall der Speisesaal,-säle 7

direct direkt *6*
direction die Richtung,-en *10*
to **discuss** besprechen *4*
dishes das Geschirr *7*
display window das Schaufenster,- *6*
distance die Entfernung,-en *3;* die Strecke,-n *8*
distant entfernt *4*
to **do** machen *1;* tun *2*
dollar der Dollar,-s *6*
door die Tür,-en *4*
downtown die Innenstadt,¨e *6*
dress das Kleid,-er *6*
to **drink** trinken *9*
to **drive** fahren *3*
to **drive around** herumfahren *7*
to **drive back** zurückfahren *10*
to **drive by** vorbeifahren *9*
driver's license der Führerschein,-e *8*
driver's test die Fahrprüfung,-en *8*
during während *5*

E

each jeder *7*
earlier vorhin *9*
early früh *9*
east der Osten *3*
easy leicht *3*
to **eat** essen *5*
eight acht *1*
eighteen achtzehn *2*
elegant elegant *7*
elevator der Fahrstuhl,¨e *7*
eleven elf *2*
employee der Angestellte,-n *6*
empty leer *5*
end das Ende *3*
to **end** beenden *10*
England England *4*
English englisch *4;* das Englisch *4*
entrance der Eingang,¨e *6*
eraser der Radiergummi,-s *8*
especially besonders *4*
essay der Aufsatz,¨e *A*
Europe Europa *5*
European europäisch *8*
even sogar *7*
evening der Abend,-e *2; this evening* ...heute abend *2*
event das Ereignis,-se *7*
every jeder *7*
everyone alle *8*
everything alles *3*

exact genau *7*
example das Beispiel,-e *7; for example* zum Beispiel *7*
excellent ausgezeichnet *10*
except außer *6*
exchange (money) der Kurs,-e *6*
excursion der Ausflug,¨e *8*
exercise die Übung,-en *4*
expensive teuer *6*
expert der Experte,-n *8*
expression der Ausdruck,¨e *4*

F

fairy tale-like märchenhaft *10*
fall der Herbst,-e *4*
family die Familie,-n *5*
famous berühmt *10*
fantastic toll *5;* phantastisch *9*
farm der Bauernhof,¨e *10*
fascism der Faschismus *7*
fast schnell *2*
father der Vater,¨ *5*
fault die Schuld *5*
favorable günstig *10*
fear die Angst,¨e *2*
feature film der Spielfilm,-e *A*
February der Februar *4*
Federal Republic of Germany die Bundesrepublik Deutschland *3*
fee die Gebühr,-en *6*
few wenige *7;* einige *7; a few* ein paar *3;* manche *8*
field das Feld,-er *10*
field path der Feldweg,-e *4*
fifteen fünfzehn *2*
figure die Figur,-en *10*
to **fill out** ausfüllen *7*
film der Film,-e *5*
finally endlich *2*
to **find** finden *4*
finish (line) das Ziel,-e *9*
to **finish** beenden *10*
first erst *5;* zuerst *5*
to **fit** passen *3*
fitting room die Umkleidekabine,-n *6*
five fünf *1*
flat flach *5*
flight der Flug,¨e *10*
to **flow** fließen *5*
flower die Blume,-n *10*
flute die Flöte,-n *8*
to **follow** folgen *7*
food das Essen *8*
foot der Fuß,¨e *3; on foot* zu Fuß *3*
for für *3;* seit *A*

foreign language die Fremdsprache,-n *4*
foreigner der Ausländer,- *10*
forenoon der Vormittag,-e *2*
forest der Wald,¨er *7*
form die Form,-en *9*
to **form** bilden *9*
formula die Formel,-n *4*
fortress die Festung,-en *10*
fountain der Brunnen,- *10*
four vier *1*
fourteen vierzehn *2*
France Frankreich *3*
free frei *7*
French (language) Französisch *6*
Friday der Freitag,-e *2*
friend der Freund,-e *1*
from von *2;* aus *2*
front: in front of vor *5*
full voll *3*
fun der Spaß *6; Have fun!* Viel Spaß! *6; It is fun.* Es macht Spaß. *8*
further weiter *4*

G

game das Spiel,-e *5*
gate das Tor,-e *10*
to **gather** sich versammeln *7*
genius der Schlaukopf *4*
gentleman der Herr,-en *1*
geography die Erdkunde *4*
German deutsch *1;* Deutsch (language) *4*
German Democratic Republic die Deutsche Demokratische Republik *3*
Germany Deutschland *3*
to **get** bekommen *2*
to **get in(to)** einsteigen *2*
to **get off** aussteigen *10*
to **get up** aufstehen *A*
girl das Mädchen,- *1*
girlfriend die Freundin,-nen *3*
to **give** geben *4*
glad froh *2*
gladly gern *4*
glass das Glas,¨er *9*
glove der Handschuh,-e *6*
to **go** gehen *1;* fahren *3; to go into* gehen über *8*
to **go back** zurückgehen *6*
to **go inside** hineingehen *7*
to **go past** vorbeiführen *10*
gold gold *4*
golf das Golf *9*

good gut *1*

goodness die Güte *7; My goodness!* Du meine Güte! *7*

grade (school) die Note,-n *4*

gram das Gramm,-e *10*

granddaughter die Enkelin,-nen *5*

grandfather der Großvater,ￜ *5*

grandmother die Großmutter,ￜ *5*

grandparents die Großeltern (pl.) *5*

grandson der Enkel,- *5*

gravy die Soße,-n *A*

gray grau *6*

great prima *3;* phantastisch *9; to be great* klasse sein *5*

green grün *6*

to **greet** begrüßen *3*

group die Gruppe,-n *B*

guitar die Gitarre,-n *A*

H

half halb *3*

ham der Schinken *A*

happy froh *2*

hard schwer *3*

hardly kaum *9*

to **have** haben *2*

to **have on** anhaben *6*

to **have to** müssen *5*

he er *1*

head der Leiter,- *9*

to **hear** hören *4*

hearty herzlich *8*

heat die Hitze *8; in this heat* bei der Hitze *8*

height die Höhe,-n *6*

Hello! Grüß dich!, Guten Tag! *1*

help die Hilfe *4*

to **help** helfen *9*

her ihr *A*

here hier *1*

Hi! Grüß dich!, Tag! *1*

high hoch *5*

highway die Landstraße,-n *10*

to **hike** wandern *6*

hill der Hügel,- *10*

his sein *5*

historic(al) historisch *7;* geschichtlich *10*

history die Geschichte *4*

hockey das Hockey *9*

home: at home zu Hause *2; to go home* nach Hause gehen *2*

homework die Hausaufgabe,-n *5; to do homework* die Hausaufgaben machen *5*

to **hope** hoffen *6*

hopefully hoffentlich *9*

horse das Pferd,-e *8*

hot heiß *7*

hotel das Hotel,-s *7*

hotel sign das Hotelschild,-er *10*

hour die Stunde,-n *2*

house das Haus,ￜer *2; half-timbered house* das Fachwerkhaus,ￜer *10*

how wie *1; How are you?* Wie geht's? *1; how many?* wie viele? *3; how much?* wieviel? *2*

Hungary Ungarn *5*

hunger der Hunger *7*

hungry hungrig *A*

to **hurry** sich beeilen *3; Let's hurry.* Beeilen wir uns! *3*

I

I ich *1*

ice cream parlor die Eisdiele,-n *2*

idea die Idee,-n *2*

identification (card) der Ausweis,-e *7*

if ob *8*

to **imagine** vorstellen *10*

immediately gleich *1;* sofort *6*

impatient ungeduldig *4*

important wichtig *8*

in in *1*

inadequate mangelhaft *4*

including einschließlich *10*

industrial city die Industriestadt,ￜe *9*

industrious fleißig *4*

information die Information,-en *10*

inhabitant der Einwohner,- *3*

interest das Interesse,-n *A*

to **interest** interessieren *A*

interesting interessant *7*

island die Insel,-n *8*

it es *1*

Italian Italienisch (language) *6*

Italy Italien *5*

J

jam die Marmelade *A*

January der Januar *4*

jeans die Jeans (pl.) *6*

to **jot down** notieren *9*

judge der Richter,- *9*

July der Juli *4*

to **jump** springen *9*

June der Juni *4*

just nur *3;* eben *4;* gerade *10; just like/as* genauso wie *4*

K

kilometer der Kilometer,- *3*

kiosk der Kiosk,-e *2*

kitchen die Küche,-n *5*

to **knit** stricken *A*

to **know (someone)** kennen *1;* wissen *3; to get to know* kennenlernen *B*

L

to **label** bezeichnen *10*

ladies' department die Damenabteilung,-en *6*

lady die Dame,-n *6*

lake der See,-n *5*

landscape die Landschaft,-en *8*

language die Sprache,-n *6*

language lab das Sprachlabor,-s *4*

large groß *3*

last letzt- *8*

to **last** dauern *3*

late spät *2; How late is it?* Wie spät ist es? *2*

late, not on time unpünktlich *5*

to **lead** führen *10*

to **learn** lernen *4; to learn by heart* auswendig lernen *4*

least: at least wenigstens *6;* mindestens *9*

to **leave** verlassen *A*

left links *7*

legendary märchenhaft *10*

length die Länge,-n *5*

to **lie** liegen *3*

Liechtenstein Liechtenstein *5*

like wie *8*

to **like** gefallen *6;* mögen *5; She likes it.* Es gefällt ihr. *6; to like to walk* gern gehen *4; Would you like to...?* Hast du Lust...? *2*

to **listen** hören *4*

little wenig *4;* klein *10; a little* etwas *2*

to **live** wohnen *1;* leben *9; living* lebend *10*

living room das Wohnzimmer,- *5*

located: to be located liegen *3;* stehen *4*

long lange *3,* lang *9*

to **look** sehen *3; Look!* Seht mal! *4; to look at* sehen auf *4*

to **look at** sich ansehen *B*
to **look for** suchen *4*
to **look over** begutachten *6;* besichtigen *10*
to **lose** verlieren *4*
    luck das Glück *2; to be lucky* Glück haben *2*
    luggage das Gepäck *3*
    luggage cart der Koffer-Kuli,-s *3*
    lunch das Mittagessen *A*
    lunch time die Mittagszeit,-en *B*
    Luxembourg Luxemburg *3*

M

to **mail (to)** zuschicken *10*
    mailbox der Briefkasten,- *7*
    mainland das Festland,-er *8*
to **make** machen *1; to make it* schaffen *9*
    man der Mann,-er *9*
    many viele *4*
    map die Karte,-n *6*
    marathon run der Marathonlauf,-e *9*
    March der März *4*
    mark die Mark *2*
    market der Markt,-e *7*
    market day der Markttag,-e *7*
    market square der Marktplatz,-e *7*
    mathematics die Mathematik (Mathe) *4*
    math problem die Matheaufgabe,-n *3*
    matter: What's the matter? Was ist los? *2*
    may dürfen *5*
    May der Mai *4*
    meal das Essen *A;* die Mahlzeit, -en *10*
    meaning die Bedeutung,-en *4*
    meanwhile unterdessen *5*
    medieval mittelalterlich *10*
to **meet** sich treffen *B;* sich versammeln *9*
    memorial das Mahnmal *7*
to **memorize** auswendig lernen *4*
    meter der Meter,- *10*
    middle die Mitte,-n *4*
    Middle Ages das Mittelalter *10*
    milk die Milch *A*
    million die Million,-en *3*
    minus minus *2*
    minute die Minute,-n *2*
    Miss das Fräulein,- *1*
    modern modern *B*

    moment der Moment,-e *3*
    Monday der Montag *2*
    money das Geld *2*
    month der Monat,-e *2*
    more than mehr als *5*
    morning der Morgen *2; this morning* heute morgen *2*
    most die meisten *7*
    mostly meistens *5*
    mother die Mutter,- *5*
    mother tongue die Muttersprache,-n *5*
    motorcycle das Motorrad,-er *7*
    mountain der Berg,-e *5*
    mouth der Mund,-er *10*
    movie der Film,-e *5*
    movie theater das Kino,-s *5*
    Mr. der Herr,-en *1*
    Mrs. die Frau,-en *1*
    much viel *2*
    museum das Museum,-seen *9*
    music die Musik *4*
    music festival das Musikfest,-e *5*
    musical instrument das Musikinstrument,-e *8*
    must müssen *5*
    my mein *1*

N

    name: to be named heißen *1; What's your name?* Wie heißt du? *1*
    name der Name,-n *1*
    namely nämlich *8*
    national flag die Nationalfahne, -n *4*
    natural(ly) natürlich *4*
    nearby in der Nähe *2*
to **need** brauchen *2*
    neighboring country Nachbarland,-er *3*
    Netherlands die Niederlande *3*
    new neu *4*
    news die Nachrichten (pl.) *A*
    newspaper die Zeitung,-en *5*
    next nächst *4*
    next to neben *10*
    nine neun *1*
    nineteen neunzehn *2*
    no nein *1;* kein *2; no time* keine Zeit *2*
    nobody niemand *9*
    noon der Mittag,-e *2*
    noon time die Mittagszeit,-en *B*
    north der Norden *3*
    North Sea die Nordsee *6*
    not nicht *1; not at all* gar nicht *4*

    notebook das Heft,-e *8*
    November der November *4*
    now jetzt *1*
    number die Nummer,- *9*

O

    October der Oktober *4*
    of von *2*
to **offer** bieten *7*
    office das Büro,-s *4*
    often oft *2;* oftmals *8*
    O.K. Gut! *1;* klar *3*
    old alt *4*
    on auf *2;* an *8*
    once einmal *3; once again* wieder einmal *3; one more time* noch einmal *5; once more* nochmal *5*
    one eins *1;* man *3*
    one-way (ticket) einfach *3*
    only nur *3;* erst *5*
    open geöffnet *B; The store is open.* Das Geschäft ist geöffnet. *B*
    or oder *5*
    orange orange *6*
to **order** bestellen *B*
    order die Ordnung,-en *10*
to **originate (river)** entspringen *8*
    other andere *4*
    otherwise sonst *9*
    our unser *5*
    out of aus *2*
    outside außerhalb *5;* ins Freie *7;* im Freien *10*
    over über *3*
to **overlook** überblicken *10*
    overnight: to stay overnight übernachten *7*
    owner der Besitzer,- (male), die Besitzerin,-nen (female) *8*

P

    page die Seite,-n *4*
    painting das Gemälde,-n *7*
    pair das Paar,-e *6*
    pants die Hose,-n *6*
    paper das Papier *8*
    paradise das Paradies,-e *6*
    parents die Eltern (pl.) *5*
to **park** parken *6*
    parking lot der Parkplatz,-e *6*
    parking meter die Parkuhr,-en *6*
    part der Teil,-e *5; for the most part* zum größten Teil *5*
    participant der Teilnehmer,- *9*
to **participate** mitmachen *9*

partly zum Teil *8*
party die Party,-s *8*
passport der Paß,¨sse *6*
to **pay** bezahlen *6*
pea die Erbse,-n *A*
peace die Ruhe *3*
pedestrian der Fußgänger,- *10*
pencil der Bleistift,-e *8*
people die Leute (pl.) *7*
per pro *10*
per cent das Prozent,-e *9*
to **perform** vorführen *10*
performance die Vorstellung,-en *5*; die Leistung,-en *9*
perhaps vielleicht *4*
permitted: to be permitted to dürfen *5*
person der Mensch,-en *6*; die Person,-en *7*
photo album das Fotoalbum,-ben *B*
to **photograph** fotografieren *B*
physics die Physik *4*
piano das Klavier,-e *8*
pink rosa *6*
to **place** stellen *A*
place der Platz,¨e *3*; der Ort,-e *10*; die Stelle,-n *9*
to **plan** vorhaben *6*; planen *B*
platform der Bahnsteig,-e *8*
to **play** spielen *5*
pleasant gemütlich *7*
please bitte *6*
pleasure die Lust *2*
plus plus *1*
police die Polizei *9*
political politisch *7*
popular beliebt *5*
population die Bevölkerung-en *9*
possibility die Möglichkeit,-en *7*
possible möglich *2*; *That's possible.* Das geht. *7*
potato die Kartoffel,-n *A*
potato salad der Kartoffelsalat *8*
pound das Pfund *10*
practical praktisch *4*
to **practice** üben *4*
practice die Übung,-en *4*; *Practice makes perfect.* Übung macht den Meister! *4*
to **prepare (a meal)** zubereiten *7*
present das Geschenk,-e *8*
to **preserve** bewahren *10*
price der Preis,-e *6*
prince der Fürst,-en *10*
problem die Aufgabe,-n *4*
product die Ware,-n *6*
program das Programm,-e *A*

to **provide** versorgen *10*
pullover der Pullover,- *5*
punctual pünktlich *2*
pupil der Schüler,- *4*
purse die Handtasche,-n *6*
to **put** stellen *A*
to **put on (clothes)** anziehen *6*; *to put on (records)* auflegen *8*

Q

quarter das Viertel,- *3*; *It's a quarter after eight.* Es ist Viertel nach acht. *3*
question die Frage,-n *A*
quick(ly) schnell *2*
quiet ruhig *4*
quite ganz *3*

R

to **rain** regnen *7*
rather lieber *5*
to **reach** erreichen *6*
to **reach into** hineinreichen *8*
to **read** lesen *4*
ready fertig *5*
really wirklich *4*; richtig *10*
reasonable preiswert *6*; günstig *10*
to **receive** bekommen *2*
record die Schallplatte,-n *8*
recorder die Blockflöte,-n *9*
red rot *4*
Red Cross das Rote Kreuz *9*
registration form das Anmeldeformular,-e *7*
to **remain** bleiben *2*
to **remind of** erinnern an *10*
to **renovate** renovieren *7*
to **repeat** wiederholen *A*
representative der Abgeordnete,-n *7*
republic die Republik,-en *5*
rest die Rast,-en *10*; *to take a rest* eine Rast machen *10*
restaurant das Restaurant,-s *7*
result das Ergebnis,-se *9*; *final result* das Endergebnis,-se *9*
right rechts *10*; *That's all right with me.* Das ist mir recht. *1*; *You're right.* Du hast recht. *3*; *That's right.* Das stimmt. *7*
right away gleich *1*; sofort *6*
to **ring (bell)** klingeln *4*
river der Fluß,¨sse *5*
room das Zimmer,- *2*

room key der Zimmerschlüssel,- *7*
row die Reihe,-n *6*; *It's his turn.* Er ist an der Reihe. *6*
ruler das Lineal,-e *8*
to **run** laufen *5*; *to run (river)* *5*
to run around herumlaufen *9*
to **run towards** entgegenlaufen *9*
runner der Läufer,- *9*

S

safe sicher *8*
sales clerk (female) die Verkäuferin,-nen *5*
the **same** dasselbe *7*
satisfactory befriedigend *4*
Saturday der Sonnabend *2*; der Samstag *2*
sausage die Wurst,¨e *A*
to **save** sparen *B*
to **say** sagen *2*
schedule der Fahrplan,¨e *3*
school die Schule,-n *2*
school bag die Schultasche,-n *8*
season die Jahreszeit,-en *4*
seat der Platz,¨e *3*; der Sitzplatz,¨e *8*
second die Sekunde,-n *2*
to **see** sehen *3*; *Let's see...* Mal sehen... *3*; *See you!* Tschüs! *2*
to **select** auswählen *B*
selection die Auswahl *6*
to **send** (zu)schicken *10*
September der September *4*
seven sieben *1*
seventeen siebzehn *2*
several einige *7*
shape die Form,-en *9*
she sie *1*
shelf das Regal,-e *4*
to **shine** scheinen *7*
ship das Schiff,-e *7*
shirt das Hemd,-en *6*
shoe der Schuh,-e *6*
to **shop** einkaufen *5*; *to go shopping* einkaufen gehen *5*
short(ly) kurz *A*
should sollen *5*
to **show** zeigen *3*
show die Vorstellung,-en *5*
siblings die Geschwister (pl.) *5*
side die Seite,-n *7*
sight(s) die Sehenswürdigkeit,-en *7*
sign das Schild,-er *7*; das Zeichen,- *9*

signal das Zeichen,- 9
significance die Bedeutung,-en 4
silence die Ruhe 3
simple einfach 3
since seit A
sincere herzlich 8
to **sing** singen B
sister die Schwester,-n 5
to **sit** sitzen 4
to **sit out** aussetzen 8
six sechs 1
sixteen sechzehn 2
to **skate** Schlittschuh laufen 9
to **ski** Ski laufen 9
skirt der Rock,¨e 6
sky der Himmel 10
slip (of paper) der Abschnitt,-e 6
slow(ly) langsam A
small klein 10
smart klug 3
snack bar die Imbißstube,-n B
to **snow** schneien 7
so so 3
soccer der Fußball,¨e 7
sock die Socke,-n 6
soft drink die Limonade,-n 9
to **solve** lösen 4
some etwas 2; ein paar 3
sometimes manchmal 4
son der Sohn¨e 5
soon bald 2; as soon as sobald 9
to **sound** klingen 10
south der Süden 3
South American südamerika-
     nisch 8
to **speak** sprechen 2
special besonders 4
special offer das Sonderangebot,
     -e 10
spectator der Zuschauer,- 9
spring der Frühling,-e 4
sport der Sport 4; kind of sport die
     Sportart,-en 9
spot die Stelle,-n 9
to **stamp** stempeln 7

stamp automat der Briefmarken-
     automat,-en 7
to **stand** stehen 4
start der Start,-s 9
to **start** starten 9
starting signal das Startsignal,-e
     9
to **start running** loslaufen 9
state der Staat,-en 3
station die Station,-en 10; der
     Bahnhof,¨e 3
to **stay** bleiben 2
still noch 2

stocking der Strumpf,¨e 6
stop (bus or streetcar) die Halte-
     stelle,-n 3
to **stop** anhalten 10
store das Geschäft,-e 6
street die Straße,-n 4
streetcar die Straßenbahn,-en 3
stretch die Strecke,-n 8
student der Schüler,- (through
     high school) 4; der Student,-
     en (at university) 4
studies das Studium,-dien 4
to **study (at university)** studieren 4
subject (school) das Fach,¨er 4
suburb der Vorort,-e 3
suddenly plötzlich 9
sufficient ausreichend 4
suggestion der Vorschlag,¨e 4
suit der Anzug,¨e 6
suitcase der Koffer,- 3
summer der Sommer,- 4
sun die Sonne 7
Sunday der Sonntag 2; on Sun-
     days sonntags 8
sunny sonnig 10
supermarket (DDR) die HO-
     Kaufhalle,-n 5
supper das Abendbrot 5
to **supply** versorgen 10
supposed: to be supposed to sol-
     len 5
to **surpass** übertreffen 9
to **surround** umgeben 10
surrounding die Umgebung,-en
     5
sweets die Süßigkeiten (pl.) 7
to **swim** schwimmen 9
Switzerland die Schweiz 3
symbol das Symbol,-e 7

T

table der Tisch,-e 5
table: to set the table den Tisch
     decken A
table tennis das Tischtennis 7
to **take (time)** dauern 3
to **take along** mitnehmen 10
to **take place** stattfinden 9
to **talk** sprechen 2; to talk about
     sprechen über 2
taste der Geschmack,¨e 8
to **taste** schmecken B
tea der Tee A
teacher der Lehrer,- 7

team die Mannschaft,-en 9
telephone das Telefon,-e 2
telephone booth die Telefon-
     zelle,-n 7
television: on television im Fern-
     sehen A
television set der Fernsehappa-
     rat,-e 7
television tower der Fernseh-
     turm,¨e 7
ten zehn 1
tennis das Tennis 9
terrific toll 5
test die Arbeit,-en 2; to take a test
     eine Arbeit schreiben 2
than als 8
thanks der Dank 10; danke 1;
     Danke schön. 5; Many
     thanks. Vielen Dank. 10
that das 1; daß 6
the der, die, das 1
theater das Theater,- 7
their ihr 4
then dann 2
there da 1; dort 3; dorthin 5; over
     there da drüben 1; there is
     (are) es gibt 4
therefore deshalb 6
they sie 1; man 3
to **think** denken 7
thirteen dreizehn 2
this dieser 3
thorough gründlich 4
thousand tausend 10
three drei 1
through durch 5
Thursday Donnerstag 2
ticket die Fahrkarte,-n 3; die
     Karte,-n 5
tide: low tide die Ebbe,-n 8
tie die Krawatte,-n 6
time die Zeit,-en 2; time(s) das
     Mal,-e 9 What time is it?
     Wieviel Uhr ist es?, 9; Wie
     spät ist es? 2; on time
     pünktlich 2
times mal 3
tired müde A
to auf 2; zu 2; nach 3; um 7
today heute 2
together zusammen 2
tomato die Tomate,-n A
tomorrow morgen 2
tonight heute abend 2
too auch 1; zu 2
top die Spitze,-n 9; to be on top an
     der Spitze sein 9; on top oben
     10

Abbreviations

A	Review Unit A
B	Review Unit B
E	Ergänzung
K	Kulturecke
L1	Lesestück 1
L2	Lesestück 2

Index

Acknowledgments

The author wishes to express his gratitude to the many people in Germany *(BRD* and *DDR),* Austria and Switzerland who assisted in the photography scenes for the textbook and the filmstrips. Particularly helpful was Panorama DDR, an organization that set up all the requested photography sessions in the German Democratic Republic. Special thanks should also go to those people who cooperated in setting up photography sessions in the other German-speaking countries: Familie Heinz Devrient (Köln), Professor Ulrich Froehlich (Würzburg), Herr Rudolf Hocker (Neustadt/Weinstraße), Herr Dieter Messner (Lienz), Herr Donatus Moosauer (Deggendorf), Herr und Frau Robert O'Reilly (EMC), Herr Horst Penner (Bergisch-Gladbach), Familie Ingomar Stainer (München), Herr und Frau Helmut Strunk (Essen).

Furthermore, the author would like to pay tribute to those professionals who contributed in the creative effort beyond the original manuscript: Rosemary J. Barry (Editor), Cyril John Schlosser (Designer) and Chris Wold Dyrud (Illustrator).

Last but not least, the author would like to thank his wife, Rosie, and his two daughters, Heidi and Marci, for showing such tremendous patience during the development of this series and for their valuable contributions before, during and after the extensive trip throughout German-speaking countries.

The following German instructors provided valuable comments for the revision of *Deutsch:Aktuell 1:*
Norma Ackley, South High School, Milwaukee, Wisconsin; *Sandra K. Benzer,* Urban Junior High School, Sheboygan, Wisconsin; *F. P. Boost,* McNary Senior High School, Salem, Oregon; *Edward H. Bray, Jr.,* Wissachickon Middle School, Ambler, Pennsylvania; *Anita Brückler,* Muskingum College, New Concord, Ohio; *Marge Burk,* Covington Latin School, Covington, Kentucky; *James Caputo,* Wooster High School, Wooster, Ohio; *Lydia Colson,* Cuyahoga Community College, Parma, Ohio; *Fred Covey,* Drake University, Des Moines, Iowa; *Leslie F. Darmek,* University of Arizona, Tucson, Arizona; *William R. Davis,* University of New Hampshire, Durham, New Hampshire; *Craig Deville,* University of Arizona, Tucson, Arizona; *Lucie M. Dilger,* Yorktown High School, Arlington, Virginia; *Lee Duty,* Sauk Prairie High School, Sauk City, Wisconsin; *Wendell Frye,* Hartwick College, Oneonta, New York; *Christa M. Fumea,* Northeast High School, St. Petersburg, Florida; *Karl-Heinz Gabbey,* Buffalo Grove High School, Buffalo Grove, Illinois; *Jacqueline S. Gnagi,* Perry A. Tipler Middle School, Oshkosh, Wisconsin; *Inez Good,* Roanoke College, Salem, Virginia; *Larry Hall,* Sewickley Academy, Sewickley, Pennsylvania; *Jerome P. Harper,* Carson-Newman College, Jefferson City, Tennessee; *Barbara A. Heck,* Arlington High School, Arlington Heights, Illinois; *Richard C. Helt,* University of Arizona, Tucson, Arizona; *Ursula F. Hildebrandt,* Libertyville High School, Libertyville, Illinois; *Frank D. Hirschbach,* University of Minnesota, Minneapolis, Minnesota; *Bradley A. Holtman,* Monroe High School, Monroe, Wisconsin; *Jörg Homberger,* Warwick High School, Lititz, Pennsylvania; *Kim P. Icsman,* Ursuline Academy, Cincinnati, Ohio; *Marie E. Ingram-Helt,* University of Arizona, Tucson, Arizona; *G. F. Jeffries,* North Hills High School, Pittsburgh, Pennsylvania; *Al Johnson,* Austin High School, Austin, Minnesota; *Thomas Kamla,* University of Scranton, Scranton, Pennsylvania; *Guido Kauls,* Minnehaha Academy, Minneapolis, Minnesota; *John Kelly,* Trinity High School, Manchester, New Hampshire; *Nancy M. King,* Parkview High School, Lilburn, Georgia; *Peter E. Klose,* Grand Blanc High School, Grand Blanc, Michigan; *George Kopecky,* West Torrance High School, Torrance, California; *Helga Lange,* Cuyahoga Valley Christian Academy, Cuyahoga Falls, Ohio; *Lowell E. Lee,* St. Louis Park Junior High School, St. Louis Park, Minnesota; *Jane Lienau,* Lutheran High School West, Detroit, Michigan; *A. H. Loewenstein,* Scottsdale High School, Scottsdale, Arizona; *Maimu Looke,* Harrison High School, Farmington, Michigan; *Mary Mateer,* DeWitt Middle School, Ithaca, New York; *Reverend J. Anthony Meis,* Bishop McNamara High School, Kankakee, Illinois; *Paul J. Nagy,* North Iowa Area Community College, Mason City, Iowa; *Lisa Oas,* Lakeview Christian Academy, Duluth, Minnesota; *Heinz J. Otto,* The Blake Schools, Minneapolis, Minnesota; *Reverend Ronald V. Perry,* Fairfield Prep School, Fairfield, Connecticut; *Martha Pleggenkuhle,* St. Ansgar Senior High School, St. Ansgar, Iowa; *Patricia Priolo,* Central High School, Scranton, Pennsylvania; *Donald E. Ruhde,* Iowa Falls High School, Iowa Falls, Iowa; *Mary Sexton,* Hamilton High School, Hamilton, Montana; *Gerlinde Sly,* Rockland Community College, Suffern, New York; *William Small,* University of Maine, Orono, Maine; *Debra Starkey,* Mitchell High School, Mitchell, Nebraska; *Michael Still,* De La Salle High School, Concord, California; *Reverend Keven Storek,* Lutheran High School, Rockford, Illinois; *Terry Mitchell Strohm,* West Chicago High School, West Chicago, Illinois; *Elvira Stromberg,* Shorecrest High School, Seattle, Washington; *Ronald Swanson,* Oshkosh North High School, Oshkosh, Wisconsin; *Ingrid von Reitzenstein,* Mundelein High School, Mundelein, Illinois; *Brigitte Wichmann,* Hanover College, Hanover, Indiana; *Hannelore Wilfert,* Russell Sage College, Troy, New York; *Tony Young,* Tokay High School, Lodi, California; *Hans R. Zumpft,* North High School, Sheboygan, Wisconsin.

Photo Credits

All the photos in the *Deutsch: Aktuell 1* (2nd edition) textbook not taken by the author have been provided by the following:

Austrian National Tourist Office: page 105 (left and bottom right)

Benkert, Christine: cover (flags)

Deutsche Bundespost: page 120 (top right)

Devrient, Heinz: page 100

Fremdenverkehrsverband Allgäu-Bayerisch e.V.: page 48

Fremdenverkehrsverband Bodensee-Oberschwaben e.V.: page 188 (top left)

Fremdenverkehrsverband Franken e.V.: page 121 (bottom right)

Fremdenverkehrsverband Lüneburger Heide e.V.: pages 109, 110 (top left), 192

Fremdenverkehrsverband München-Oberbayern e.V.: cover (top), pages 110 (center right), 249 (left)

Fremdenverkehrsverband Rheinland-Pfalz e.V.: pages 11 (left), 12, 76 (right)

German Information Center: pages 77 (both), 161 (top right and left), 180 (left), 191 (top right), 213 (center left and bottom right), 233 (top left), 237 (top right), 238 (top right)

German Rail: pages 53 (top and center left), 54 (bottom left and right)

Informations- und Presseamt Dortmund: page 166 (right)

Inter Nationes: page 249 (bottom right)

Landesfremdenverkehrsverband Baden-Württemberg e.V.: cover (center), pages 13, 30 (left), 58, 89 (right), 110 (center left), 191 (center and bottom right), 233 (bottom right), 237 (bottom right), 238 (top left)

Lufthansa German Airlines: pages 54 (top left), 180 (right), 188 (right), 247 (bottom right)

Moosauer, Donatus: pages 86 (both), 146 (both), 191 (top left)

Panorama DDR: pages ix (center right), 49 (right), 83 (top left), 162 (top left and bottom), 209 (top right and left), 213 (center right)

Presse- und Informationsamt der Bundesregierung (Bildstelle): pages ix (top left), 49 (left), 76 (left), 161 (bottom right), 191 (bottom left), 213 (bottom left), 214 (right top and bottom)

Stokes, Jim: page 243 (top right)

Swiss National Tourist Office: pages ix (bottom left), 110 (top right), 133, 139 (all), 213 (top right), 237 (top left)

Verkehrsbüro der Stadt Ulm: pages 29 (left), 158, 214 (top left), 238 (bottom center)